By the Time
We Got to
WOODSTOCK

★ ★ ★ ★ ★ ★ ★ ★ ★ ★ ★

By the Time We Got to WOODSTOCK

★ ★ ★ ★ ★ ★ ★ ★ ★ ★ ★ ★ ★

The Great Rock 'n' Roll Revolution of 1969

BRUCE POLLOCK

Backbeat
Books

An Imprint of Hal Leonard Corporation
New York

Published in 2009 by Backbeat Books
An Imprint of Hal Leonard Corporation
7777 West Bluemound Road
Milwaukee, WI 53213

Trade Book Division Editorial Offices
19 West 21st Street, New York, NY 10010

Printed in the United States of America.

Book design by Publishers' Design and Production Services, Inc.

Library of Congress Cataloging-in-Publication Data

Pollock, Bruce.
  By the time we got to Woodstock : the great rock 'n' roll revolution of 1969 / Bruce Pollock.
     p. cm.
  Includes bibliographical references (p.   ) and index.
  ISBN 978-0-87930-979-4 (6 × 9 pbk.)
  1. Rock music—1961–1970—History and criticism.   2. Nineteen sixty-nine, A.D.   I. Title.
  ML3534.P6248 2009
  781.6609'046—dc22

                                                        2009018213

www.backbeatbooks.com

For Barbara, Becky, Lisa, Eric, and Violet—
for always listening when I ramble

Contents

★ ★ ★ ★ ★ ★ ★ ★ ★

Contents

PART TWO

Opiates for the People

Author's Note

★ ★ ★ ★ ★ ★ ★ ★ ★

THE NON-ATTRIBUTED QUOTES in *By the Time We Got to Woodstock* were all taken from interviews I conducted, either especially for the book or during the course of my long and estimable career as "the next-to-last of the rock journalists." Several were submitted in their entirety as written pieces at my request and edited for publication.

Good Times/ Bad Times

★ ★ ★ ★ ★ ★ ★ ★ ★ ★ ★ ★ ★

> *It was the best of times, it was the worst of times, it was the age of wisdom, it was the age of foolishness, it was the epoch of belief, it was the epoch of incredulity, it was the season of Light, it was the season of Darkness, it was the spring of hope, it was the winter of despair, we had everything before us, we had nothing before us, we were all going direct to Heaven, we were all going direct the other way. . . .*
>
> from *A Tale of Two Cities* by Charles Dickens

THE PERIOD STARTING IN WASHINGTON, D.C., right after the election of Richard M. Nixon on November 4, 1968, and concluding with four deaths at Kent State in Ohio at the hands of the National Guard on May 4, 1970, was a time in the annals of rock 'n' roll like no other, in which hope grappled with despair, wisdom debated foolishness, belief and incredulity shared meals at the same communal table, and the forces of darkness escalated their counterassault on the light-bearing counterculture as dusk fell on Aquarius.

After the crushing defeats and confusions of 1968, 1969 would be a year of radical and profound personal risks, changes, and choices in the way music was perceived, written about, experienced, exploited, played, and disseminated, containing key releases by artists of unparalleled promise and uncommon achievement working in dozens of sometimes overlapping genres with ferocious pride born of rabid competition and massive stakes.

Prior to this season of political retribution, turmoil on the streets, men on the moon, acid in the drinking water, and escalating war overseas, the nascent Baby Boom generation had turned the power of its numbers and the potency of its idealism into an unmatched alliance between the popular and the revolutionary, the elite and the mainstream. Standing astride the barricades at every turn—social, emotional, political, artistic—the musicians and bands of 1965–1968, in the songs they sang, the albums they delivered, and the causes they espoused, were the only artists who consistently stood atop the mountain, commandeered the stages at the most important rallies, and issued all the crucial manifestos. In 1969, they all came tumbling down, seemingly at once.

How else to explain the strange arrangements in the wind as one era ended and another began, typified by Elvis Presley's return to Memphis in January and Bob Dylan's duets with Johnny Cash in Nashville in February? The Beatles played their last live performance as a group on a rooftop at Apple Studios in London on January 30, famously ending with the arrival of the police. The Rolling Stones' lead guitarist, Brian Jones, announced his departure from the band in June and was discovered floating in his swimming pool a month later, his death labeled "misadventure." Led Zeppelin made a career of "misadventure," paving the way for the heavy metal onslaught of the 1970s with albums *Led Zeppelin* and *Led Zeppelin II* in February and November. The peaceful Commencement Day vibes of Woodstock in August gave way to the murder of a gun-wielding spectator at the Altamont Speedway in December. In the meantime, the United States thrilled the world with moon landings in July and November, for a moment changing the subject on the streets and campuses of America from the bombing of Cambodia in March, the My Lai Massacre exposed in November, and the ominous draft lottery set to start rattling numbers in December.

The twin delivery systems of FM radio and the rock press graduated from underground status to play in the major leagues with the big boys, and in 1969 the suits moved in, just as the album and the album track sought to take over from the single as the preferred source of rock 'n' roll information—art, inspiration, and politics. Instigated at regular hysterical intervals by passionate 15,000-word essays of the newly crowned arbiters of the Alternate Culture in *Rolling Stone*, *Cream*, *Crawdaddy!*, and the *Village Voice*, this new counterculture quickly grew beyond the walls of the college gymnasiums and renovated movie theaters accustomed to housing them, exploding into the open fields at 100,000 a pop at outdoor festivals through the summer. Dubbed by Jimi Hendrix as his "sky church," the fanatic followers who made the season such a success celebrated themselves in August at the Woodstock Festival in Bethel, New York (two births, three deaths, 177 arrests) before officially burying themselves in December at the Altamont Speedway in Livermore, California (one homicide, three other deaths).

Bethel and Livermore were not the only two cities mythically joined at the fractured hip in 1969. New York City and San Francisco were still battling it out for the hippie overflow as flocks of the deflowered children of 1967 migrated from San Francisco's Golden Gate Park to Tompkins Square Park on New York's rent-friendly Lower East Side. But Los Angeles to the south was also deriding the San Francisco dream as so much summer-break posturing in the face of its own more legendary mystique, at least until former Beach Boys protégé Charles Manson put a permanent scar on the Hollywood sign with his mad rampage through Benedict Canyon in August, set to the tune of the Beatles' "Helter Skelter."

Politically, Cambridge and Berkeley in the wake of the Nixon election were scarier than ever, with the radical Weathermen and the entrenched Students for a Democratic Society leading undergrads and outside agitators from coast to coast in battles with the police, most notably at Harvard Yard and People's Park, in April. In June, the Weathermen battled SDS in Chicago and took over the ever more fractionalized party of protest, while the theater of the absurd trial of the Chicago Eight (soon to be Seven) played there for sixteen weeks, starting in September, captivating an untrusting youth that already thought itself beyond astonishment and cynicism. Prior to speaking at her Wellesley College commencement in Massachusetts a few months earlier, the president of college government and presiding officer of the college senate, Hillary D. Rodham, asked her classmates for their major concerns about life in these perilous times. They told her to talk about the lack of trust permeating society.

In Ann Arbor, John Sinclair of the White Panthers adopted an irrepressible rock band, the MC5, hoping to up the cause of noisy Revolution, while in Detroit, Diana Ross of the Supremes adopted an irresistible pop/R&B band, the Jackson 5, hoping to save the increasingly dysfunctional Motown family. Nearby, Iggy Pop's antic Stooges and George Clinton's frantic Funkadelic were preparing their reactions. *The Stooges*, released in August, was one big step toward punk. *Funkadelic*, released the following March, was a great leap forward for funk.

Meanwhile, the Elvis Presley comeback trail stretched from Memphis to Las Vegas, where it settled at the Las Vegas International Hotel for the month of August. On Broadway, *Hair! A Tribal Rock Opera*, which had moved there in 1968, continued its profitable attempt to put a winsome face on the counterculture—scoring several hit songs in 1969 for its efforts. Pete Townshend's own rock opera, *Tommy*, arrived in June (scoring Pete a bigger knockout than his purported takedown of Abbie Hoffman, the Yippie mouthpiece, at the Woodstock Festival in August). But Hollywood's chilling *Easy Rider* (made by Bob Rafaelson with profits derived from the TV show *The Monkees*) hit the mark more squarely when it debuted in July, with its vision of doomed hippies and its eclectic soundtrack. Not surprisingly, "Ballad of Easy Rider," its melancholy theme by the Byrds, with uncredited editorial help from Bob Dylan, failed to make the Top 40. In August, Arlo Guthrie starred in *Alice's Restaurant*, the movie of his song, detailing his and a male generation's angst-ridden relationship with their local draft boards. Joni Mitchell summed up the era here with "Songs to Aging Children Come," an anthem more properly dour than the sprightly epic she wrote a few months later, "Woodstock."

This is not to exclude the infamous Zip to Zap Festival of Light that was scheduled to take place on the weekend of May 10 and 11, in the tiny mining town of Zap, North Dakota, population 250, but was canceled when the town's two taverns ran out of beer and 30,000 rioting students had to be quelled by the National Guard. This ensured it would rank as only slightly less of an inadvertent generational symbol than the crowds of aimless teens milling in front of Pandora's Box, the Sunset Strip nightclub immortalized by Stephen Stills in "For What It's Worth" in 1966.

The signal anthem of 1969 was Dino Valente's "Get Together," which finally peaked as a hit in September by the Youngbloods. But like the earlier "The Age of Aquarius," a No. 1 hit in April by the 5th Dimension—and like the Summer of Love itself—the song's message of belief, light, hope, and most of all togetherness was delivered to the masses long after its meaning had been thoroughly defiled.

Newly liberated solo performers as disparate as Lou Reed (formerly of the Velvet Underground) and John Sebastian (formerly of the Lovin' Spoonful) bore witness to Lou's cry of "Wow, there are a lot of us." Commenting on an early performance of the Velvet Underground, Lou said, "It was a show by and for freaks, of which there turned out to be many more than anyone suspected." To which John might have responded, "You guys are beautiful," as he blissfully observed the same phenomenon a few years later while hosting the Woodstock Festival on a triple dose of acid, courtesy of the former comic Hugh Romney, a.k.a. Wavy Gravy.

But the truth outside the castle walls was a lot bleaker. Nineteen-sixty-nine was the year in which John

Lennon and Paul McCartney couldn't stand to be in the same recording studio with each other, especially when Yoko Ono was camped out in a corner in her bed. Janis Joplin left the protection of Big Brother to fend for herself as a reigning rock goddess in a fickle world. Frank Zappa left the Mothers of Invention. Jimi Hendrix left the Experience. The Famous Flames left James Brown. The songwriting team of Holland, Dozier, and Holland left Motown after a bitter lawsuit. Jim Morrison left his pants on a stage in Miami. And Simon wasn't any too thrilled with Garfunkel.

Despite the conciliatory "Bridge over Troubled Water," recorded in 1969, first performed on the TV special *Songs of America* in November and a No. 1 hit by February 1970, Simon knew the run was over. "As the relationship was disintegrating, the album was selling ten million copies," he told me. "And by the time I decided I was going to go out on my own, you can imagine how difficult it was telling the record company there wasn't going to be any follow-up to an album that sold ten million. But for me it really saved my ass, because I don't think we could have followed it up."

He could have been speaking for the era itself, which had reached lunar heights in its anger, intensity, creativity, exposure, and ultimate effect on its audience. Where else could it go from there but into ego trips, animosity, litigation, overdoses, violence, and retaliation? In San Francisco all the hippest radical kids were getting guns (to shoot each other or *the man*, who knew)? One of them showed up at the concert in nearby Altamont. In Los Angeles the blissful surf turned monstrous. By this point many of the brightest stars were lighting out for other territories. Even the Grateful Dead had painfully decided it was time to get their act together and make it into a business. As Simon observed during that same interview, "Sooner or later you become the mainstream."

And sooner or later all eras end, as the acid-washed folk rock of the Alternate Culture gave way in 1969 to the bubblegum and heavy metal of the next wave of high school adherents.

Nevertheless, the stories of these artists and how they worked and played together, lived, loved, got loaded, got busted, and created these watershed songs and albums under such duress more than befit the ending of an era of extremes. In 1969, experimentalism and virtuosity reigned supreme, from the Eastern eloquence of Kaleidoscope to the East Coast experimentations of the Rascals to the progressive rock of Yes and King Crimson. Guitar explorations abounded, from Jimi Hendrix, Frank Zappa, and John McLaughlin with Miles Davis's band to Johnny Winter, Michael Bloomfield, and Carlos Santana. Yet there was room for the profane weirdness of the Fugs and David Peel, as well as the Archies.

In 1969, two of Frank Zappa's all-time favorite albums came out within a couple of months of each other—*Philosophy of the World* by the Shaggs in April and *Trout Mask Replica* by Captain Beefheart in June—both inspiring eloquent misinterpretations in the rock press, the one going on to become a certified masterpiece, the other merely certifiable. While thousands of album-loving, FM-listening, war-protesting members of the Alternate Culture marched on Washington in October to protest the war, two months shy of the draft lottery, the AM radio staple Top 40 seemed to have weathered the album cut storm, with future classics by the Beatles and the Stones going head to head with the Temptations, Creedence Clearwater Revival, the 5th Dimension, Tommy James, Elvis Presley, Bob Dylan, Aretha Franklin, Sly Stone, Led Zeppelin, and the Jackson 5.

Memories may differ about the potency of the drugs, the tactics of the Weathermen and the Black Panthers, the trials of the Chicago Eight (Seven), Sirhan Sirhan and James Earl Ray, the My Lai massacre, the Manson murders, or the varied approaches to dealing with the draft. But the music is conclusive, a mirror of its time in a time of passion, rage and changes.

It was also a time when the apparently vast budget of the average record buyer was tested on an almost weekly basis. . . .

PART ONE

No Easy Way Down

★ ★ ★ ★ ★ ★ ★ ★ ★ ★ ★ ★ ★ ★

CHAPTER ONE

Nixon's Coming

★ ★ ★ ★ ★ ★ ★ ★ ★ ★ ★ ★ ★

LIKE MOST SELF-RESPECTING RESIDENTS of Greenwich Village, I awoke on the morning of November 5, 1968 flat on my back on a mattress in a sleazy rooming house. I was listening to the prostitute on the other side of the wall argue with her latest client about the going rate—they were perhaps the only two in the neighborhood unfazed by the results of the presidential election of the night before, which had not been finalized until the wee hours. Although in the hectic, draining final months leading up to this contest, the skirmish between Richard Nixon and Hubert Humphrey had been characterized by radical and moderate liberals alike as "six of one, half a dozen of the other," those lifelong Democrats among us who retired for the night with Humphrey a hair ahead were rudely and profoundly awakened by the news that the Daley operation in Chicago, as if to atone for its role in JFK's squeaker of 1960 (over the same Nixon), had shifted the election to the enemy while we peacefully slept. Having endured those eight years in rage and exile, watching the children of the left proceed to freak out in his absence, like a gang of juvenile delinquents in a class led by the substitute teacher in the movie *Blackboard Jungle*, Nixon was now more than ready to provide a severe directional tilt to the cosmic pinball machine, the walls of which we'd all been happily bouncing against since that epic defeat.

Living in Greenwich Village, as I had since the fall of 1966, I had no firsthand knowledge of the Nixon constituency, the fabled "silent majority," except for random brushes with the occasional authority figure during my biannual, tentative forays past Fourteenth Street to labor in the mailrooms and typing pools of New York City long enough to qualify for another package of unemployment benefits, so I could continue working on my endless novel (about a writer working on his endless novel) and my Dylanesque (or at least Paul Simonesque) song lyrics. Milling around at night with other semi-starving artists at the clubs and watering holes of MacDougal Street, I'd failed to pick up on the zeitgeist as it whistled in the wind just above my head. It would have served me well to remember a trip to San Francisco I made in 1968, when one of the residents at the house where I was staying on Haight Street scoffed at what I smugly called my New York State Creative Writing Grant. "After the revolution there will be no unemployment insurance," he said, advising me in the same sentence to get myself a gun.

In New York City, few of us had guns. But then, San Francisco was always a much more radical place than the West Village. LSD had been in vogue at Stanford in nearby Palo Alto since the early '60s. The rock groups there, fortified by mind-altering acid, were at the front lines of every political battle, from student strikes to radio station strikes, as chronicled in the pages of the upstart *Rolling Stone.* "The support which has been given all radical causes by rock groups, particularly San Francisco rock groups, is incalculable," wrote Ralph J. Gleason, a *Rolling Stone* cofounder and columnist, in the *Drama Review.* "I mention this not to lavish credit on the bands but to point out that every cause goes to them for help. The reason is the power of the music.

"'Lighting a joint is a revolutionary act,' Leary says, and there is a deep truth in this," Gleason continued, "since the act puts the actor outside the law from that time on. But I think the whole body of rock music, spreading out from the center, with Dylan, the Beatles and the Stones, involves its audience in an even more fundamental confrontation with society. It says you are, all of you, wrong."

By 1969, the rock 'n' roll constituency was as vast as its taste for communism, socialism, utopianism, solipsism—let alone a unified vision of revolution—was unquantifiable. Many a Washington Square regular believed in the same essential antiwar, pro–civil rights issues, but that's about as far as it went, even in '68, when the Beatles preached moderation in "Revolution" and the Rolling Stones fanned the flames with "Street Fighting Man," released a month after the convention and banned in Chicago.

And now, concurrent with Nixon's arrival, other competing voices reentered the conversation, with responses that might have been laughed out of the room, if not the universe, in 1964, when Barry Goldwater took but six states in his quest to stanch the rising tide of high-decibel rock 'n' roll rebellion.

"The coup de grace, according to the swingers at *National Review*, is that 'Revolution' puts down the Maoists," wrote Gary Allen in *American Opinion*, a monthly journal of the John Birch Society. He went on,

> The Beatles are simply telling the Maoists that Fabian gradualism is working and that the Maoists might blow it all by getting the public excited before things are ready for revolution. The song makes it perfectly clear that the Beatles are on the side of and working for the revolution and that their war is going to be successful. In short, revolution takes the Moscow line against Trotskyites and the Progressive Labor Party, based on Lenin's *Leftwing Extremism: An Infantile Disorder.*

To whom another *Rolling Stone* preeminence, Greil Marcus, being the only one in the room to make sense of that, might have been replying in his thoughtful book *Rock and Roll Will Stand*:

> Rock 'n' roll is not a means by which to "learn about politics," nor a wavelength for a message as to what is to be done or who is to be fought. It is, at times (especially in such moments as August, 1968), a way to get a feeling for the political spaces we might happen to occupy at any particular time. Rock 'n' roll music and a rock 'n' roll song—a record—keeps those spaces open. If we can keep moving in that space opened up by a song that brings us a joke on ourselves and a sense of the doubts we might try to hide, we have a chance at an honest response to the coldly serious New Left and the fascism of the old guard.

As resonant and nuanced as this approach might have been, many an apolitical rock 'n' roll slob, waking up on his mattress the day after the election, had to countenance the notion (if only subconsciously) that Susan Huck, writing in *Review of the News*,could well represent the wave of the future in her assessment of the captains of our beloved music industry.

"What they're grabbing for are minds," she wrote. "They want to con these kids into enslaving themselves to drugs, sex and revolution. They want to talk them into destroying their own society and heritage, in the perfectly asinine expectation that some Utopia will spring full-blown from an alliance of old perverts and spoiled brats."

In the meantime, Bob Dylan took to the hills with his band, leaving behind only the songs on *Nashville Skyline* as cryptic clues to his disappearance, his mind-set, his political affiliations. In Detroit, just as Motown was finding its social conscience, fans of the MC5, exhausted from continuously kicking out the jams, were opting to vegetate with the Stooges and Alice Cooper or in front of the tube watching Elvis's triumphant return or Grace Slick in blackface on *The Smothers Brothers Comedy Hour* in '68, or the moon walk, *Bewitched*, or *The Brady Bunch* in '69. While Led Zeppelin lit a flame to the Urban Blues Revival in '69, Richard Nader's doo-wop raiders co-opted Madison Square Garden for an Oldies Revival.

As usual, self-preservation ruled, followed closely by self-interest and self-justification. Many of the Aged of Aquarius had bolted from the bandstand bandwagon way before "The Age of Aquarius" by the 5th Dimension hit No. 1, their flowers from the Summer of Love neatly folded into their graduation yearbooks. Others chose to celebrate one more time at Woodstock before commencing the long strange trip to adulthood. For a lot of them politics was strictly theater, especially as practiced by Abbie Hoffman of the Youth International Party. But so was rock 'n' roll, never so clearly epitomized as when Pete Townshend of the Who at that famous assemblage clobbered Hoffman with his guitar, yelling, "Get off my stage." As the December 1 draft lottery approached, while some waited in fear or marched in protest, others made plans for attending the Rolling Stones' free concert at Altamont, where Mick Jagger's battle was not with a spindly geek like Hoffman, but rather with a whole tribe of Hell's Angels. As history notes, unlike Townshend, he failed miserably.

Personally, in 1969, like the Lovin' Spoonful of '65, I still believed in a music that could "set you free." Like Neil Young, I woke up every afternoon "Expecting to Fly." Like the Byrds as scripted by Gerry Goffin and Carole King, I knew I "Wasn't Born to Follow." Like Dylan, in D. A. Pennebaker's scathing tour documentary *Don't Look Back*, I didn't. All I needed upon rising was a fifteen-minute fix of a bawling Janis Joplin in "Down on Me," segued into the mournful "Down River" by David Ackles, into Tracy Nelson's thunderous "Down So Low" by Mother Earth, to maintain my melancholy resolve. A late-afternoon break consisting of the stoic "This Is My Country" by the Impressions, melding into Richie Havens's stark "The Klan," into the healing "Abraham, Martin and John" by Dion, into the motivating "Time Has Come Today" by the Chambers Brothers, capped off by the surging "Pride of Man" by Hamilton Camp, was all the politics I found necessary to preserve the status quo—at least until my unemployment checks ran out.

But Dave Van Ronk, the Mayor of MacDougal Street, host of the weekly hoot I staunchly attended every Tuesday night at the Gaslight Café, friend and protector of Dylan, bawdy, rowdy, cowlicked howler of the blues, was much more astute than I when it came to the realities of the larger world. "Thermidor had arrived," he intoned as a comment on the election's aftermath, when I interviewed him in the early eighties. It was during the month of Thermidor in the French Revolutionary calendar that the political pendulum of the era swung, in 1794, from the incipient revolutionaries back to the more moderate right. "Everyone who was involved in folk music certainly felt it," Dave said. "The whole left wing wave had passed."

Flat on my back (listening to the radio) was as good a position as any to absorb the news of 1969. More trusted an ally than network television or the *New York Times*, radio, or, more specifically, FM radio, had been a vital link to the progress of the Alternate Culture, starring rock 'n' roll's agenda for world domination, since the summer of 1966, when WOR-FM took on the established AM/Top 40 giants with a stunning revolutionary repertoire of wall-to-wall album cuts—sans deejays! For two months the music played nonstop and unidentified while I listened entranced and liberated on a different mattress at a friend's apartment in Brooklyn. It was like stumbling onto something magical and subversive, a station with no rules, obviously too good to last, like the broken pay phone in the neighborhood that dispensed a dollar and a half in quarters after every local call.

Later it would be revealed that WOR-FM was only revolutionary by accident; the union was simply finalizing the deejay's contracts with the station. In fact, all those loyal, ecstatic fans of the original formless format wound up serving as tools of management, which compiled their frenzied letters to send to advertisers during the height of the negotiations. I would also discover that the first song ever played on the station was "Wild Thing" by the Troggs, which was already No. 1 on the charts, subversive only to those who preferred the previous middle-of-the-road programming.

It's quite possible the repertoire was not as I've always remembered it, either, i.e., consisting solely of great, largely unknown tracks from Buffalo Springfield, Love, the Jimi Hendrix Experience, Country Joe and the Fish, Circus Maximus, the Chambers Brothers, the Mothers of Invention, Al Kooper's Blood, Sweat and Tears, the Jefferson Airplane, Moby Grape, the Merry-Go-Round, the Velvet Underground, the Blues Project, the Paul Butterfield Blues Band, Mother Earth, and the Grateful Dead. A playlist from music director Scott Muni's first day on the air after the strike ended in October reveals an unsettling mix of slightly edgy rock and your regulation middle-of-the-road pop and R&B—starting with "I Can't Control Myself" by the Troggs into "Come On Up" by the Young Rascals, "Black Is Black" by Los Bravos, "Look Through My Window" by the Mamas and the Papas, and "If I Were a Carpenter" by Bobby Darin, into "I Just Don't Know What to Do with Myself" by Dionne Warwick. Also included were commercials for aluminum siding, the Pepsi Generation, the movie *Dead Heat on a Merry-Go-Round*, and the U.S. Army. Deejay Johnny Michaels followed "Scottso" with "I'll Be There" by the Four Tops, "Mickey's Monkey" by the Miracles, and Nancy Sinatra singing "In Our Time."

Within a year Muni and compatriots Rosko and Johnny Michaels would be on the much more authentic WNEW-FM, which had started playing the kind of progressive album mix mentioned above as far back as October of 1967. One of WNEW's early settlers, Pete Fornatale, explained to me:

Rosko quit on the air on a Monday night in October. Instead of being content to build the beautiful thing they had going [with free-form album cuts], WOR brought in this clown Bill Drake, who was basically a Top 40 czar, who brought in all the bells and whistles of Top 40, so Rosko quit on the air. I'm teaching high school on Long Island to avoid the draft and still doing the show I'd started in 1964 on [the college station at Fordham University] WFUV. I invited him on the next Saturday to talk about why he had quit.

Rosko was an articulate man, a passionate man, and he laid out his case. Unbeknownst to either of us, George Duncan and Nat Asch, general manager and program director of WNEW, were listening to see how he would handle himself. Well, they heard him but they also heard me. They hired Rosko immediately.

About a month after he started, when all of that hippie sponsorship came through, they hired Jonathan Schwartz and then Scott Muni and then, on January 1, the Nightbird, Alison Steele, who was the only one held over from the station's previous format of all-women deejays. As they moved into 1969, Mike Jahn, the *Times* music critic, did some part-time stuff. Zacherle came aboard. [Record producer] Richard Robinson was a weekend person.

And then in July someone quit, someone got fired, and someone was on vacation, and they were stuck for two midnight-to-six shows, Saturday night into Sunday and Sunday into Monday. And the PD gave me a call. I went into the studio on the twenty-fifth to sit in with Rosko. It was the night that Teddy Kennedy went on national TV to talk about Mary Jo Kopechne. Man had landed on the moon four or five days earlier, Kennedy is making an idiot of himself on national television, and I'm sitting there with Rosko. The next night, after the midnight news I do my first show at WNEW-FM. I played "Sing This Song All Together" by the Rolling Stones, followed by "You Can All Join In" by Traffic.

Thus the art of the segue, variously practiced elsewhere, on tiny signals, over public radio or barter stations, with limited range and influence, had arrived at the largest stage in the world. "If you were marked by Elvis and the Beatles and you got to your college campus and had an opportunity to infiltrate the radio station, you had the opportunity to treat radio not as a business but as an art form, to treat it as a canvas," said Pete. "At WNEW I went in there every day and had a blank canvas and it was up to me to use the colors." When his first set on the air was over, as instructed, Fornatale looked at the log to see which commercials were scheduled. "Some were prerecorded on cartridges," he said, "but the one live commercial for the first break was for the Woodstock Music and Art Fair, less than a month away—seven dollars a day, but if you bought all three days, eighteen dollars."

Throughout 1969, with the tears of the Martin Luther King and Bobby Kennedy assassinations and the tear gas of Chicago—followed by the inconceivable election results—still stinging, the mission of the Alternate Culture as advanced by the *Village Voice, Rolling Stone, Fusion, Crawdaddy!,* and the rest of the nascent rock press would need a beacon in the night like WNEW-FM more than ever. With no false modesty, Fornatale recalled,

If you lived in New York in 1969 or '70, WNEW was the station you listened to. While we were doing it I guess it was like eye of the hurricane. It wasn't in the front of our consciousness. But one of the station's characteristics was a seriousness of purpose. Somehow or another, you knew that there was a huge difference between the loudmouthed AM deejay, Bruce Morrow, zipping into this identity of cousin Brucie, with all of the elements of performance that involves, and what you were doing by going in, being yourself, and talking about things that you cared about that went beyond the paycheck. There was never any dictating about your position on things or causes. We used to arrange for buses to go down to the big antiwar demonstrations in Washington. Even though we were the strangest of bedfellows: the general manager George Duncan was an ex-marine; he certainly did not buy into any of the politics, or even maybe the passion of the music. He came from another generation entirely. But the notion was *we can make a little money from these punks playing Phil Ochs and Bob Dylan.* The other part is, when you ain't got nothing you got nothing to lose.

Progressive FM radio sold albums and filled convention halls. There were no focus groups. We were the focus group. I remember one night the promo guy from Atlantic comes in with a test pressing of *Led Zeppelin II.* This is sometime between 10 P.M. and 2 A.M. and he just shows up with an acetate and I immediately dropped the needle on "Whole Lotta Love." The Crosby, Stills and Nash debut—everybody knows every track on that album because of a loose, undefined, unplanned conspiracy of journalists, deejays, and concert promoters. It was organic and it was very real and very powerful, more powerful than we realized. The biggest mistake I made was thinking this was going to go on forever.

A comment from Paul Simon speaks even more directly to the crossroads the generation that came of age with rock 'n' roll in the 1950s had reached by the end of the '60s:

> For me the significant change occurred around 1969, after I wrote "The Boxer." At that point I stopped smoking grass and I never went back. I told a friend of mine, a really good musician, that I had writer's block, and he said, "When are you going to stop playing this folkie shit, all the time the same G to C chords? You could be a really good songwriter, but you don't know enough, you don't have enough tools. Forget about having hits—go learn your ax." So I started to study theory. I began listening to other kinds of music—gospel, Jamaican ska, Antonio Carlos Jobim. Gospel was easy for me to feel at home with because it sounded like the rock 'n' roll I grew up with.

Similarly, having reached for and attained so many exhilarating creative peaks during the last few years, a momentarily winded generation was now confronted by a stark, dramatic crossroads. Get back to your roots, preferably in some secluded two-room country shack with a year's worth of canned food stockpiled in the extra room, or pick up a weapon—to join the Revolution as espoused by the Weathermen but seemingly disdained by the Beatles, or to fight in Viet Nam as espoused by Richard M. Nixon.

Nixon invited James Brown to perform in D.C. during the ceremonies leading up to his inauguration—along with Dinah Shore, Lionel Hampton, and Tony Bennett. An avowedly apolitical performer who claimed he never voted, Brown suffered some fallout in the black community for accepting this invitation, although Brown himself had seemingly forecast it in "America Is My Home," a jingoistic anthem released the previous May whose lyrics would have befitted a patriotic country music type like Merle Haggard. Brown's exhortation to his constituency at the inaugural ball—"Say It Loud—I'm Black and I'm Proud," the song he wrote to quell a nation's unrest after the Martin Luther King assassination—was at odds with Nixon's own message, which praised the "silent majority" and advised the protestors to "lower [their] voices." Unfortunately, students at the University of Massachusetts, Penn State, Howard University, the University of Wisconsin, and Harvard University were too busy sitting in, rioting, occupying buildings, and taunting the administration and the police to heed Nixon's warning.

By the end of 1970, James Brown would be joined by Elvis Presley as a charter member of the Nixon rock 'n' roll fan club. The Hubert Humphrey fan club, meanwhile, consisted of at least one member, Tommy James. Humphrey in fact wrote the liner notes for *Crimson and Clover,*one of Tommy's three big albums of 1969, which lost out in the next year's Grammy Awards to Johnny Cash's liner notes for Dylan's *Nashville Skyline.* According to Tommy,

> For me, 1969 really started with the presidential campaign of 1968. The first thing we did was a rally in Manhattan. Several candidates were there, including Robert Kennedy and Eugene McCarthy. We set up our equipment and started to play and a

whole bunch of hippies are yelling, "Sellout!" We did a twenty-minute set and we left but we ended up being put on a list for the Democratic Party. We were asked if we could go to L.A. to appear at some of the festivities during the primary at the Ambassador Hotel. We had to turn it down because we were playing in Dallas, Texas, of all places, at the World Teen Fair. Back in New York that night I walk into my apartment just in time to turn on the primary from L.A. and Bobby Kennedy gets killed.

I was hit very hard. A big part of the '60s for me had been Robert Kennedy. We all believed back then a leader could actually change things. To me, getting Bobby Kennedy in the White House was all about getting the Kennedy thing back. That's what the '60s were about, if you really get down to it, trying to get that thing back that we had before JFK was killed. When Bobby was gone I personally went into a real funk and stayed that way for weeks.

Some time later, we get a call up at Roulette from Hubert Humphrey's personal assistant, Ursula Culver. She asked if we would be interested in coming out on the campaign and playing for Humphrey. At that moment I didn't know if I wanted to or not. I was still torn up about Kennedy. But then I got to thinking, anything to keep Nixon out of office. So we said yes. Then we watched the convention in August up at my apartment while we were writing and we saw the night the thing exploded and all the kids getting beat up. We go, "Holy shit, what have we gotten ourselves into?" The country was so torn apart. A couple of nights later, at two or three in the morning, Humphrey gives his speech where Chicago's Mayor Daley got real mad at him.

We met Humphrey out on the campaign the following week. I think the first gig was at an airplane hangar in Wheeling, West Virginia. We ended up playing a whole bunch of gigs with him. We had our own twelve-passenger Lear Jet compliments of Butler Aviation out at LaGuardia airport so we could join the campaign whenever we had a chance. We'd play the gigs and we'd all stay at the same hotel. He'd be up late at night and ask us to come up to his suite and we'd talk. One time he told us how he was going to end the war with a national referendum. Another time he said he wanted me to be President's Advisor on Youth Affairs.

We were with him at the Remington Hotel in Minneapolis on the night of the election. When Humphrey went to bed he was ever so slightly ahead of Nixon. And then, all of a sudden, the voting machines broke down in Cook County, Chicago. Two hours later, the voting machines come back on and Nixon was declared the winner. Well, obviously that was Daley. He was pissed at Hubert Humphrey and everyone calling him a Nazi at the convention, so I think he basically threw the election to Nixon. Everybody thought Humphrey would do a recount. He said, "No, our country's been through enough. Nixon's our president now."

That was the moment the '60s ended, if you really want the truth. That was the moment where all the hope of the '60s was gone.

Nevertheless, Tommy James and the Shondells had one of their most productive years in 1969. The band released five singles and every one was a million-seller, starting with "Crimson and Clover," which hit No. 1 in

February. They outsold the Beatles that year as far as singles, and for good measure their three albums went platinum.

"January was a quiet month for us," Tommy said. "And then in February, all hell broke loose. 'Crimson and Clover' goes number one. I do *The Ed Sullivan Show* first week of February. And then I have to go for my draft induction physical!"

Tommy gives his mentor at Roulette, the notorious music man Morris Levy, all the credit for his subsequent escape from the jaws of the war machine.

"Morris was on the board of directors of the Chemical Bank," Tommy laughed. "You talk about the cat guarding the milk. One of his best friends on the board is the head of the Selective Service in New York and he gets me out. So Morris probably saved my life."

Understandably, Tommy and the band preferred the relative safety of the road, touring for much of the year. This was the year of the outdoor festival, when many in the youth culture, aged eighteen to twenty-three, having no magnum opus to complete and no desire or ability to fire a gun, decided instead to party. From coast to coast at one event after another, defiance and dread joined hands in a weird death waltz as they waited for the hammer to fall. Tommy James's year included a stop at the Atlanta Pop Festival on July 4, but not Woodstock. He explains,

> All the festivals of 1969, including Woodstock, felt more like wakes than celebrations. In August, "Crystal Blue Persuasion" had just gone No. 1. We had two gigs three weeks apart in Hawaii. When we crunched the numbers it was cheaper to stay there than go back and forth from New York. We were in a

twenty-two-room mansion at the foot of Diamondhead when I got a call from my secretary at Roulette. She says Artie Kornfeld, a friend of mine who was one of the principals of Woodstock, called and said there's going to be this big gig at a pig farm in New York and they'd really like you to be there. I said, "Wait, a minute, you're asking me to leave paradise, fly six thousand miles to play a freaking pig farm? I tell you what, if we're not there, tell them to start without us." We knew by the first day of the festival we'd really screwed up bad.

When 1969 ended the garage door slammed shut. I know there's this romance about the '60s, but for most of us who were there, there was a lot of pain, a lot of feelings we could never get back again.

As if to underscore Tommy's contention, by the time the populace had a chance to vote again in 1972 (with the voting age now lowered to eighteen), all the bills of the '60s were cashed in by Nixon's armies, as the Democrats, led by the hapless George McGovern, proceeded to lose forty-two of the forty-three states they'd won in '64 over Barry Goldwater.

Thermidor was here to stay.

CHAPTER TWO

Goin' Up the Country

★ ★ ★ ★ ★ ★ ★ ★ ★ ★ ★ ★ ★

"**Y**EAH, DYLAN WAS REAL AND the Beatles were plastic," said Roger McGuinn, founder of the Byrds, when I asked him about the musical shift in 1964 from rock 'n' roll to folk rock brought about by the Beatles' influence on Bob Dylan and vice versa. "Then the Beatles got more authentic and Dylan got more Top 40." When I prodded McGuinn further about Dylan's influence on the generation and the culture, specifically the Alternate Culture he'd supposedly spoke for and then abandoned for the woods, I'd clearly crossed a line

"People imagined all these things going on," he said with disdain. "'Oh, this guy's a great spokesman, a great artist.' I think it was definitely an overestimation of the people involved. The fact is, it's just punks trying to play music, usually."

Punks trying to play music I could accept gladly. But why in 1969 were all these punks suddenly so enamored with country music? The simple answer, of course, was to blame it all on Bob Dylan, who scheduled a return trip to Nashville in February of 1969 for the recording of his first pure country album, *Nashville Skyline.*

Dylan had been recording in Nashville since *Blonde on Blonde* in 1966. The follow-up, *John Wesley Harding*, released at the end of 1967, contained a couple of country songs, but veered more toward the mystic West, as epitomized by all those faces in the trees on the album cover and the great "All Along the Watchtower" inside, whose two approaching riders (or was it writers?) had to be Dylan and Allen Ginsberg, right? But *Nashville Skyline* went way too far: not only a country album, but a putrid country album. It was hardly on a par with Waylon Jennings or Merle Haggard or Willie Nelson or Tom T. Hall or Johnny Cash, who mangled the opening cut, "Girl from the North Country." It went downhill from there.

There were many schools of thought as to Dylan's condition in 1969 propounded in the coffeehouses of the MacDougal Street he'd left behind, the primary one being the "vegetable theory." This theory, unlike the bogus "Paul is dead" rumors that circulated later in the year about Paul McCartney, was based on nothing as tangible as backward masked lyrics; in fact, it was based on nothing at all but gut feelings (and perhaps a few old candy wrappers unearthed by Dylan garbologist A. J. Webberman). Those of us stranded without a compass in the West Village, as the world and the music scene turned to the East, seeing no direction home without our spokesman to lead us, reckoned that he'd been so mangled and internally bruised by his 1966 motorcycle accident that he'd totally lost his edge, to say nothing of his voice, let alone his mind. The simplistic ditties he offered the world when the album was released in May were actually the best his enfeebled brain could now create, probably the best he'd ever again be capable of producing. The *John Wesley Harding* album was probably stitched out of old stuff lying around half-baked and half-finished; *Nashville Skyline* was the true Dylan now, the only Dylan we had left. If there were to be any other Dylans in our lifetime it would have to be one of those "New Dylan" types floating around, David Blue, say, or Loudon Wainwright.

Of course, those who were privy to Dylan's jam sessions at Big Pink in 1967 with his former backup band, the Hawks, soon to become the Band, knew better. These few intrepid musicologists had already sampled some of the deceptively tangy and indubitably rootsy fare on bootleg editions of *The Great White Wonder*, not officially released until 1975 as *The Basement Tapes*, with quality odes like "Tears of Rage," "I Shall Be Released," "The Mighty Quinn," and "This Wheel's on Fire." But even that could be accounted for in the vegetable theory, which allowed Dylan the occasional gem of old but not the ability to distinguish between what was genuine and what was god-awful. And there was no one in the entourage with the clout or the confidence to advise him. Robbie Robertson was a hired hand. Dylan's constant foil and companion, Bobby Neuwirth, was there strictly for the entertainment value. His manager, Albert Grossman, definitely couldn't be trusted. (The vegetable theory was only confirmed by the appearance of *Nashville Skyline*'s demented follow-up, *Self Portrait*, in 1970).

The more paranoid among us had an even worse prognosis: that Dylan had pulled a J. D. Salinger or a Sandy Koufax. At the height of his fame he'd just decided that he'd had enough. Sure, he knew the difference between good and bad; in fact, he was writing better songs than ever, but he'd developed such a disdain for his audience, the counterculture in particular, that he'd be damned if he was about to deliver any of his best stuff to the marketplace. The genuine article he would continue writing for himself and his friends, stockpiling songs like canned food for future generations as yet unborn and untainted by his manufactured legend. The brain-dead country songs and covers he would release for public consumption, year after year until we finally got sick of them, sick of him, and just went away. The 1966 motorcycle accident, in this context, might not have been so serious after all; it could have been a grisly ruse designed to help him effect his (drifter's) escape. (This theory was again confirmed by his ghastly and goofy appearance on the first installment of *The Johnny Cash Show* on ABC-TV on June 6, along with Doug Kershaw, Fanny Flagg and—amazingly—Joni Mitchell).

Or maybe, the more cerebral among us thought, Dylan was trying to tell us something. That it was time to grow up and become the mainstream, echoing what Paul Simon went through after "The Boxer," when he decided to immerse himself in gospel music. As Dylan had turned his back on the folk crowd once he'd conquered the form, most notably symbolized by his amped-up appearance at the '65 Newport Folk Festival playing "Maggie's Farm" alongside guitarist Michael Bloomfield and guitarist-cum-organist Al Kooper—he'd turn-turn-turned again, from folk rock to country music, a genre despised by the intelligentsia, this time motivated by no less a Beatlesque (if not Bunyanesque) figure than Elvis Presley.

In the same way that Dylan had followed the Beatles on the record charts of 1964, he might have easily been struck by an item in the trades describing Elvis's sojourn on January 13, 1969 to American Studios in Memphis, to record there for the first time since his legendary Sun Records days of the mid-'50s (polishing off "Long Black Limousine" and "This Is the Story" on his first day of work). The country vibe was obviously in the air, put there by, among others, Dylan's longtime cohorts, the Byrds, whose *Sweetheart of the Rodeo* came out in the tragic summer of '68, containing country fare like "I Am a Pilgrim" and Gram Parsons' "Hickory Wind," and Big Pink Dylan covers like "You Ain't Going Nowhere" and "Nothing Was Delivered."

McGuinn himself had wanted the band to turn in the opposite direction, toward the kind of Coltrane-inspired jazz that influenced "Eight Miles High." But he lost this particular power struggle to mercurial new sideman Gram Parsons, even though Parsons' '68 release *Safe at Home*, by his short-lived International Submarine Band (featuring classic country tunes like "I Still Miss Someone" and "Miller's Cave" as well as his own "Luxury Liner," soon to be covered by Emmylou Harris), had gone nowhere. In March of 1969 the Byrds sang "Drugstore Truck Driving Man" and "Old Blue" in *Dr. Byrds & Mr. Hyde* and then "Jesus Is Just Alright," as well as the mournful theme for *Easy Rider*, which came out in July, featuring the Band's "The Weight" on the soundtrack.

Not surprisingly, the Band's guitarist and main songwriter, Robbie Robertson, weighed in on the subject:

When *Blonde on Blonde* came out a lot of critics wrote, "This is the worst stuff I've ever heard in my life." And then the world changed. With time, everyone started to say, "No, no, no, that was good all along. I didn't mean what I said." People changed their stories on it—audiences did, critics did, everybody did. It was the same thing with *Music from Big Pink*, 'cause by then everybody had turned up to ten. Everybody was playing loud and violently and we were writing patriotic songs about family and this was exactly what you didn't write about. Everybody was wearing psychedelic clothing and polka dots and we looked like Amish people. We were completely against the grain and did not know for one second that what we were doing was going to fit in at all. All we knew what that it was true to our hearts and we had to depend on those instincts.

Musically, I thought, these guys are playing a million notes a second and it's beginning to bore me. Jamming became very unimportant in my life. So I just went the other way. I remember after we made that album, Eric Clapton, who I'd just met, told me, "This album has made me disband Cream, because I don't believe in what we're doing anymore. Hearing the record made me feel that what we were doing was no longer valid."

Obviously, Bob didn't need a weatherman (or Robbie Robertson) to know it was a good time to change direction, with *Nashville Skyline* becoming one of his biggest albums, thanks to some blushing praise in the rock press. "Bob Dylan's ninth album poses fewer mysteries and yet, paradoxically, offers greater rewards than any of his previous work," Paul Nelson started off his ecstatic if largely incomprehensible *Rolling Stone* review—which he would retract at a much later date. Shaking his head as he perused the review over his morning coffee, Dylan must have sighed deeply, wondering what else on earth he had to do to turn his rabid fans against him. It was surely then or a short time later that the light bulb called *Self Portrait* emerged as his last possible exit visa.

Elvis, too, got a pretty good career boost out of his sentimental journey to Memphis. Putting down tracks for six weeks, he nailed such gems as "In the Ghetto," released in May, which became his biggest hit since 1965, "Rubberneckin,'" "Don't Cry Daddy," "Kentucky Rain," "Hey Jude," and "Suspicious Minds," which became his first No. 1 since 1962, arriving on the charts November 1, the same week that Merle Haggard's hippie-bashing anthem "Okie from Muskogee" debuted at No. 91.

In July the King made another comeback, this one to Las Vegas—his first time there since a disastrous stint in '56, remembered primarily for his encounter with Freddy Bell and the Bellboys in the lounge of the Frontier hotel, joking their way through a version of Big Mama Thornton's recent R&B hit, "Hound Dog." That song was written by the young L.A. team of Jerry Leiber and Mike Stoller, who would soon move to the Brill Building in New York City and make a cottage industry out of songs for Elvis Presley's movie career, which also came to an end in 1969 with *The Trouble with Girls*, the film that gave us Elvis at his most annoyed in the Mac Davis–Billy Strange number, "Clean Up Your Own Backyard."

Country music in general experienced a comparable crossover surge in 1969, as befitting the swing to the political right, with sixteen songs hitting the year's Top 20 as opposed to six in 1968. Nothing was as big as '68's two No. 1s, "Honey" and "Harper Valley PTA," but Johnny Cash's "A Boy Named Sue," written by *Playboy* illustrator and humorist Shel Silverstein, wound up at No. 2. Glen Campbell had a big year with the songs of Jimmy Webb,

"Wichita Lineman," and the vaguely antiwar "Galveston." Dusty Springfield, the soulful chanteuse formerly of the folk group the Springfields, had a breakthrough session in Memphis late in '68 that resulted in the country-flavored pop/soul masterpiece *Dusty in Memphis*, produced by Jerry Wexler—from which came the indelible "Son of a Preacher Man," soon covered by Aretha Franklin, for whom it had originally been written. In addition to "Suspicious Minds" and "In the Ghetto" (recorded at the same American Studios as Dusty), Elvis scored earlier in the year with the inspirational "If I Can Dream," the closing song of the 1968 TV special that opened the gates to his 1969 resurgence. The great Joe South picked up a well-deserved Grammy for "Games People Play," Kenny Rogers brought well-deserved royalty checks to Mel Tillis ("Ruby, Don't Take Your Love to Town") and Mike Settle ("But You Know I Love You"), and Roy Clark played a whole lot of fiddle on "Yesterday When I Was Young." From Dylan's aforementioned *Nashville Skyline* came his first Top 10 hit since 1966 (and the last of his career), "Lay Lady Lay," a tune turned down by the Everly Brothers as too suggestive. But the true iconic moment of the year must be reserved for Tammy Wynette's Top 20 showing with "Stand by Your Man," a retrograde sentiment at least on a par with Merle Haggard's "Okie from Muskogee," taking on the nascent proto-feminist movement as much as Merle challenged the fading hippie ethos.

But even fading hippies got that country feeling in 1969, induced perhaps more by the demise of the social and sexual revolution than by any special chord changes proffered by the likes of Dylan or McGuinn. Such was the case with Tracy Nelson, leader of the San

Francisco psychedelic blues/rock outfit Mother Earth, as she surveyed the rubble of the Free Love movement:

> Here I was right in the middle of all these people who were always proselytizing. If you didn't embrace this euphoria and this totally useless, pointless lifestyle you were a schmuck and they let you know it. They were very condescending. In the meantime they were living like animals, begging for money on the street. The women were literally kept barefoot and pregnant and in the kitchen making herb tea for the guys. Either that, or they were this bizarre kind of whore image, just the total earthy sexual persona. They felt they had the world by the tail and the answer to everything. I felt they were full of shit.

Hence the sneaky, ironic title of Mother Earth's debut album, *Living with the Animals.* In 1969 they recorded some tracks for the follow-up, *Make a Joyful Noise*, in Nashville, with stellar sidemen like Pete Drake on pedal steel, Ben Keith on dobro, and Elvis veteran D. J. Fontana on drums. Tracy enjoyed the Nashville experience so much, and so dreaded a return to San Francisco, that she stayed on at the farmhouse the group had rented in Mt. Juliet, Tennessee, after the songs were completed. In short order she fell in love with the countryside and country music, driving home the point with an album called *Mother Earth Presents Tracy Nelson Country Music*, recorded in 1969, featuring another Elvis vet, Scotty Moore, playing on her version of "That's All Right." A quick scan of the track list also reveals at number four, yes, a cover of Tammy Wynette's "Stand by Your Man."

Even ascendant hippies, riding the coattails of the Acid Revolution, were not immune to country's calming charms. Country touches abound on the Jefferson Airplane's often-strident *Volunteers*, recorded throughout 1969, from the opening gospel-inflected bars of "On the Farm" to the closing crescendos of "We Can Be Together," based on a bluegrass lick. Jorma Kaukonen and Jack Cassady were already deep into their side project, the rootsy acoustic Hot Tuna. Country Joe redefined his nickname by going to Nashville to record an album of Woody Guthrie songs. Jerry Garcia already had a country rock outfit on the side by '69 in the New Riders of the Purple Sage. On their own 1970 release, *Workingman's Dead*, the Grateful Dead indulged their never-disguised penchant for American roots music with tunes like "Casey Jones," "Dire Wolf," and "Cumberland Gap." In the ashes of no less a cultural touchstone than Buffalo Springfield, the country rock band Poco arose, after much behind-the-scenes corporate bartering between Atlantic Records and Columbia Records. In the ashes of Moby Grape, after a stay in Bellevue, Skip Spence went to straight to Nashville to record *Oar*.

Weakening Los Angeles' claim as the Nashville of the West, the Nitty Gritty Dirt Band briefly broke up in '69, after they lost Jackson Browne to a solo career and a string of albums, including *Live* (at the Troubadour), failed to follow up on the success of their '67 hit "Buy for Me the Rain." But they'd be back the next year after covering Jerry Jeff Walker's "Mr. Bojangles," previously a turntable hit in New York City launched by the underground radio station WBAI.

Meanwhile, right about the time Dylan was packing his bags for Nashville, the Byrds, with Roger McGuinn now finally in total control and surrounded by three new members, were releasing *Dr. Byrds & Mr. Hyde*, featuring

McGuinn's collaboration with now ex-member Gram Parsons on "Drugstore Truck Driving Man." Right about this time, Gram himself was emerging from a house in California's San Fernando Valley with another former Byrd, Chris Hillman, carrying tunes like "Sin City," "Hot Burrito No. 1," and "Christine's Tune" for *The Gilded Palace of Sin*, the first album by their new group, the Flying Burrito Brothers, soon to become a landmark among musicians still flocking to the Coast to partake of the new decade's mellower, nonconfrontational vibe.

As the Band proceeded with all due haste toward their self-titled follow-up to *Music from Big Pink* (recorded at Sammy Davis Jr.'s house in L.A.), the folk singer Phil Ochs belatedly joined the roots brigade, if only in the spirit of self-parody, with the sadly prophetic *Rehearsals for Retirement*. Ochs never made it through the '70s, taking his life in mid-decade. Roger McGuinn, surveying the failure of *Dr. Byrds & Mr. Hyde*, found his own way to escape.

"I did a lot of cocaine," he said. "There were times I wouldn't pick up a guitar for weeks."

By the end of that decade, both he and Dylan found God. But McGuinn never recaptured the particular lightning he held in a bottle from 1965 through '69. "It was kind of a renaissance period," he said. "I guess since it faded out, the incentive to do stuff like that has gone with it. It's kind of like a spiritual thing, like an atmosphere that's created that inspires people to artistic creativity and achievement and when that breaks there's no motivation to do that for a while. And then it comes back. I'm waiting for it to come back."

CHAPTER THREE

The L.A. Trip

★ ★ ★ ★ ★ ★ ★ ★ ★ ★ ★ ★ ★

ALTHOUGH THE TRIBAL ROCK OPERA *Hair!* was a New York City phenomenon, opening Off Broadway in '67 and eventually landing on and wowing Broadway in '68, its biggest hit—1969's top song, the 5th Dimension's version of "Aquarius/Let the Sunshine In"—was pure California. Beyond the stage of the Biltmore Theater, only there was astrology taken so seriously. Even the governor's wife, Nancy, was into it. The latter-day hippies so central and celebrated in *Hair!* were a California creation as well. Although a close reading of the rock 'n' roll scriptures reveals the term showing up in a 1963 song by the Orlons—about a place in Philadelphia where "all the hippies meet" called "South Street"—these were a different breed of greasy-haired mini-hipsters. Aspiring gangster and pre-gangsta wannabes, pejoratively dubbed in jazz circles since the '40s, the South Street strain were the antithesis of what hippies would later symbolize: multicolored dope-smoking philosophical flakes who tore off their clothes and burst into song every five minutes or so.

This would not have bothered Galt MacDermot, the R&B and jazz fan who composed all the music for *Hair!* "I was not involved in the counterculture of the play at all," he said. "I'd never heard of hippies. I'd heard of beatniks, but I thought that was over. Personally, I think the music of that period was over too by 1969. The music from '64 to '68 was phenomenal. *Hair!* was written in 1967. Everybody remembers '68, nobody remembers '67. I was too busy doing *Hair!* to listen by that time."

Most of the crucial events in the life and death of the hippie happened while MacDermot was at the office in '68. "Martin Luther King was shot while we were in rehearsal," he said. "There were quite a lot of black kids in the show and they were upset—everybody was upset. And then Kennedy. But when you're doing a show, that's what you're doing. By that time the show was already written; we weren't trying to add anything new."

Hair! opened on Broadway on April 29, midway between those two defining tragedies. As he'd been doing since its inception, Galt played piano in the band. "The idea was to have a rock 'n' roll band. That was what they told me, a rock 'n' roll band onstage. They didn't want Broadway singers; they wanted pop and soulful singers. I was a big fan of R&B, so we were really on the same wavelength from the start."

The Canadian MacDermot met the New York City actors/lyricists James Rado and Gerome Ragni at the April-Blackwood offices of publisher Nat Shapiro, who was also coauthor of a book of jazz interviews, *Hear Me Talkin' to Ya,* with Nat Hentoff. MacDermot had originally looked him up hoping to talk about jazz. Rado and Ragni approached Nat much in the manner of the reigning rock stars of the day, armed with lyrics and little else. "Nat said, where's the music? And they said we'll write that when we get into rehearsals," Galt recounted. "Nat said, no, you have to have it written beforehand." That's when he recommended Galt.

"I read the lyrics and really liked them. They were nicely written; they knew exactly what they were trying to say. I myself had no knowledge of theater. I was just doing the music as best as I could. When we originally did the show with Joe Papp in '67, the kids were much younger and not as experienced; later the melodies were always adapted to the performers."

After doing the show for three months MacDermot retired from the grueling public spotlight. "I was thirty-eight years old by that time. I said, I can't keep doing this." What he did next was the score of the movie *Cotton Comes to Harlem*, followed by the musical *Isabel's a Jezebel*, which flopped, followed by *Dude*, Gerry Ragni's failed follow-up to *Hair!*

But the outsized success of *Hair!* in 1969 would be enough to cover a multitude of artistic choices, as it collected a total of four Top 10 songs, including "Aquarius/ Let the Sunshine In" in April, "Hair" by the Cowsills in May, "Good Morning Starshine" by Oliver in July, and "Easy to Be Hard" by Three Dog Night in September. "Where Do I Go/Be In/Hare Krishna" by the Happenings bombed in August, as did Carla Thomas's earlier version of "Where Do I Go" in August of '68. Nat Shapiro's personal friend Nina Simone hit the bottom 10 in January of '69 with "Ain't Got No/I Got Life" but fared a lot better with it in England.

Among the many people calling the publisher in 1968 for a lock of *Hair's* mystique was the L.A. producer

Bones Howe, who'd been working with the 5th Dimension since engineering "Up Up and Away" for their first album in 1967. He'd produced hits for the Turtles ("It Ain't Me Babe") and the Association ("Windy"), and had been a personal guest of Lou Adler at the Monterey Pop Festival, where he'd been perhaps the only West Coast guy in attendance to appreciate Laura Nyro's gruesome performance. Later he delivered Laura's "Stoned Soul Picnic" to the 5th Dimension, which became their biggest R&B hit. He was shuttling back and forth between his home in L.A. and the studio in New York working on the vocals for the *Stoned Soul Picnic* album when the group told him they wanted to do "Aquarius." He recalls,

> The thing that bothered me about it was that there'd been other releases of "Aquarius," and none had done anything, so I was concerned about what we would do that would be any different. I went to see the show and there's a place where they do "The Flesh Failures" and at the end of the song is just a three-bar repeated thing of "Let the sunshine in" where Ragni was swinging across the stage on a chandelier and there was all kinds of craziness going on. That really stuck with me and I came out of the theater saying, I wonder if I could stick that on the end of "Aquarius" and make that the ending.

That the Age of Aquarius announced to mainstream America by the song (harmony, understanding, sympathy, trust, mystic crystals, revelations) had already given way to Richard Nixon's vision of law and order troubled Bones Howe not in the least. "I was in my thirties then; I was never part of that culture," he said, echoing Galt

MacDermot. "But I made records they liked. I spent my life in the studio. Sometimes I went to the Trip and the Crescendo and all of those places on Sunset Strip because I worked with so many of those people. I was the engineer on 'Eve of Destruction' when the Mamas and Papas came to sing backup vocals. I was there the first night they were there and did their first three albums."

Neither did the fact that the 5th Dimension's year, which began by celebrating the Age of Aquarius, ended with their recording of Laura Nyro's desperate call to "Save the Country"—a song she'd written in '68 soon after Bobby Kennedy was assassinated and put on her thrilling 1969 album, *New York Tendaberry*. For Howe it was just another career milestone:

> Clive [Davis] wanted me to record "Save the Country" with Laura as a single and I was able to do it in L.A. using my rhythm section. The trouble was, I found out later that she wasn't going to include it in the album. She was excited about it when she did it. But when she stepped back and listened to it she said, wait a minute, that's not me. It was too produced, too pop for her. She wanted to do "Save the Country" just sitting at the piano. She said, "You make records that sock it to the people. I can't sock it to the people. I just don't do that."

A few years before she died in 1997 at the age of forty-nine, I had the opportunity to interview Laura Nyro over the phone. Shortly thereafter I met her backstage at a Newport Folk Festival. "People who follow their own convictions all have to go through certain obstacles," she said in an ethereal voice. "I don't think I'm different from other people who are searching . . . to be happy, really. And I'm kind of happy now."

She certainly wasn't happy in the 1960s.

> Right after Peter, Paul and Mary recorded a song I wrote called "And When I Die," the '60s started spinning me into a whirlwind, and outside of some recognition for my music, I felt like I was living inside a hurricane. My rhythm of life was more of a free-spirited one and then it changed. I felt like I was losing the rhythm of my youth, because so many things were happening at the same time. I needed to find some peace and experience other things in life without a bunch of people breathing down my neck.

Among those people was rock 'n' roll super agent, manager, and soon-to-be mogul David Geffen. Famously protective of his clients' interests and even more famously devoted to Laura, he spent the rest of the '60s religiously scouring the terrain for land mines in the wake of her epically strange performance at the 1967 Monterey Pop Festival.

One such potential land mine was perceived to be an up-and-coming soulful young thrush who'd made a name for herself in Frank Zappa's heady troupe the Mothers of Invention. Unfortunately, that name was Uncle Meat. After storming out of her Zappa-produced sessions in L.A. for her first album while debating that very topic, Sandy Hurvitz, soon to become Essra Mohawk, returned to Greenwich Village, where one day she received a phone call from Laura herself, offering aid and comfort as well as access to David Geffen's Rolodex.

"They got me a contract with Reprise and then sat on me for a year and a half," Essra told me, in explanation for why her excellent and now highly revered *Primordial Lovers* wasn't released until April 1970.

While at work on this album, Essra married her record producer, the prolific Frazier Mohawk (*née* Barry Friedman) and lived in a house in Laurel Canyon, L.A.'s famed bohemian enclave, not far from where her former mentor and tormentor, Zappa, had set up riotous shop in Tom Mix's log cabin, replete with zonked-out freaks and hippies; gorgeous, compliant groupies who would soon become recording artists (the GTOs); wall–to-wall music; and Tony the Wonder Horse buried under the bowling alley in the basement. After Zappa and family moved out, the new place to congregate, fornicate, harmonize, and get loaded belonged to Mama Cass, late of the disbanded Mamas and the Papas, none of whose three singles released in 1969 did any better than Top 30, despite the hopefully titled "It's Getting Better."

It was Cass Elliot who introduced David Crosby and Stephen Stills to Graham Nash in 1968, when the three were untangling their previous commitments to the Byrds, Buffalo Springfield, and the Hollies, respectively. Groups were like marriages in the California hills in that freewheeling era, always trembling on the brink of adultery and divorce. Graham Nash moved in with Joni Mitchell (and immortalized their Laurel Canyon digs in "Our House") while David Crosby was still in the picture. Crosby had already written "Triad" about a completely different potential threesome. The domestic arrangement certainly didn't harm Mitchell creatively, although Crosby, who'd produced her first album, did step aside in favor of Paul Rothschild (who'd worked with the Doors and the Paul Butterfield Blues Band) for 1969's *Clouds*, featuring "Chelsea Morning," "Both Sides Now," and "Songs to

Aging Children Come," which was prominently heard over the closing credits of the movie *Alice's Restaurant* in August. By Mitchell's third album, *Ladies of the Canyon*, written through 1969 and released in April of 1970, she was still thinking fondly of Nash, referencing him in the song "Willy," although he had by then moved up the coast to San Francisco with Crosby. The album was more famous for "Big Yellow Taxi" and "The Circle Game," Joni's answer to fellow Canadian Neil Young's oft-used B-side, "Sugar Mountain."

Rolling Stone's itinerant banjo-picking reporter Happy Traum, who caught up with Joni early in 1969, described the house with painterly precision: "There are antique handbags hung on a bathroom wall, a hand-carved hat rack at the door; there are castle-style doors and Tiffany stained glass windows, a grandfather clock and a Priestly piano. . . . Joni is in the kitchen using the only electric lights on in the house. She is making crust for a rhubarb pie." If it seemed a shame to intrude upon such an idyllic setting with messages from the shrill outside world, Joni was the first to agree. "It's good to be exposed to politics and what's going down here," she told Traum, "but too much of it can cripple me. And if I really let myself think about it, the violence, the sickness of it all, I think I'd flip out."

Further up the Laurel Canyon road, a normal, modest, balanced former Brooklyn girl and 1650 Broadway staffer named Carole King was undergoing a seismic love affair of her own, leaving her songwriting partner and husband Gerry Goffin behind for the romance of becoming a rock star at the age of twenty-seven in a band called the City with James Taylor's Flying Machine guitarist Danny Kortchmar and King's second husband, bassist Charley Larkey. "With [publishers] Don Kirshner and Al Nevins I was always singing on demos," Carole told me. "To me, what I was doing with the City and then on *Writer* was another collection of demos. Even *Tapestry* was still demos in my mind."

Nevertheless, Taylor managed to cajole King out of her tremendous stage fright for long enough to tour with him in his backing group, surrounded by Kortchmar and Larkey, as well as drummer Joel O'Brien and Ralph Schuckett on organ, with Abigale Haness providing additional vocals. This same backup group, minus King, would record albums for Atlantic in 1970 and 1971 under the name Jo Mama.

Meanwhile, Gerry Goffin was suffering from writer's block, brought about only in part by the breakup of his marriage with King. "First it was pop lyrics," he said, "then all of a sudden poetry got involved and there's a big difference between being a pop lyricist and being a poet—which blew my head a whole lot. Being a poet is much harder. I wanted to be a poet, but I wasn't able to, so I gave up."

Which is just like Gerry to discount the poetic gems he and Carole were coming up with in 1968 and 1969, among them a couple the Byrds made into classics, "Goin' Back" and "Wasn't Born to Follow," topped only by the era's ultimate dirge, "No Easy Way Down," which Dusty Springfield sang on *Dusty in Memphis*.

Essra Mohawk was too preoccupied making her album, she claimed, to be much involved in the extravagant Laurel Canyon lifestyle, the orgies seemingly taking place behind every unlocked door and naked window. Instead it was heroin, another of the era's tragic excesses, so abundant in the constant party life of the neighborhood, that eventually derailed her career. "I was off and on a junkie for four years," Essra reflected when I interviewed her at her parents' house in Philadelphia. Taking a longer view of herself and the era, she continued:

> We were all adolescents forever. We were allowed to remain children longer than any other generation in history. So we didn't know responsibility. We didn't know caution. We only knew freedom. What's wrong with all these people older than us? Don't they know how to be free? Then we found out, if we lived long enough, that there were things they were hip to that we'd better get hip to. So I personally feel grateful I didn't make it then because I know what I would have done with my success. I would probably be dead.

By mid-1969 the orgy scene had moved, en masse, to Shady Oak, former Monkee Peter Tork's legendary party pad, whose living room sported a 6' × 9' picture window overlooking the San Fernando valley and whose fifty-foot pool usually sported an uncounted array of nude girls swimming as if choreographed by Busby Berkeley in a film by Kenneth Anger. In this case, though, the film being played on the 10' × 12' wall of the movie room was probably *Easy Rider*, if not *Head*, the demented Monkee epic of 1968 whose every frame Tork has memorized.

Other than his admitted addictions to sex, alcohol, and lavishing money on total strangers, Tork was an early adapter of the Aquarian lifestyle celebrated in *Hair!* and lived to its fullest for a few years by some elite musicians and their wasted hangers-on in Laurel Canyon. Tork says,

> I brought some sugar cubes with me when I left New York in 1965. I'd heard they deteriorate at room

temperature, so I took two. Acid does not deteriorate at room temperature. I had a classic experience. I looked in the mirror and saw my mother. I dove out the front door in Long Beach at two in the morning hollering. I fell into a pumpkin patch and finally had a sense of there being a cosmic pattern. I didn't see God in the sense that Jesus came to me or I saw a man with a beard in a chair high in the sky, but I did have a sense of a driving, patterned force being the sum total of all the benevolent intelligences now or ever on the face of the earth.

As a result of this and comparable experiences, Tork was able to blissfully adapt to the ending of the Monkees in 1969 as well as to the notion that he'd way overpaid for his fabulous house that had once belonged to the skinny comedian Wally Cox. He and his pregnant girlfriend headed east with the idea of becoming organic farmers and rented out the house to a previous competitor for the role Tork landed in *The Monkees*, Stephen Stills, who used it as, among other things, a place for Crosby, Stills and Nash to rehearse for their upcoming first two live gigs, first in Chicago and then the next day at the Woodstock Festival.

When I interviewed him years later, he was living in a friend's room in New York City apart from his wife and child. Tork did not totally disavow his youthful vision:

I thought the new dawn had come. So did everybody else. We thought that everything was going to be roses from here on out. But you have to do that. Those of us who were young and innocent and open and thrilled to be part of the age were not able— couldn't have mustered the vision—to see that it was a passing thing that would eventually turn around. There were a lot of little societies where people knew if they flipped out their friends would take them to the beach and let them watch the ocean roll. Then you began to find what we call lame heads. At first head was a compliment. Anybody who smoked grass was all right with me. I saw it as a vindication of my way of life. Then I began to perceive that it was not a matter of everybody finally waking up to themselves, but rather of simply following the style of the day.

Among the most dangerous of the lame heads circulating through the California musician community was the ex-con Charles Manson, who arrived in San Francisco just in time for 1967's mythic Summer of Love, fresh from a stint in Terminal Island prison, where he'd unsuccessfully lobbied against his own release. Quickly amassing a harem befitting a Mormon sultan, he decided he might as well become a rock star and journeyed down the coast to Los Angeles. With a madman's energy and a threatening demeanor that made Mick Jagger seem like Don Knotts, Manson also managed to charm or intimidate a number of music business heavies, among them Neil Young, who brought Manson's tape to his label, Reprise; record producer Terry Melcher (the Byrds, Paul Revere and the Raiders), who visited Manson once to listen to him perform; and Beach Boy Dennis Wilson, who wound up putting his name on Manson's creepy "Cease to Exist," changing the first line to "Cease to resist" and the title to "Never Learn Not to Love," which appeared as the B-side of the late '68 single "Bluebirds over the Mountain" and then on the Beach Boys' *20/20* album, released in March of 1969.

Interviewed by Keith Altham for *Rave* two months after the album's release, Wilson spoke mystically of his new buddy and sometime houseguest from Hell. "Charles Manson, who is another friend of mine, says he is the devil. He sings, plays, and writes poetry and may be another artist for Brother Records." At the time Wilson was living in a furnished room in the apartment of his friend Gregg Jakobson, the man who introduced Manson to Terry Melcher, having essentially been forced out by Manson and his harem. This motley zombie-eyed bunch, according to David Toop in *Collusion*, "occupied Dennis's house, wrecked his uninsured Mercedes Benz, used his Rolls Royce for supermarket garbage runs and dumped him with the largest gonorrhea bill in history."

In keeping with the mellowness of the era, soon to be destroyed by Manson and his "family," Wilson saw his displacement in philosophical terms. "There's a piano in there and a bed and that's all I need," he told Keith Altham. "People fill their lives and their rooms with so much stuff that they don't need—watches, furniture, cars—and they pour their life into keeping and acquiring these things. I could live anywhere I want and my favorite place is that little room."

The re-titled and rewritten "Never Learn Not to Love," which also contains the Mansonesque sentiment, if not actual line "submission is a gift," was either a kind of barter payment or down payment on Wilson's current and future largesse, or the result of an outright sale. According to Toop, "Dennis is quite clear that Manson sold the song for money and wanted no credit." In any case, Charlie couldn't have been too pleased with a rewrite that watered down his demonic tone to the stuff of pop palaver.

According to writer David Dalton, who also lived for a while in Wilson's spacious cabin (but not at the same time as Manson), after Wilson received a silver bullet in the mail from Manson, he slept with a gun under his pillow. "This is Southern California, baby," Dalton wrote in *Mojo.* "Worlds collide. Surf boards and Sufis, kitsch and apocalypse, dune buggies and doomsday cults live right next door to each other."

The August '69 massacres eventually attributed to Manson and his devotees "[were] not Old Hollywood," experimental filmmaker Kenneth Anger wrote in his book *Hollywood Babylon.* "What befell the red house on Cielo Drive resembled the devastation caused by a jet plane crash: the Bad Ship Lollipop piloted by Uncle Sugar, Charlie Manson—programmed puppet, deus ex garbage can." For a time, though, before Manson was put away, the gruesome nature of the unsolved murders terrorized the previously insulated, immune community of loving freaks and hippies that made up the L.A. scene, laying waste to the already fading good vibrations.

"It was saturnalia time in Hollywood, a very grim feast of the meaningless," Robert Stone wrote in his memoir of the period, *Prime Green.*

> The youngsters disappeared from the boulevard as though the bad father of the feast had eaten them. For some time Manson went uncaught and the police put out false leads. Before his capture, the most extraordinary speculations as to motive and perpetrator went around. The most unsettling involved the number of people who suspected one another of having a hand in the murders.
>
> Then the Manson Family went down, and the theorizing and the interpretations exfoliated. Nixon

had done it. Why? To embarrass the antiwar movement. . . .

This was not the most far-fetched of the notions being bandied about in the aftermath of Manson's capture. The idea that he was being framed by the LAPD for his long hair and his stoner's jargon was a shared belief in certain demographic precincts, among them the offices of *Rolling Stone*. David Dalton pitched the story as the classic cops vs. the counterculture. Jann Wenner bought it.

Outlining his interpretation of four Beatles songs from the White Album—"Rocky Raccoon," "Blackbird," "Helter Skelter," and "Revolution No. 9"—during a prison interview, Manson didn't appear to author Dalton as any more delusional than your average tripped-out hippie. "The music is bringing on the revolution, the unorganized overthrow of the establishment," Manson told him, espousing a common enough 1969 formulation. "The Beatles know, in the sense that the subconscious knows."

Eventually, Dalton had to discard his presumption of Manson's innocence, but not of his dark, Aleister Crowleyesque powers. "Appearing with almost supernatural precision in the last months of the '60s, he seemed to call into question everything about the counterculture," he wrote in *Mojo*."His malign arrival synchronized so perfectly with America's nervous breakdown that it is hard not to bestow occult meanings."

A short time later, Dennis Wilson was telling David Toop in *Collusion*, "I'm the luckiest guy in the world, because I got off only losing my money."

Another frequent visitor to Dennis's cabin, Bobby BeauSoleil, was not as lucky. Like Manson, he came to

Los Angeles after spending the Summer of Love in San Francisco, a nineteen-year-old virtuoso in an outfit called the Orkustra that also featured David LaFlamme, later of It's a Beautiful Day fame, headlining an event called the Invisible Circus, a typical San Francisco night of music, poetry, theater, and free love presented by the Diggers and the Sexual Freedom League. This is where he was discovered by the visionary filmmaker Anger, whose *Scorpio Rising* from 1963 was one of the first films to successfully and viscerally utilize vintage rock songs in its score.

According to David Toop, Anger instantly saw Beau-Soleil as the lead actor for his newest work of modern voodoo, to be entitled *Lucifer Rising.* Soon they were living together at Anger's place and BeauSoleil had left the Orkustra to form a new group, called the Magick Powerhouse of Oz, especially for the purpose of scoring the eventual film. According to writer Michael Moynihan, the band "became a sort of underground legend despite the fact that no one ever heard a single note of their music." This bizarre but typically '60s oversight should have been rectified at the new Straight Theater on the night Anger was scheduled to present footage and music from *Lucifer Rising,* but instead it ended with Anger accusing BeauSoleil of stealing the 1600-foot print of the film.

From here on, the story gets hazy.

Anger left for London and BeauSoleil for Los Angeles, where he may have lived for a time with Love's Arthur Lee, whom he knew from his stint in one of Arthur's previous bands called the Grassroots (not *the* Grassroots). Eventually he fell in with Charles Manson and his docile followers at the Spahn Cowboy Ranch, a desolate communal dude ranch for wasted hippies, where, among the other things he did for money, he made a porno flick entitled *The Ramrodder*. According to some reports, it was then that he delivered Anger's film to Manson, who demanded $10,000 for its return.

Drug dealing was also a potentially lucrative sideline for many an indigent hippie, but when BeauSoleil procured some bad mescaline for the Straight Satans, a motorcycle gang that hung around the ranch soaking up the sun with Manson and clan, not being your typical weekend hippies in from the suburbs, they demanded their money back. Paying a visit to the negligent dealer, Gary Hinman, along with two of Manson's female acolytes, BeauSoleil had to call in the reinforcements, the reinforcements being Charles Manson, who slashed Hinman with a machete. Still lacking repayment, and with the bloody dealer threatening to call the authorities, BeauSoleil finished the job himself, on the night of July 27. He was arrested for the murder on August 6 and eventually sentenced to life in prison.

Some in Manson's circle still claim the atrocities committed in Benedict Canyon on August 9 were a cover-up designed to protect BeauSoleil.

In the meantime, Anger returned from London to present his newest film, *The Invocation of My Demon Brother*, scored by Mick Jagger and containing footage of BeauSoleil, as well as the Rolling Stones in performance. According to Deborah Allison, writing on the Senses of Cinema Web site, when the film was initially shot, "Anger's conception of Lucifer was still closely tied to the figure and force of Mars. The invocation is a battle cry in a period of transition between an old order and a new."

A big fan of Jimmy Page's (and Ozzy Osbourne's) favorite cult hero, Aleister Crowley, Anger once said, "I have one product that I'm selling, the twentieth century's most misunderstood genius, Aleister Crowley." In an interview with *Spider Magazine*, referenced by Deborah Allison in her essay on the Senses of Cinema Web site, Anger also revealed a debt to astrology linking him to his younger brothers and sisters of the counterculture: "The age that ended in 1962 was the Piscean Age . . . which was the age of Jesus Christ," he commented. "Where the Piscean Age was ruled by Neptune, the planet of mysticism, the Aquarian Age is ruled by Uranus, the most erratic planet of all   it's the sign of the unexpected, revolution. . . ."

Still obsessed with *Lucifer Rising*, the original theft of which BeauSoleil adamantly denied, Anger next went to Jimmy Page for the soundtrack. But when Page bailed after several songs, BeauSoleil reached out from Tracy Prison to send Anger a demo of his work with the Freedom Orchestra, eventually resulting in the soundtrack that accompanied the film's showing at the Whitney Museum in New York in 1980.

Exactly when the missing tapes finally surfaced is unclear. According to Michael Moynihan's liner notes on the Anthology Recordings Web site, BeauSoleil gave the tapes to David LaFlamme in 1967. LaFlamme promptly forgot about them for thirty years. When the items resurfaced, among them was *Lucifer Rising*. But Moynihan was much more interested in the music, which was "the only audio document ever made by the Magick Powerhouse of Oz. It was a live room recording that had been done in the Straight Theater, engineered by Brent Dangerfield. BeauSoleil was as surprised as anyone to learn of its existence." In the end, "Kenneth Anger and Bobby BeauSoleil managed to craft a peerless work of dark psychedelia, a volcanic expression of triumphant spiritual freedom."

A somewhat more down-to-earth but equally revealing portrait of a neighborhood now full in its decline was provided to me by the former lead singer of the Boston band Ultimate Spinach, Ted Myers, who arrived in the Land of Pipe Dreams just about this time, hoping to get a new lease on musical life after the hugely hyped "Boss Town Sound" went bust.

> I had no intention of going to L.A. It was San Francisco and Berkeley I was interested in. I landed in Berkeley and checked into the Berkeley Inn on Telegraph Avenue. That's where I ran into an aspiring writer named Don, who had a master's in psychology. He was an escapee from the University of Chicago postgraduate program. Two months shy of his doctorate he decided to drop out to pursue his real love, writing song lyrics, poetry, and children's books.
>
> The first thing that happened was the People's Park riots, which broke out shortly after my arrival and were taking place right outside my window. Tear gas and bullets flying, cops shooting at kids, kids throwing rocks and bottles, newsmen shooting film out my window . . . this was the shit! After a week in California I decided I wasn't going back to Boston. But Don and I soon realized if we were going to have a go at the music business we would have to move to L.A. Don had some friends from U of C who had a house in Laurel Canyon. Right away I knew if I had to live in L.A., this was where I wanted to be. To me, coming from East Coast big cities, the quaint, narrow, winding streets of the Canyon looked like something out of Disneyland. And there were lots of beautiful young girls walking and hitchhiking all

over that fabled oasis of hipness and free love right in the middle of crass L.A.

We saw an ad for a groovy house on Kirkwood Drive whose owner was a glamorous if over-the-hill French actress named Françoise. At $175 a month it was a bit pricey, but we managed to scrape up the rent. Soon afterward we were joined by another friend of Don's from Chicago, a songwriter named Tommy. Tommy crashed in the living room, I got the one bedroom, and Don, recluse that he was, was quite happy with the little room out behind the garage.

But by the summer strange, dark events were beginning to occur: the Harry Houdini house on Laurel Canyon Boulevard burned down. I'll never forget coming around the bend and seeing the flames reaching to the sky. Then came the Manson family murders. We took these portents of doom as signs the times ahead might not be as rosy as the past few years.

Françoise took a shine to us and would bring us various household items, seeing that we had barely a stick of furniture. One day she brought us three of the strangest looking coffee mugs I have ever seen. Each mug had a face . . . and these faces looked truly malevolent. What with all the voodoo in the air, we took it into our heads that the mugs were evil spirits, and our landlady was a witch. She had planted these things on us to watch us—maybe to put a hex on us. I constructed a little home for them out of a shoebox. I cut a little window for each face. Then I set them on a pedestal inside a clothing closet. You had to peel back the clothes, but once you did, there they were, peering out at you.

Almost immediately, bad things started to happen. Darlene, a seventeen-year-old unwed mother we had picked up hitchhiking, who made porno movies for a living, brought a guy over who was dying of a heroin overdose. We walked him around the living room for hours, pouring coffee down his throat to keep him awake. Strangely, it worked; he didn't die. A few days later, he came back to thank us for saving his life. And a few days after that, he came back, broke into our house, and stole my guitar.

Now, I was in no position to buy a new guitar. Besides, that was a 1950s Gibson J-50; you don't just stumble across one of those every day. As I was a singer/songwriter and professional musician by trade, this guy had ripped off my livelihood. I had no choice: I had to go after him and get my guitar back. Darlene told us that his junkie friends hung out in a sort of basement underneath the Canyon Country Store. Armed only with a hunting knife and insane determination, me and my two buddies invaded their lair. Fortunately, his friends turned out to be a bunch of wimps and spilled the beans almost immediately. They were pretty sure their pal was going to try to hock my ax in a certain pawnshop on Western Ave.

Bright and early the next morning, still packing our collective blade, we staked out the pawnshop. We sat there for hours, waiting for him to show up, but nothing happened. By noon we got tired of waiting, and decided to ask the owners if they had seen him. As we entered, we were instantly in the sights of two very large guns. Both proprietors had us in their crosshairs. Seeing us approach from across the street, I guess they thought we meant to hold them up. Realizing this, I did some fast talking, after which they lowered the firearms, turned, and produced my guitar from behind the counter. The bastard had beaten us there! It cost me forty dollars to get it back.

Clearly, it was time to do something about the mugs, but what? We took them to a guy someone had recommended as a bona fide psychic and warlock. He confirmed that they were indeed the source of our bad luck, but he cautioned us not to simply destroy them. They had to be disposed of in a very specific manner. We had to bury them, following a ritual, complete with chanting incantations that he laid out to us. It had to take place at dawn. The designated morning was fittingly misty and gray. We dug a hole of the prescribed dimensions in our backyard. Next, the shoebox was brought out. The windows had been taped up. Kabalistic symbols had been inscribed in Magic Marker on the outside of the box-cum-coffin. Then, amidst the solemn chants that had been written out for us, we lowered the three malevolent gnomes into the sod, and quickly covered them over.

I wish I could say that was the end of my bad luck in 1969, but weird occurrences continued to plague us, right into the '70s. Perhaps the mugs reached out from their shallow grave to keep us under their collective whammy. Or perhaps a series of bad decisions, fueled by poverty and substandard drugs, conspired to bring us down. One thing was for sure: the Age of Aquarius had certainly ended—just as it was dawning.

CHAPTER FOUR

If You're Leaving San Francisco

★ ★ ★ ★ ★ ★ ★ ★ ★ ★ ★ ★ ★

"I'LL TELL YOU WHAT I SAW WHEN I went to San Francisco," Frank Zappa told me in 1974:

> Whereas in Los Angeles you had people freaking out; that is, making their own clothes, dressing however they wanted to dress, wearing their hair out, being as weird as they wanted to be in public and everybody going in separate directions—in San Francisco I found everybody dressed up in 1890s garb. It was like an extension of high school where one shoe is the 'in' shoe. It was in the same sort of vein, but it was the costume of the 1890s. In San Francisco they had a "more rustic than thou" approach. It was cute, but it wasn't as evolved as what was going on in L.A.

Limited to Zappa's musical operation, and assuming he wasn't just putting me on, I'd have to agree. The San Francisco groups were basically updating American roots music with the aid of Timothy Leary's proselytizing, Owsley Stanley's chemicals, the unprecedented largesse of city officials, the biweekly pep talks in *Rolling Stone*, the major label establishment windfalls, and promoter Bill Graham's relentless work ethic. As epitomized by his labels Straight and Bizarre, which lurched from the sublime to the ridiculous, as his own Mothers of Invention were apt to do in any given performance, Zappa backed up his words with action, if not necessarily ready-for-prime-time music with commercial potential.

Having pronounced 1969's after-school experiment in humiliation *Philosophy of the World* by the Shaggs from New Hampshire one of the greatest albums ever released, Zappa had included on his own 1968–69 roster ultimate weirdness from the sad likes of Wild Man Fischer (*The Wild Man Fischer Story*), the cross-dressing bar band Alice Cooper (*Pretties for You*), the creative doodling of his in-house groupies, Girls Together Outrageously, a.k.a. GTO (*Permanent Damage*)—who were, supposedly, very good dancers—and the under-produced Uncle Meat album by Sandy Hurvitz, the future Essra Mohawk, entitled *Sandy's Album Is Here at Last*. But Zappa also greenlighted *Trout Mask Replica* by Captain Beefheart, generally regarded as one of the era's landmark masterpieces, as well as several albums by the tragically gifted Tim Buckley, who died of an overdose in 1975 (*Blue Afternoon* and much of *Lorca* and *Starsailor* were all recorded during the same four-week period in 1969).

Commenting on the vocalizing on Buckley's *Starsailor*, one reviewer said, "It sounds as if his liver is being torn out." Some critics still find the Beefheart album inscrutable and un-listenable. But others realize how magically evocative its creative landscape was. "What the critics failed to see was that this was a band with a vision," Lester Bangs wrote in a review in *Rolling Stone*, "that their music, difficult, rough and raucous as it is, proceeded from an original consciousness."

"I'm a great poet," Beefheart, a.k.a. Don Van Vliet, told writer Miles in *Zig Zag* in 1969, proving it time and again throughout the album he'd just finished. "Better than those cats like Ginsberg, because I let it flow. I can't stop it. I've got books and books of stuff. I'm a great horn player—I've already exhausted the instrument. I've done everything that can be done with it. Really, I need a whole new art form."

Nevertheless, considering his tongue-in-cheek penchant for artistic subterfuge, one has to wonder if even Zappa, like many another '60s visionary, knew what he had when these unique artists handed in their finished products.

With all due respect, then, a few years later I consulted Jefferson Airplane co-founder Marty Balin for his impressions of San Francisco in its rustic heyday. He said,

> It was a great feeling at first. I remember talking to a guy at *Time* magazine when it was just hitting and Haight Street was like a tourist attraction and people were dressed in colorful costumes like you see at the Renaissance Fair. I said it's great you're publicizing this and telling people about all this spirit and everything that exists here. He looked at me and said, "Fastest way to kill it." He sure was right.

Grateful Dead lyricist Robert Hunter shared this assessment, if a bit more poetically. "As soon as the TV cameras screwed down on it the vampire began to drink and only those with self-contained blood units survived intact," he commented. "It was ugly to watch the efficiency with which that scene was dismantled. The Abyssinians came down like wolves upon the fold. There was no bone worth picking not stripped clean and the marrow sucked."

Marked by the folk rock exploits of the We Five, the tense dynamics of Marty Balin and Grace Slick in the Jefferson Airplane, the unrestrained pyrotechnics of Janis Joplin in Big Brother and the Holding Company, the melodic political satire of Country Joe and the Fish, and the easy, flowing acid vibes of the Grateful Dead, San Francisco didn't need John Phillips's blatant hippie travelogue "San Francisco (Be Sure to Wear Flowers in Your Hair)," as sung by Phillips's onetime partner in the Journeymen, Scott McKenzie, to claim the mantle of hip supremacy from Los Angeles in 1967, the success of that year's Monterey Pop Festival notwithstanding. With its pioneering ethos of the Gold Rush days, its beatnik ambience enshrined at City Lights, the rampant drug experimentation taking place among the literati at Stanford (in the process of being memorialized for all time by Tom Wolfe in *The Electric Kool-Aid Acid Test*), the surgically enhanced Carole Doda dancing topless at the Condor in North Beach, and the preponderance of glassy-eyed homegrown bands, San Francisco was the easiest of marks for the invading record executives and vice versa.

"When I first went to L.A. to negotiate a contract I walked into an office and the guy asked me what I wanted, and I said we want $50,000," Marty Balin said. "He said, 'Okay, what else do you want?' Done. I had said it jokingly and he said okay. I didn't know what else to say."

A short time later, the next big buzz on the street was for Moby Grape. Witnessing their rehearsals, Sam Andrews, Janis Joplin's guitarist in Big Brother and the Holding Company, declared they were "better than the Beatles." Naturally, the suits descended, checkbooks open wide. Columbia Records eventually won the rights, celebrating with an extravagant shindig for the press at the Avalon Ballroom at which 10,000 purple orchids floated down from the ceiling. "There were 700 bottles of wine and no corkscrew," according to David Fricke's liner notes to their boxed set. Stumped as to which of the five best tunes on the album to pick as the band's first single, the label went for the unprecedented strategy of releasing them all at once: "Hey Grandma," "Omaha," "8:05," "Fall on You," and "Sitting by the Window" all stiffed.

By 1969, the group had fractured, with the increasingly drug-addled drummer Skip Spence doing a stint in Bellevue. Upon his release, like many a wounded San Francisco head, he went to Nashville to record a solo album, *Oar*, which was described like so by Greil Marcus in *Rolling Stone*: "Sometimes his playing is about as good as Wild Man Fischer and sometimes he's perfectly brilliant. 'War in Peace' is pure San Francisco in its sound, but San Francisco long after the scene and Spence himself have passed from it, a slow aging glimpse of what the music was all about." Neither of the Grape's two 1969 releases, *Moby Grape '69* and *Truly Fine Citizen*, cracked the upper hundred of the album chart.

According to Lillian Roxon's *Rock Encyclopedia*, the Steve Miller Band, recently relocated to San Francisco from Chicago, hauled in a bigger take than anyone. "He was besieged with offers to record from a variety of labels.

After holding out for months he eventually succumbed to one of the biggest royalty advances in the history of rock—$50,000 plus a $10,000 bonus, plus a five-year contract and an offer to record in any part of the world the band chose."

Although Miller released three respectably selling albums between November '68 and December '69, he was hardly recouped, producing but one chart single, "Living in the USA," which failed to break out of the bottom 10.

Former blues singer Tracy Nelson had known Steve back in Chicago, where Miller used to sit in with the masters of the Southside like Muddy Waters, Buddy Guy, Otis Rush, and Howling Wolf. "They thought he was amusing," she told me. "When he came to San Francisco and put together a group right away, that got me kind of excited. He made a statement to me at one point that this is the happening music; this psychedelic stuff is really what's grabbing people. He really did recognize the trend as something that was going to have significance, whereas I had written it off."

With Miller's help, Tracy formed Mother Earth and got signed to Mercury Records. "I went from earning $30 a week to $65,000 a year," she said. "And of course we gave it all away. We were so democratic and everybody got a cut. We lived high off the hog on the road. The money was just there and it was always going to be there. It made me think I could jerk off and do whatever the hell I wanted to and get away with it."

Mother Earth did not have someone like Bill Graham guiding them. Grace Slick told me,

Bill's instinct was always "you better keep at it, you better get it while it's hot." We always thought he was nuts, going crazy trying to get the bucks, not because he was totally money-oriented but just because Bill's instinct was to make sure of everything, watch everything, control everything, it could all fall apart at any second. We didn't have that attitude. We had a looser attitude. I was never determined to be a great singer; basically I was determined to be a great fuck-off.

This was a common attitude among the newly ordained San Francisco rock elite that Tracy Nelson, for one, found debilitating:

I was contending with a lot of hassles dealing with the musicians, trying to keep them from each other's throats, trying to keep everybody from getting drunk all the time on gigs, dealing with promoters who treated me like garbage. Also, I had no recognition at the time of the kind of conflict that goes on when you work with male musicians. They would get defensive and snotty and I didn't understand why they would come down on me so hard for doing what I thought had to be done.

By the end of 1969 Tracy was in living in Nashville, having fallen in love with the place when she stayed on to make a country album after the band finished recording *Make a Joyful Noise*.

In a similar fashion, Janis Joplin had to grow up in a hurry after she left Big Brother and the Holding Company at the end of '68, just two months after *Cheap Thrills* hit it big, in a move that drew the wrath of her San Francisco audience. But, as Janis told David Dalton in *Piece of My Heart: The Life, Times and Legend of Janis Joplin*, it was way past time for a change.

What drove me crazy was that I couldn't dredge up any sincerity in the music anymore. Maybe it was that everybody got too lazy, which I think is definitely true. I kept singing the same old songs every night. Finally I said to myself, listen, man, you consider yourself a singer, but you're nothing but an actor. I wasn't doing anything but standing still. So I quit. Lots of people think it was a mistake and it well may have been a mistake. Those guys in Big Brother certainly loved me more than anybody else ever will. And that showed on the stage. But we were enacting it up there, man, we weren't lovin' each other. We knew when the lights went on it was a show.

With Michael Bloomfield and Nick Gravenities of the Paul Butterfield Blues Band doing the recruiting, the Kozmic Blues Band took shape, allowing Janis to spend much of 1969 blessedly out of town, starting small in Rindge, New Hampshire, before moving on to Boston and New York City, returning home in March to generally miserable reviews. Europe in the spring was a tonic for her and the band, enabling them to enter Hollywood Studios on a high. The ensuing *I Got Dem Ol' Kozmic Blues Again Mama!* was a smash, with the title cut Janis's most heartfelt and revealing composition since "Down on Me."

The Grateful Dead, meanwhile, threw all their money back into the band and lived on workman's wages, especially after drummer Mickey Hart's father, Lenny, a former owner of a drum store then touring as an evangelist, replaced Bill Graham as their manager in 1969 and systematically ripped them off for a year before absconding to the beaches of Mexico with his bank teller girlfriend. "How naïve are these guys?" Phil Lesh wrote in his memoir, *Searching for the Sound: My Life with the Grateful Dead.*"The truth is we didn't really care about any of those details, partly out of laziness and partly because deep down we all feared that delving too deeply into the business end might compromise the music somehow."

At that point, their main concern as a band was the ongoing issue of how to translate their epic, mesmerizing live performances within the confines of the recording studio. Jerry summed it up in his typically metaphorical fashion. "What I do is sort of a Zen thing," he explained. "It's Zen and the Art of Notesmanship. It really has to do with the moment and the live situation. Recording is like building a ship in a bottle. Playing live is like being in a rowboat in a storm. I find I'm much less emotionally suited to building ships in bottles."

The Dead solved their problems by recording two albums in 1969, *Aoxomoxoa* (an unpronounceable palindrome, the meaning of which has been parsed to death by egghead Deadheads on several continents) and *Live/Dead*, released at the end of the year but recorded the previous winter and spring at the Avalon Ballroom and the Fillmore. Of the many shows they played at the Fillmore in 1969, one spring gig that probably didn't make the record was nonetheless of major significance in that it provided Phil Lesh the opportunity to capture in his book about as eloquent a description of the LSD experience from a musician's perspective as has ever been published.

Somehow we managed to start playing. It was as if the music was being sung by gigantic dragons on the timescale of plate tectonics; each note seemed to take days to develop, every overtone sang its own song, each drumbeat generated a new heaven and a new earth. We were seeing and singing the quantum collapse of probability into actuality—it was frightening and exhilarating at the same time. At one point, I looked over at Jerry and saw a bridge of light like a rainbow of a thousand colors streaming between us; and flowing back and forth across that bridge: three-dimensional musical notes—some swirling like the planet Jupiter rotating at 100 times normal speed, some like fuzzy little tennis balls with dozens of legs and feet (each wearing a different sock), some striped like zebras, some like pool balls, some even rectangular or hexagonal, all brilliantly colored and evolving as they flowed, not only the notes that were being played, but all the possible notes that could have been played.

Not long thereafter, the Dead were called into service in their role as community fund-raisers to play a benefit at Winterland for the 400 people who had been busted at People's Park in Berkeley a few days before. It was a stellar lineup, including the Airplane, Santana, and Bill Graham's recent San Francisco Records signing, Aum. As reported by Michael Lydon in his book *Rock Folk*, it was not their best performance.

"Maybe they were a bit tired of being taken for granted as sure fire deliverers of good vibes, drained by the constant expectations," he wrote. "Or it might have been cynical: a benefit for those Berkeley dudes who finally learned what a park is but are still hung up on confrontation and cops and bricks and spokesmen giving TV interviews and all that bullshit. The Dead were glad to do it, but it was one more benefit to bail out the politicos."

The siege of Berkeley by the California Highway Patrol, the Alameda County Sheriff's office, and the National Guard over the use of a piece of land owned by the University of California, destined to become a ball field and a parking lot, but at that moment being co-opted by the community of flower-bearing hippies and rally-crying Yippies, was emblematic of the new turn in the struggles between the counterculture and the authorities trumpeted by Nixon's "law and order" administration and Governor Ronald Reagan's simmering (and by and large accurate) conviction that the Berkeley campus had long been "a haven for Communist sympathizers, protesters, and sex deviates."

The first full-blown riot, on May 15, with chanting residents and students facing the buckshot and tear gas of the police in the attempt to "take back the park" that Reagan had ordered fenced in and stripped of flowers, resulted in the death of a student, the blinding of an innocent bystander, and at least 128 injuries. A week later, at a Sproul Plaza memorial for the victims, the National Guard attacked again, arresting hundreds, tear-gassing thousands. A near state of martial law prevailed for several more weeks in what was truly the flower children's last hurrah, as the stakes were raised once again on the limits of freedom in the land of the free. Said San Francisco resident Jon Levit, a former hippie who later became a cop himself, and then a novelist,

> I had friends involved in the People's Park fiasco. One of my roommates, a white guy with a huge Afro, and his girlfriend borrowed a baby and posed for a PR picture wearing bandoliers and holding weapons. To them, it was more theater than anything else. I remember friends of theirs talking about how they'd had enough and how they were going to teach

'those pigs' a lesson, by violent means if necessary. I mentioned in a friendly manner that they were crazy if they thought they could fight the police. Cops, they said, oh, no, we're talking about those pigs in (the Revolutionary Youth Movement).

Country Joe and the Fish guitarist Barry Melton told me,

I remember being in those People's Park demonstrations. We were walking down University Avenue and some part of the group we were walking with broke off and ran to the car dealership across the street and started smashing windshields, which inevitably brought the riot squad down the street in the opposite direction with tear gas and billy clubs drawn and set the stage for a violent confrontation. I'd say the majority of the people I was marching with weren't looking for any kind of violent confrontation, but it only takes ten dedicated agitators in a crowd of 2000 to turn things violent.

Now, depending on your view, that could have been CIA provocateurs or quite frankly ultraleft fringe groups. There are a lot of things that happened during that period that in retrospect were insidious but at the time maybe we weren't paranoid enough to understand their implications. For instance, I don't associate being busted necessarily with a federal agenda. But the thing that really was part of the federal agenda is that when Nixon finally did get in, we were audited by the IRS, and the guy kept coming back and back and back and there was really nothing there. When our bookkeeper turned to him and said, "Why are you doing this? We've been through this twice," basically he said, "I have my orders."

Deep into recording their *Volunteers* album at Wally Heider's state-of-the-art studio in San Francisco at the time, the Jefferson Airplane had obviously taken in the mood of the street, the mood of the people, and the mood of the government, as evidenced by the incendiary "We Can Be Together," with its up-against-the-wall mentality. Perhaps the only people who didn't see the Airplane as spear-carriers in the youth revolution after that were the members of the band themselves. "If people saw us as political, then that's their misconception," Paul Kantner told writer Jeff Tamarkin for the album's liner notes. But then he added, most revealingly, "We didn't see a need to correct that, because there was a certain value in it." Taking refuge in the convenient rationalization that he was merely reporting the news, not commenting on it, Kantner continued, "Rather than a call to arms, it was a call to attention to what's going on around you and maybe you have to foment in your own mind something to do about it that's coherent, rather than responding in the old tried and true ways. That's reconstruction."

By the time the album came out in November, the Airplane were one of the few groups in the area still espousing the medicinal benefits of togetherness; even the Diggers had taken to the hills. By then the mantle of togetherness had moved east, where, according to *Newsweek*, the event that "may well rank as one of the most politically and sociologically significant of the age," the Woodstock Festival, had taken place. Against all odds it was "the moment when the special culture of the U.S. youth of the '60s openly displayed its strength, appeal and power."

Having long since dubbed rock "the anthem of revolution, one long symphony of protest . . . the proclamation of a new set of values," in most other important ways Jann Wenner, San Francisco's version of *Citizen Kane's* Charles Foster Kane, diverged radically from the hippie culture showcased so lovingly at Woodstock. As reported by Sam Anson in *Gone Crazy and Back Again: The Rise and Fall of the Rolling Stone Generation,*

> There were no psychedelic graphics to be found in *Rolling Stone's* pages, no items from the Underground Press Service, no ads for sexual emporiums, all of which sustained what Wenner called the hippie press. His own magazine, he insisted from the beginning, had to be distributed legit, like *Time,* not hawked on street corners as the hippie papers were. Hippies did not work, did not want money, and Wenner believed devoutly in both.

Fittingly, as far back as its 1967 beginnings, Wenner staffed his paper mostly with serious-minded professionals: cofounder Ralph Gleason wrote for the *San Francisco Chronicle;* early editor John Burks had been a reporter for the *Oakland Tribune;* staffer Michael Lydon wrote for *Newsweek;* the first record review editor was a Cambridge intellectual, Jon Landau; and Greil Marcus taught American studies at Wenner's alma mater, Berkeley. A bit loopier than the others, Charles Perry was future LSD magnate Owsley Stanley's roommate; moreover, he first turned Stanley on to the mythic drug that made so many things seem possible. Another early arrival, Ben Fong-Torres, came from the phone company, where he'd served as editor of its corporate magazine.

"I had been an editor, a columnist, and a reporter for the paper at San Francisco State, so I had been writing for three years," Fong-Torres told me. "The phone company allowed me to get involved with writing feature stories for a magazine. I learned how to edit. I learned color printing. I learned design, traveled, and it paid a decent salary. We did a special issue on the history of San Francisco, and I sat with S. I. Hayakawa at San Francisco State and wrote about what was going on there."

As opposed to the more infamous Berkeley, San Francisco State, being a commuter college, slid under the radar for much of the time Ben Fong-Torres was in attendance. Yet, he noted,

> We were one of the first colleges on the West Coast to organize a civil rights contingent to go to Montgomery to march in support of the people there. We supported Cesar Chavez and the farm workers. We hosted speakers who were proposing the legalization of marijuana, staged a number of town halls presenting information about the war in Vietnam, and had a Sexual Freedom League as an official on-campus organization. Being in San Francisco, that was part and parcel of the culture.

As, of course, was rock music. Fong-Torres continued,

> Big Brother and the Holding Company, when they first got their singer from Texas to join them, came to San Francisco State and did their first rehearsals on campus. That was partly because the Albin Brothers were students and there were always folk festivals on campus, which were of course hyphenated with rock, blues, and gospel. One day there was a free noon concert in front of the men's gym that featured a band called Great Society, so Grace Slick made one of her first public appearances at San Francisco State. The Airplane was hired by San Francisco State

to play at a kind of alternative Homecoming Ball in 1966. I have a classic Fillmore-style poster of that concert. Dan Hicks was a student there and he joined the Charlatans. There are lots of connections between the campus and what was going on around town.

Aside from the bands and their attendant trips festivals, nothing going on around town was bigger than *Rolling Stone*. "My roommates and I had read several issues of the paper when it first came out," Ben said. "We would pass it around like a joint. I didn't have any idea of how big it might get, but it covered the scene from New York to London, and it was based in San Francisco, so there was an obvious bias toward the local bands. The first page of the first issue had a filler item about a local radio station KFRC that would never have made the front page of *Billboard*."

After successfully pitching an item for the Flashes column about Chicago's Siegel-Schwall Blues Band, who were in town for a free concert promoting a Dick Clark–produced hippie movie, *Psych Out*, starring Jack Nicholson, Dean Stockwell, and Susan Strasberg, he soon latched onto a beat of his own, when the pioneering underground FM station KMPX went out on strike.

It was the first hippie labor strike. Longhairs versus the owner, who wouldn't pay the disc jockeys more than minimum wage even though they were bringing in tons of new advertising and making the station more money than ever. Previously it had been a barter station. Now it was a real radio station and they were not rewarding their staff, so they walked out. It became a massive public strike, with bands showing up on the street to support them. I wound up writing most of the reports because their main reporter got fired some-where along the way. During that process I got to know Jann and whoever else was around.

Profiles of Gordon Lightfoot and Joni Mitchell fol-lowed. "At that point Jann trusted me enough to do a large piece on the third wave of the San Francisco sound. It was a very long report on what was going on in the city in terms of record labels glomming onto acts, building studios, and sending producers to San Francisco to further take ad-vantage of what was happening here."

In March of 1969, he was offered a staff position.

I was making about seven to eight hundred dollars a month at the phone company, which was pretty good money in 1969. Jann said, "I can give you five hun-dred." It was horrible money, but I said okay. Even when I joined, the paper was popular enough around certain circles, that I knew it was the right move. Like any rock 'n' roll phenomenon, once people realized that there was something going on, just like at the Fillmore and the Avalon, or as it was at the creation of free-form radio, they wanted to make it known that they were supportive of it. They would show up at the ball-rooms and buy the albums. It was that sense of com-munity that made it so we knew right away there was tremendous appreciation of *Rolling Stone.*

Through 1969, that appreciation, as with all under-ground movements, was largely word of mouth, just as the magazine's survival in those days was largely hand to mouth. Said Ben, "From May 1969 to April 1970 we worked out of a rent-free loft atop a printing plant on Bran-nan Street, next door to a slaughterhouse, with a few desks we bought from Goodwill Industries, so we were really funky, although in a classy way. Jann and his wife Jane always had a sense of décor and decorum about them. There still was a look about the place."

In 1970, the larger world began to catch on when the *Columbia Journalism Review* did a profile and a design magazine took notice of some of the groovy things *Rolling Stone* was doing, such as its unusual size and unorthodox bimonthly publication schedule.

> These were things that happened because Jann didn't know better. He just said, "I'm too anxious to do a monthly thing, let's come out every two weeks." He said, "What does this press do? We do tabloids, we do quarter fold. Oh, okay, we'll do that then, instead of just a regular magazine, we'll fold it over twice like some British tabloid." I think it was just that Jann didn't have much choice in the matter.
>
> The mainstream press was not doing anything we were interested in. Jann was always looking at British papers like *Melody Maker*. We also kept an eye on *Crawdaddy!* and *Creem*. But we made an effort not to cover the same stuff or follow their stories. Jann definitely tried to avoid being pinned with the underground press image.

As much as *Rolling Stone* struggled to go mainstream, by 1969 the San Francisco scene was desperately trying to return to its underground roots. The Airplane split with their manager, Bill Graham, the only man in town whose megalomania rivaled Wenner's. Jorma Kaukonen and Jack Cassady got more and more into their acoustic side project, Hot Tuna. Another of Graham's former clients, the Grateful Dead, decided to try their hand at running the Carousel Ballroom. It was, according to Robert Sam

Anson, a particularly hippiesque disaster, featuring a motley group of tenants, including the Hell's Angels and the Black Panthers. "Brawling was common, arrests frequent. On one occasion, a group showed up and paid their admission with parts of a freshly butchered lamb. Another time, some overly enthusiastic music lovers built a small bonfire in the middle of the hall. The Carousel folded after thirteen weeks."

"It didn't help to have a hundred thousand cars driving down Haight Street all day long," rock 'n' roll manager Travis Rivers told me.

> There was a CBS documentary that came out implying that all this art and music and poetry was coming out of the minds of people who were totally fucked up on drugs. So kids thought, wow I can just get stoned and all this wonderful stuff will come out. So we ended up with all these mental cripples on the street. And then they started ripping one another off, because it costs a lot of money once you get strung out on speed.

A week after the grisly murder of pregnant actress Sharon Tate and her friends in the Hollywood Hills, with the killers still at large, the Woodstock Festival, a continent away, did its best to put a smiley face on the California experience. But it had no chance. For the Grateful Dead, it was a particularly creative and technical disaster. The Airplane's set came and went without incident. Country Joe and the Fish delivered their by now perfunctory off-color cheer on cue. Barry Melton reflects,

> For our band particularly that was a time of change. During the recording of *Here We Go Again*, earlier in

the year, our rhythm section had departed. The band at Woodstock is not the happy-go-lucky group of guys from Berkeley that appeared at Monterey in 1967. We had become professionals on some level, even though by today's standards we were almost tribal in our lack of sophistication. Generally, we take the things we love and we ruin them by turning them into our profession, and music is no different. We'd all been stirred by the fires of idealism, what music could do in terms of social change, by Pete Seeger and a bunch of lofty thoughts about how folk music could change the world. But what happens when you do it on the road for 300 days a year for a couple of years is in some sense you turn into a person out there making a living and the idealistic is lost to the pragmatic.

If you really want to see the idealism of the '60s and what it was all about for me, go look at the movie *Monterey Pop*, where the police chief happily welcomed all the hippies. It was love, peace, and understanding for three days. Everybody's smiling and they all look happy and there's this sense of idealism; everybody is dreamy-eyed, saying things in retrospect that could probably be termed asinine. Actually naïve is a better word, although sometimes they could be interchangeable. There's a naïve quality to *Monterey Pop* in 1967 as one approaches the Summer of Love. By Woodstock everybody's kind of hard already and you have Bill Graham talking about digging trenches, Leningen verses the ants, setting fires. This generation of idealists had turned into a group of folks ready to fight back.

The careers of two San Francisco bands were kicked into overdrive that weekend: Santana and Sly and the

Family Stone—three if you want to count Crosby and Nash of Crosby, Stills and Nash, who had only recently relocated to San Francisco.

Santana's percussive, Latin-flavored rock was tailor-made for audiences of 100,000 or more, as I could attest, having caught their free concert in Central Park a week before Woodstock, with drummer Michael Shrieve in particular imprinting "Soul Sacrifice" on my brain. In *Bill Graham Presents: My Life Inside Rock and Out*, Carlos Santana told Robert Greenfield that Woodstock was a "disaster area."

> I had taken some mescaline and just at the point that I was coming onto it, this guy came over and said, "Look, if you don't go on right now, you guys are not going to play." I had played loaded before, but not to that big of a crowd. I just prayed the Lord would keep me in tune and in time.
>
> A lot of people played really bad. They got pretty wasted before they got out there and they didn't sound very professional. The peak for me was Sly Stone, bar none. He took over that night.

A former San Francisco deejay and the producer of the early folk rock classic "Laugh Laugh" by the Beau Brummels, Sly was an especially beloved figure among the town's leading tastemakers, as much for his larger-than-life fashion sense as for his searing psychedelic funk. In his book *Mystery Train: Images of America in Rock 'n' Roll Music*, Greil Marcus called Sly

> an outrageous showman whose style was a combination of Fillmore district pimp gone stone crazy and Fillmore Auditorium optimism with a point to it. A

cultural politician of the first order, Sly was less interested in crossing racial and musical lines than in tearing them up.

In the manner of the very greatest rock 'n' roll, Sly and the Family Stone made music no one had ever heard before.

In his book *Rock and Roll: The 100 Best Singles,* *Crawdaddy!* founder Paul Williams placed Sly's "Thank You (Falettinme Be Mice Elf Agin)" among the four best singles of 1969. "It's clear that Sly Stone—along with James Brown and very few others—invented the future. Funk, rap, hip hop; it's all there, a radical departure from everything soul music and rock and roll had been, less obvious now only because Motown and the rest of the industry began copying and learning from Sly the instant they heard him."

Dave Marsh put five Sly and the Family Stone songs into his *The Heart of Rock and Soul: The 1001 Greatest Singles Ever Made*, including the aforementioned "Thank You," approaching it from a starkly different angle.

He sat down to write a song and poison spilled out. Set it to one of the grungiest guitar-bass riffs he'd ever devised, a slinky, sinister beat, then picked up the tempo just a hair. Got more specific as the verses progressed, drew more blood from the shards of his own hopes and career, mocked his own songs.

No one caught on. The record went straight to Number One. No one heard him.

Sly's signature moment at the Woodstock festival had to be his performance of "I Want to Take You Higher," a tune that debuted on the B side of his 1969

Come together? For the Beatles, 1969 was the time of the season when tension ran high. (Photofest)

A Summer of Love reject, Charles Manson carved his bloody initials on the era nonetheless. (Photofest)

For an unparalleled experience, Jimi Hendrix was the guitar equivalent of a walk on the moon. (Warner Bros/Photofest)

According to Carlos Santana and many another venerated rock commentator, Sly and the Family Stone stole the show at Woodstock. (Warner Bros/Photofest)

By the end of 1969, even Jerry Garcia and the Grateful Dead realized they had to enter the mainstream. (Warner Bros/Photofest)

Typified by Lou Reed's facetious peace sign, the Velvet Underground led the '60s counterrevolution. (Photofest)

The man couldn't bust our music. The MC5 did it all by themselves. (Photofest)

Riding the next wave of the blues, Led Zeppelin would rule the '70s. (Photofest)

In 1969, Tommy James and the Shondels had a bigger year on the singles chart than the Beatles. (Photofest)

All Phil Spector wanted was to be free. That's not how it turned out to be. (Photofest)

As seen in the movie *Alice's Restaurant*, in an attempt to avoid the looming draft lottery, starting in December 1969, American men went nuts. (UA/Photofest)

Many people thought Dylan had become a vegetable in 1966; this 1969 appearance on Johnny Cash's TV show did nothing to prove otherwise. (ABC/Photofest)

"Made it, Ma! Top of the world!" said Janis Joplin. It wouldn't last.
(Photofest)

single "Stand" and then reappeared as its own A-side a year later to capitalize on the Woodstock vibes (and the *Woodstock* film). As in his earlier "Higher" from his debut album, Sly's mission was clear in this song and in his music. And at Woodstock he nearly accomplished what 10,000 Yippies had failed to do a year before at the Pentagon: mass levitation. But how much higher could a generation go before it cracked the sky, the rubber band split, and the dream exploded back to earth like so many raining purple orchids?

As the memory of Woodstock faded, the plucky City by the Bay, city of love-ins and be-ins and trips festivals, was still looking for something to cure it, define it, right the wooden ship. As it happened, Michele Hush, my first editor at *Rock Magazine*, was there at the time, sort of.

> After a weekend with the Girl Scouts at Camp Blue Bay on Long Island when I was eleven or so, I realized any event that lacked indoor plumbing was not for me. So, when I was offered a ticket to Woodstock, I thought about the mud and crud and decided to go to San Francisco with my friend Gene instead. I was imagining a return to a place where Owsley Stanley was making acid, incense was in the air, and every few weeks or so the biggest San Francisco bands, from the Dead to the Airplane to Big Brother, played somewhere for free. We soon realized things had changed radically since 1967, when everything seemed fairly innocent and rather magical (although that might have been the acid). In 1969, whether you walked down Haight Street or Telegraph Avenue in Berkeley, you immediately noticed that the kids peddling acid tabs were gone and the dope dealers, nodding junkies and scary speed

freaks had taken their place. Given the general ugliness of the vibe and the word that Hell's Angels would be present at Altamont, Gene and I decided we would skip that event, too.

What we did attend was the First Annual Holy Man Jam, in October, produced by the Family Dog. New York cynics that we were, it never occurred to us that the "holy man" aspect might be serious. It's a Beautiful Day topped the bill and I'm sure they played for a while, but my memory of their performance is overpowered by visions of Timothy Leary and Alan Watts and a succession of extravagantly dressed members of exotic religions, from Tibetan monks to Sufis to Hari Krishnas to the Church of Satan, who took turns working their particular mojos.

I particularly remember a group of monks in long, dark robes who tolled strange, eerie bells for about a light year longer than the time it might take for a soul to make a round trip to eternity. My personal last straw was a ridiculous guy with a Satan-style moustache and goatee who danced up to me in a slinky, snaky way and offered me an apple (which I took as a painfully obvious reference to the Garden of Eden).

The Holy Man Jam apparently lasted for three nights, but my friends and I were out of there after less than one. All the way home, people talked about Satanic rituals and infant sacrifices; it seemed like everybody knew somebody who knew somebody who knew somebody who had witnessed something unspeakable somewhere in Marin County.

The Kinks were coming to the Fillmore West in late November, and I was more than psyched for some velvet pants and Davies brothers antics. But when the news about the arrest of the Manson Family hit the media around then, it just seemed to be more evidence that it was time to get the hell out of California.

Pushing doggedly forward, as if to prove Jann Wenner's long-held contention that only the West Coast knew how to throw a proper rock festival, San Francisco, with the unblinking eye of the media upon it and America wandering through its streets by day, the tear gas falling from above, looked to the Rolling Stones (of all people) to save them, and the Hell's Angels (of all people) to protect them. Moreover, because of various permits falling through and other logistical nightmares, they had only about a day and a half to prepare it. Even a legendary optimist like Jerry Garcia, noted friend of the Angels, knew this was a bad idea. "It was in the air that it was not a good time to do something," he told Robert Greenfield in *Bill Graham Presents: My Life Inside Rock and Out.* "There were too many divisive elements. It was too weird. And that place, God, it was Hell." Emmett Grogan, founder of the Diggers, was just as prescient. "He wrote on the bulletin board up at Alembic, where we were rehearsing and a lot of the planning was going on," Garcia said, "First Annual Charlie Manson Death Festival.' *Before* it happened."

Barry Melton commented,

I remember all of 1969 as a difficult time. You have this culture of violence taking hold, not an expectation of violence but an awareness that violence could be a component of almost any situation. Our band was formed in a cocoon where violence wasn't part of the equation, and 1969 was marked by a number of violent events. Altamont was one of them. People's Park was one of them.

We played a concert at San Jose State with Ike and Tina Turner and there was some huge confrontation between the Hell's Angels and people in the crowd and we were at a loss as to whether to stop the music or keep on playing. We didn't know how to handle it. We were used to gathering large crowds of essentially peaceful people, antiwar people, people who had directly moved over from the civil rights movement of the early '60s, which was intended to be a nonviolent movement. By the time you get to the end of the '60s, you're seeing the Black Panthers; you're seeing a different kind of confrontational model take place. It's like, we tried to be nonviolent and it didn't do us any good, so now we're going to confront you. It's certainly harder to get out there and play when there's a potential for violence.

Marty Balin was there with the Jefferson Airplane that bleak day at the racetrack when 300,000 came to pay homage to the authors of such anthems as "Street Fighting Man," "Gimme Shelter," "Midnight Rambler," and "Sympathy for the Devil," and both he and they left battered and broken. The moon was in Scorpio, always a bad sign.

Although Balin and crew had bowed out before the fatal event, the trouble started early. The Angels had undoubtedly already consumed most of the 100 cases of beer that was their payment. They waded through the swelling crowd of tripping hippies wielding their customized pool cue like scythes as they defended what was most important to them: their motorcycles, their manhood, their status in the Brotherhood, American values, and Mick Jagger, probably in that order.

"There was a fight going on when we started to perform," said Balin. "They were beating this guy up and the audience just stepped back and watched it happen, so I jumped down and they stopped. But when I went back and we started to perform again, the same fight started up. So I joined in again and I got knocked out. That was end of our performance."

And the end of an era? "Altamont," Bill Graham intoned. "The word conjures up an event which was more costly to rock 'n' roll than any single day in the history of entertainment."

Michael Lydon came at it from a more literary angle, speculating in an early 1970 issue of *Fusion* that Tom Wolfe knew what was going to happen when he ended *The Electric Kool-Aid Acid Test*, at least two years before, with Ken Kesey chanting, "We blew it," not once but *nine times* (and in CAPS). "Kesey said it, of course, not Wolfe, but Wolfe made it a book's last sentence, not Kesey," wrote Lydon. "Maybe Kesey thought it for one night (who doesn't) but it summed up the whole journey for Wolfe. Tom Wolfe says he thinks the bus has gone astray, blown it, and that Kesey, who started the bus, knows it."

In 1969, Lydon pointed out, this idea would be repeated by Peter Fonda in the last frame of *Easy Rider*, making it an even more fitting epitaph for the escaping generation, many among them looking for nirvana anywhere but in San Francisco. Melton reflected,

> Everybody was reaching out to some extent that year. Joe McDonald cut a Woody Guthrie album with Nashville musicians on it. I did a soul and blues album with the Chess house band in Chicago.

I had loved the old R&B and blues stuff from the Chess library and since I had enough money to get anybody I wanted to back me up, I did that. In a way it was living out my fantasy. Vanguard let Joe and me both do solo albums wherever we liked, to placate us. The record company was trying to hold the band together.

I think our first two albums were almost like indigenous music of some kind; they might as well be field recordings of poor kids from the Bay Area making, for want of a better term, garage band music on a shoestring, fifty percent idealism and fifty percent some musical training. There was a similarity to the sound of all those bands, because we all knew each other and jammed with each other. And we all came into national prominence within about a year of each other. That means we all started to get money within the same period of time, and with money, depending on how much you had, a lot of personal options opened up. Money is kind of an insidious agreement in any art form. What gets maintained is a more commercialized version of whatever you were doing. *Here We Go Again* has orchestrations on it. That's because we had enough money to have orchestrations, so we had orchestrations. I always tell my friends in the Grateful Dead they're kind of lucky they were still starving back then. If we had remained unsuccessful and starving perhaps the band would still be together.

Any time you're intensely in the public eye, unless you're extraordinarily well grounded, or you have people familiar enough with the phenomenon to help shield you from it, you lose your perspective. It's hard to stay grounded when everybody wants to screw you or get you high. There's a whole substratum of people who want to sell you things or they've figured out some scheme to make you and them rich. As someone in the middle of a maelstrom, I definitely wanted to get the hell out of there. I couldn't think of anything I wanted to do less than be a famous guy.

In his essay, Lydon mentions what some regard as a significant flaw in Wolfe's portrait of the era. "Wolfe made his basic mistake in seeing Kesey as the central figure," Lydon wrote. "It was Cassady, they say, Cassady was the man. If so, Wolfe made a mistake that Kerouac didn't make. Kerouac knew it was Neal Cassady twenty years ago."

As the decade turned, and a generation longed for a simpler time of simpler heroes, slouching toward San Francisco to be reborn, they might have been better off remembering the recently deceased Kerouac's own closing lines about Cassady (a.k.a. Dean Moriarty) from a previous generational epic, *On the Road*, published in 1955: ". . . . just before the coming of complete night that blesses the earth, darkens all rivers, cups the peaks and folds the shore in, and nobody, nobody knows what's going to happen to anybody besides the forlorn rags of growing old, I think of Dean Moriarty, I even think of Old Dean Moriarty the father we never found, I think of Dean Moriarty."

CHAPTER FIVE

East Is East

★ ★ ★ ★ ★ ★ ★ ★ ★ ★ ★ ★ ★

WHILE "THE AGE OF AQUARIUS" STARTED on Broadway and found its ultimate fame in Los Angeles, 1969's other most emblematic hit song, "Get Together," began in San Francisco and wound up in Greenwich Village, inside the well-traveled guitar case of its author, Chester A. Powers, known professionally as Dino Valenti, one of the more mercurial and difficult characters in an era loaded with mercurial and difficult characters.

San Francisco folk icons the Kingston Trio, whose manager, Frank Werber, bought the rights to the song from Valenti in 1964, were the first to perform "Get Together." Next came versions by actor/folksinger (Bob) Hamilton Camp (whose career arc spans appearances on *The Andy Griffith Show* and *Desperate Housewives*) and the Chad Mitchell Trio with John Denver sitting in for the drug-busted Chad Mitchell. Another Werber-managed Bay Area group, We Five, released it late in 1965, as a follow-up to their Top 10 hit, "You Were on My Mind," with Beverly Bivens handling lead chores on both songs (it barely dented the Top 40). But it didn't become an official San

Francisco anthem until the Jefferson Airplane's 1966 version on their debut album, *Takes Off*. In 1967, H. P. Lovecraft, a Chicago band on their way to San Francisco for the Summer of Love, and, on the East Coast, the Youngbloods, led by Jesse Colin Young, both put it on their respective debut albums.

But 1969 was its best year, with Los Angeles recordings by a group called Smith on their album *A Group Called Smith* and on the Carpenters' debut, *Ticket to Ride*, not to mention fading New York folk-scene recordings by Carolyn Hester in *Coalition* and Bonnie Dobson in *Bonnie Dobson*, along with a garage band version by the Cryan Shames on *Synthesis*. The tune also shows up on David Crosby's early Byrds sessions, Judy Collins's Newport set, Nick Drake's home tapes, John Denver's outtakes, and a set of rare Fairport Convention sides, all of which earned Valenti nothing more than another ego massage, which, by most accounts, he needed a lot less in those days than a fat royalty check, having been just released from prison, where he'd spent the previous eighteen months on a drug charge.

Once out of jail, Valenti fled San Francisco's noxious orbit, reneging on his long-ago promise to join Quicksilver Messenger Service and taking their guitarist Gary Duncan with him to Greenwich Village to form a new band. They arrived to find the famous neighborhood in a massive state of social and creative unrest. Nevertheless, on June 28, 1969, as the country counted down the days to the Apollo moon launch, and in Bethel, New York, two men with unlimited capital attempted the even more challenging task of persuading the skeptical townsfolk to permit them to stage the outdoor rock concert to end all outdoor rock concerts, Valenti saw the

Youngbloods' 1967 version of "Get Together" reenter the charts (sparked by its use as a promo for the National Conference of Christians and Jews) on the very same night that a bunch of frustrated gay men and women started throwing bricks at the police and burning trash cans in front of the Stonewall Tavern on Christopher Street.

In a scene reminiscent of the speakeasy days of Prohibition, a police raid on the Genovese family–owned bar went awry when the formerly docile patrons refused to submit to the customary if humiliating drill of lining up outside to provide proper identification. The taunts and antics of those milling outside the club escalated madly in a matter of minutes until the surging streets were filled with songs and shouts of pride and anger, as "We Shall Overcome" and "Gay Power" formed a mythic medley in a massive coming-out party easily as immense in its impact as what was planned for later in upstate New York. Allen Ginsberg, a Christopher Street resident, took in the scene; Dave Van Ronk, a regular Christopher Street drinker, was arrested.

For Van Ronk it must have seemed like a poignant flashback to the 1960 folksinger riots in Washington Square. It was the same riot police, and the same kind of staunchly weird community of outcasts singing "We Shall Overcome," that ultimately prevented a roadway from splitting the park in two and led to the great Urban Folk Scare of the 1960s, which Dave presided over from his perch at the Gaslight Café on MacDougal Street. Sadly, the 1969 riots over several days at the end of June were the most activity the West Village had seen since 1967.

"We had five or six real fat years," Van Ronk told me. "Some people bought houses in the country, some people built recording studios, some people acquired expensive drug habits. And all of it was taken for granted." By 1969, St. Marks Place in the East Village had replaced MacDougal Street as the happening gathering place for restless fashion plates and music fans. The Electric Circus had the Velvet Underground and more; the Fillmore East had double and triple bills like you wouldn't believe: B. B. King/Johnny Winter/Terry Reid; The Mothers of Invention/Buddy Miles Express/Chicago; Blood, Sweat and Tears/Jethro Tull/Albert King; Buddy Rich/The Grassroots/Spirit; Joni Mitchell/Joseph Cotton/Taj Mahal—and that was only January through April.

"I remember going somewhere on the train with Tom Paxton in 1969," said Van Ronk about the cultural seismic shift. "We were discussing the business and he said, 'I saw this great cartoon in the *New Yorker* last week: one brontosaurus was talking to another, saying "I don't know about you, but frankly this cold snap has me a little worried." Van Ronk cackled. "I've always been a doom crier. For years I'd been predicting grass growing on MacDougal Street, so I think it gave me some satisfaction."

But even the notoriously cynical Van Ronk, who died in 2002, had to admit the scene had been pretty special in its day. "We were very conscious something important was going on. Essentially, everybody was performing for everybody else. The community was the audience that counted. To get the approval of Joni Mitchell was infinitely better than a three-page review in the *Times*. And, of course, Joni herself was working for the same approval."

Perhaps needing more approval than most, Phil Ochs, the most political of the folk singers, turned out to be among the most fragile. By 1969 he was predicting his own decline in the gloomy *Rehearsals for Retirement* and his actual demise in the next year's countrified *Greatest Hits*. "I recently came to the conclusion that Colonel Parker knows more about organizing America than Angela Davis or SDS," he said in reference to the latter work, when I interviewed him in 1974, two years before he committed suicide.

> In terms of changes in America, you have to reach the working class, and to me, Elvis Presley, in retrospect, is like a giant commercialization of the working-class singer. His gold suit was Parker's idea, a cheap icon of all America has to offer. That was part of the idea behind my *Greatest Hits* album. The key songs would be "My Kingdom for a Car" or "Gas Station Women." I mean, "My Kingdom for a Car" could be done by Jerry Lee Lewis.

As besieged by writer's block as he was at the time, Ochs could not discount his past achievements, summing them up to me, in his trademark rapid-fire delivery, in a kind of eulogy in advance.

> That period in the Village was incredibly exciting, super euphoric. There was total creativity on the part of a great number of individuals that laid the bedrock for the next ten years. For me, songwriting was easy from 1961 to 1966 and then it got more and more difficult. It could be alcohol; it could be the deterioration of the politics I was involved in. It could be a deterioration of the country. Basically, me and the country were deteriorating simultaneously and that's probably why it stopped coming. Ever since the late '60s what's constantly on my mind is discipline, training, get it together, clean up your act. I haven't been able to do it yet, but the impulse is as strong

as ever. To my dying day I'll always think about the next possible song.

But the important thing to bear in mind in terms of a whole life, you take a person's whole life and whether it's ten years or sixty years and say, what has this person done, what has he accomplished, if anything? He's now dead, what has he left behind him of value? And I think the people who made that contribution in the '60s can rest on that.

Eric Andersen, who often followed Phil on the same stages in one Village coffeehouse after another, was a good deal less effusive when I met him at the El Quixote bar of the Chelsea Hotel. This was the legendary edifice where Leonard Cohen immortalized Janis Joplin in "Chelsea Hotel No. 2," Joni Mitchell celebrated the view from her window in "Chelsea Morning," and Jack Kerouac wrote the hippie bible, *On the Road*.

"I can't look at the '60s with much lucidity," he said. "It was a crazy era and the streets were kind of clouded over. You could see the forces of repression at work, but the ones who were fighting that repression couldn't agree with each other. So it was a negative time with everybody vying for attention and getting caught up in their own ego trips."

It's no surprise that Andersen's 1969 was filled with three unremarkable albums: his last on Vanguard, *A Country Dream*, in which he followed Bob Dylan's large footprints to Nashville; *Avalanche*, his first lackluster effort for Warner Brothers; and *Eric Andersen*, his last for Warner Brothers. "America is a place where in order to succeed you almost have to become a parody of yourself," he said.

By the time Jack Kerouac died of complications due to booze in Florida on October 21, 1969, at the age of forty-seven (three days after "Get Together" spent the last of its seventeen weeks on the charts) he was less a parody of himself than a caricature, having completed a ludicrous 360, coming out in favor of the war and against the Alternate Culture, claiming the hippies had co-opted his message and destroyed it. By the time Janis Joplin died of a heroin overdose at the Landmark Hotel in Hollywood on October 4, 1970, she was well on her way to becoming, according to a cover story in *Rolling Stone*, this generation's Judy Garland—who herself had succumbed to drugs and suicidal impulses on June 22, 1969 (only a week before "Get Together" started its mythic run).

Culminating the week the Miracle Mets finished their miracle season on October 16 by defeating the Baltimore Orioles five to three in the famed "shoe polish" game, the championship season of "Get Together" encompassed an otherwise psychotic summer, including a leap from No. 74 to No. 64 the week ending July 18, as Teddy Kennedy was driving off a bridge in Chappaquiddick, Massachusetts, killing his aide Mary Jo Kopechne, two days before men landed on the moon. The week ending August 9, while Charles Manson was on his killing spree in the Hollywood Hills and 400,000 delirious souls trekked through the Catskill Mountains on their way to Woodstock, while the wild winds of Camille whipped through the Southland, "Get Together" moved inexorably from No. 29 to No. 21. Finally, on September 6, the day after Lt. William Calley went on trial for six counts of murder during the My Lai Massacre, "Get Together" reached its peak position of No. 5, two slots ahead of "Lay Lady Lay" by Bob Dylan and just behind "Green River" by Creedence Clearwater Revival, "Sugar Sugar" by the Archies, "A Boy Named Sue" by Johnny Cash and, up at the top, "Honky Tonk Women" by the Rolling Stones (still three months away from Altamont).

Oddly enough, and in spite of Altamont, Dino Valenti and guitarist Gary Duncan returned to San Francisco in 1970 to belatedly join Quicksilver Messenger Service for *What About Me* and *Just for Love*, both released that year, and a few other albums, none of which would restore Valenti to the relevance and acclaim he (among few others) felt he so richly deserved.

If the effort to stay relevant wound up driving Phil Ochs to suicide, in the aftermath of his own form of self-parody, appearing on the cover of *Greatest Hits* in an Elvis-style gold suit, other former denizens of the MacDougal Street era were similarly groping for a way up and out. Dave Van Ronk founded the ill-fated Hudson Dusters, which drained his bank account. The pristine Carolyn Hester, first wife of author/folksinger Richard Fariña, went oddly psychedelic on the less-than-memorable *Coalition*. Andersen's three muted efforts of 1969 have already been noted. Janis Ian, still living down her teenage Greenwich Village success with "Society's Child," a non-autobiographical song about interracial courtship that actually crashed the Top 20 in 1967, put out a reasonably good album that stiffed in 1969, perhaps ironically titled *Who Really Cares*. Buffy Sainte-Marie, the preternaturally gifted Cree Indian folksinger of "Universal Soldier" and "My Country 'Tis of Thy People You're Dying" fame, soared to the limits of her already ungodly voice in the echo-drenched *Illuminations*, which attracted few in her audience. Said Sainte-Marie,

> Let me tell you about American audiences. They mostly want to hear things that sound like they've

heard them before. My songs are always at least two years ahead of their time. For two years I was criticized for writing "Universal Soldier." For two years I couldn't sing "Now That the Buffalo's Gone" on television. Two years after I'd written it they finally let me sing it. Everybody wanted to be an Indian, right? But they wouldn't let me sing "My Country 'Tis of Thy People You're Dying" because it was too strong. Two years went by, now that's all they want me to sing.

I wrote "Until It's Time for You to Go" and the folkies called me a sellout. I wore sparkles on my clothes and tight satiny dresses and high heels because that's the way I felt, and it was the wrong way to feel at the Newport Folk Festival, because it wasn't what Joanie and Bobby were wearing. My songs are a collective reflection of my entire personality. If someone were to say they didn't think I should sing this or that because I sang something else that they liked better and they only think I should write one kind of song, it would just make me laugh.

Tim Hardin, Fred Neil, Richie Havens, and John Sebastian, frequent Village regulars at the Night Owl Café, were meandering down decidedly different roads in 1969. On the heels of Harry Nilsson's success with Fred's wistful "Everybody's Talkin'" in the Oscar-winning movie *Midnight Cowboy*, Neil's earlier *Fred Neil* album was re-released as *Everybody's Talkin'*. Anything that could bring songs like "The Dolphins" to a wider audience can't be bad, yet neither version of the album sold. Never an ebullient guy, Tim Hardin was described in a review for *Suite for Susan Moore* as "dark, somber, strange, drowsy and obtuse." *Richard P. Havens, 1983*, a double album that leaned toward uninspired Lennon and McCartney covers as opposed to the majestic Dylan covers on which Richie's fortune had been made, was already off the charts by the time of his legendary Woodstock appearance. *Stonehenge*, coming out a few months after Woodstock, featured his worthy take on "It's All Over Now, Baby Blue," but was otherwise dominated by pedestrian originals.

John Sebastian had taken a bunch of hard knocks by the end of the '60s, leading to the breakup of the wonderful Lovin' Spoonful, primarily over a drug-related incident where they were perceived to have turned in their supplier, a countercultural no-no that soured their image among the cognoscenti. "In later years Ralph Gleason wrote a very good piece on the whole thing, which to my mind set things right," Sebastian said, "but it was way too late. That piece doesn't click in anybody's mind, like 'Oh yes, The Vindication of the Lovin' Spoonful by Ralph Gleason, of course.'"

While the Joe Butler–led Spoonful were putting out *Revelation Revolution '69*, Sebastian was in Sag Harbor, New York, entertaining friends like David Crosby, Stephen Stills, and Graham Nash, and working on a solo album. "The folks at MGM said, 'Great, another Spoonful album.' I said, 'Hey, guys, this is a solo album.' MGM said, 'No, we're putting it out as the Spoonful.' And I said, 'Then you're not putting it out.'" Following protracted legal disputes, the album wound up coming out on Warner Brothers . . . and MGM. "So, not only did I lose a lot of momentum," said Sebastian, "but then people were going, 'Which is the real album?'"

In the meantime, Sebastian's musical wanderings took him even farther afield of the folk scene than any of his cronies, landing him, briefly, on Broadway, where he supplied the words and music for the show *Jimmy Shine*, which accumulated 166 performances at the Brooks Atkinson Theater between December 1968 and April 1969, featuring Dustin Hoffman in the title role. Sebastian remembers,

> I told them I was writing songs for them. I had written half the songs already. Just by coincidence they fit in. I wrote one or two for the show, custom made, and they were so awful they were great. One was "There's a Future in Fish, Mr. Shine," which was sung by the guy who used to play one of the uncles on the Molly Goldberg radio show.
>
> You see, they weren't sure whether to consider me important or not, because they weren't sure whether they wanted it to be a musical. So they were telling me, this isn't a musical, it's only a show with music in it. They wanted to have music in it, but they didn't want to spend the money to have music in it. It was a bunch of people trying desperately to adjust to this new thing. They said, "*Hair!* made it; maybe we should pay attention to him." I'd say, "All right, guys, you don't have to give me an orchestra or anything, all I need is a four-piece band." And they'd say, "How about a three-piece band?"
>
> Here's another thing they did. I had a song in there that they cut in half. The guy they assigned me to teach the song to could not sing. Hence they said, "Okay, we'll cut the song in half and he'll sing half on his entrance and half on his exit." And I said, "Okay, guys, I'm just going to go ahead and make the record my way and make a recording of it." The song is "She's a Lady." It's a nice song. It has impact on stage. It stops a show or two now and then in my shows. So I knew the song was valuable and I also

knew that none of the people there saw the value, forget musical, the dramatic value of the song. So it was at that point that I became discouraged by the people around me.

But even on the other side of the Fifth Avenue dividing line that separated the rowdy East Village from the more staid West, some signature artists were having problems as the '60s crashed at their feet. The formerly incendiary Velvet Underground issued the relatively quiet *The Velvet Underground* in 1969, as if announcing the party was already over. By the time they released *Loaded* in 1970, founder Lou Reed was gone (although the album did feature the indestructible "Sweet Jane"). It would be years before their accomplishments would be acknowledged by a new generation. Even by 1967, however, the party was a decided downer, filled with hard drugs and hard rock dirges like "I'm Waiting for My Man" and "Sister Ray," the opposite of the sunshine, love, peace, and flowers proffered by the Grateful Dead and the rest of the San Francisco bands.

"When we went out to Frisco Bill Graham was doing his Fillmore and had his light show, right?" Reed told me. "We saw a picture of the Buddha and we said, 'That's got to go.' Graham said we were the lowest trash ever to hit San Francisco."

Graham was joined in this viewpoint by *Rolling Stone* eminence Ralph Gleason. Said Reed with a smirk,

When Gleason reviewed us, I'll never forget it—he said the whole love thing going on in San Francisco has been partially sabotaged by the influx of this trash from New York, representing everything they had cured. Let's say we were a little bit sarcastic about the love thing, which we were right about, because look what happened. We knew that in the first place. They thought acid was going to solve everything. You take acid and you'll solve the problems of the universe. We just said, bullshit, you people are fucked. That's not the way it is and you're kidding yourself. And they hated us.

On St. Marks Place, they fit right in between the Ukrainian drunks and tourists in from New Jersey. "It was a show by and for freaks," said Lou, "of which there turned out to be many more than anyone suspected."

Many of these freaks also loved the clownish Fugs, who formed out of the Peace Eye Bookstore on Second Avenue and were led by the poets Tuli Kupferberg and Ed Sanders. With their amateurish lack of chops and wholesomely profane lyrics celebrating boobs, drugs, and Swinburne, the Fugs were chafing inside the essential psychic dilemma of whether to quit, get better, or follow Ed Sanders into country music. On their 1969 release, *The Belle of Avenue A*, they seemed to traipse down all three paths at once, with Tuli contributing political and poetic odes like "Chicago" and "Flower Children" and Sanders yodeling in preparation for his next album, *Sanders' Truckstop.*

An elder statesman, three years older than Allen Ginsberg, Tuli knew they'd reached a crossroads. "I always thought of us as theater," he said. "I felt we should be buffoons. I was afraid we'd get lost in trying to become fine musicians."

The Fugs played their last concert at Rice University in February of 1969, capping a career that virtually defined defiance in the face of all creative odds, taking the movement as high as it could go, and, in some cases, at the Pentagon for instance, even a little bit higher. "I'm amazed we never got arrested," said Tuli. "We'd constantly be amazed at where we were going to play and finding hippie radicals when we got there." Such was the case in Appleton, Wisconsin, where Senator Joseph McCarthy was buried. It was McCarthy's relentless search for Communists during his televised hearings of the '50s that laid the foundation upon which the '60s counterculture was built.

Traveling with the Fugs that day was Allen Ginsberg. Said Tuli,

> Ginsberg wanted to do a thing on McCarthy's grave, so about fifty of us went out in an open truck in the middle of the winter and we were going to do some kind of Buddhist thing for the elevation of his soul to the next stage. We brought flowers and candles and the highlight of the whole thing was when some young girl lay down on the grave to give him some affection. This was completely misinterpreted by a reporter as our pissing on his grave. And it went out over Paul Harvey's noon news broadcast out of Chicago.
>
> We got this call later at the hotel: "You better leave; we think you may be arrested." So we left in the middle of the night, taking the student who'd brought us, and we traveled in this secret caravan to Madison. Once we got to Madison it was like we'd just reached the revolutionary Zion.

Tuli was justifiably proud of the Fugs' output. "We felt our songs were as great as any being written. We were saying what had to be said." Nonetheless, he was not surprised by the outcome of the movement itself.

As I look at it now, a common basis for a lot of the mistakes was that, since it was so much of a youth movement, people didn't realize that what's wonderful at nineteen may not be what you would want when you're thirty or thirty-five. Politically, the movement was never able to affiliate with the vast majority of people who were not nineteen, who had problems with work and family, education. It said, this was life, when maybe it was just youth.

I was ten to fifteen years older than some of those people. Some of the things they did shocked me at first. I couldn't see the physical destructiveness of the drug thing. I was terrified by the loss of control. Self-destruction is not particularly charming, although sometimes it was accidental. The young people just didn't know the dangers. Some of them woke up dead.

Followers of the Fugs' school of theatrical non-musicianship were legion on the Lower East Side, where the possibility of finding a six-room apartment for fifty-seven dollars a month made making actual money from your music that much less of a priority. How else to explain David Peel, whose abrasively obnoxious but not unfunny *Have a Marijuana* set back the cause of thoughtful pot smokers everywhere? Peel went on to have an inexplicably illustrious career as the virtual Lenny Bruce of rock, spending 1969 making *American Revolution* (Buddah, 1970), which contained such subtle anthems as "I Want to Get High," "Legalize Marijuana," and "Oink Oink Oink." On the strength of this, no less a revolutionary couple than John Lennon and Yoko Ono promptly signed him to Apple Records and put out *The Pope Smokes Dope* in 1972, while worthy releases from real poets like Allen Ginsberg and Lawrence Ferlinghetti, let alone Lenny Bruce himself, moldered on Lennon's dormant Zapple.

Peel's eventual label mates on Apple, Elephant's Memory, were actually real musicians, a beefy psychedelic horn band that went on to back up John and Yoko on their first somewhat normal album, 1972's *Sometime in New York City*. But their best work was their forgotten 1969 debut, also called *Elephant's Memory*, a couple of tracks from which landed in the *Midnight Cowboy* soundtrack: "Jungle Gym at the Zoo" and "Old Man Willow," although my favorite track remains "Crossroads of the Stepping Stones."

Then there were the Godz, whose music ranged from the unbearable to the god-awful, but who were somehow allowed to put out at least six albums, including 1969's *Third Testament*, which one critic admitted was not up to their usual standard. Then again, this was the year of the painfully amateur Shaggs' *Philosophy of the World*, which found critics falling all over themselves trying to out-hip one another in their ability to be in on and above the joke—if it was a joke—at the same time. Years later, the *New Yorker* dispatched Susan Orleans, author of the acclaimed book *The Orchid Thief* (upon which Charlie Kaufman's sensational movie *Adaptation* was based) to New Hampshire to interview a couple of the band members and attempt to explain the phenomenon, as if she were Joan Didion slouching to Bethlehem in the pages of the esteemed *Saturday Evening Post* (news flash: the *Saturday Evening Post* went under in 1969).

Of course, only in 1969 could the line between "savant" and visionary be so often and so willfully blurred. Lothar and the Hand People come to mind, Theremin-toting innovators whose 1969 release, *Space Hymn*, inspired by the moon landing, has sadly never found its way onto CD. However, their first album, *Presenting . . . Lothar and the Hand People*, earned high praise from Lenny Kaye, writing in *Rolling Stone* early in 1969. "It is electronic country, a kind of good-time music played by mad dwarfs. It may be strange that New York, the city which deifies speed and insanity, could produce this music, but it is as if Lothar and the Hand People have gone through this madness and come out on the other side, smiling." And Lenny was not alone in his adoration. According to an article in the *Denver Post*, "High-fashion photographer Richard Avedon took their pictures for free, in exchange for the group playing at his son's high school graduation party." Richard Pryor opened for them, Jimi Hendrix sat in on rehearsals, Keith Richards bought them drinks, and Jonathan Richman played them his early songs. But the best was when their single "Machines" was rated on *American Bandstand.* "Dick asked two kids what they thought of it and both said they hated it," Hand Person Paul Conly remembered. "Dick said, 'What would you rate it?' and one kid said, 'What's the lowest I can give it?' That was the highlight. That was about as good as it gets."

Sometimes sharing sidemen—and a warped theatrical vision—with the Fugs, Peter Stamfel's existential bluegrass outfit the Holy Modal Rounders released *The Moray Eels Eats the Holy Modal Rounders,* on which playwright Sam Shepard plays the tambourine (his next gig would be as screenwriter of Antonioni's misguided generational statement *Zabriskie Point*). The leadoff track from this ineffably strange album, "Bird Song," would go on to a legendary life of its own due to its appearance in the *Easy Rider* soundtrack. But Stampfel has always claimed the album was really more the vision of its producer, Frazier Mohawk—whose vision also obviously included the ineffably strange warbler Essra, a personal rock music dream girl of mine ever since I saw her singing as Uncle Meat with the Mothers of Invention at the Garrick Theater on Bleecker Street in 1967.

Nineteen-sixty-nine was an odd year for my rock music dream girls anyway, with Essra getting married, Maria Muldaur of the Jim Kweskin Jug Band following her husband Geoff and the group's messianic banjo and harp player Mel Lyman to a communal cult in Roxbury, Massachusetts, Carole King divorcing Gerry, Grace Slick taking up with Paul Kantner while she was still married, Joni Mitchell effortlessly segueing from David Crosby into Graham Nash, Mama Michelle Phillips retiring, Linda Ronstadt leaving the Stone Poneys, Tracy Nelson moving to country music, Cher heading to Las Vegas, Laura Nyro retreating behind her smoky mystique, Buffy Sainte-Marie going off the deep end, and Brigitte Bardot releasing an album with sex fiend Serge Gainsbourg, containing the original version of the steamy "Je T'aime . . . Moi Non Plus" covered by Serge with his new wife Jane Birkin, in a version that went to No. 1 in England in 1969 soon after it was banned.

Even Alix Dobkin, Gaslight Café proprietor Sam Hood's tempting wife, whom he occasionally prodded into performing, came out right around this time as a lesbian.

Reportedly murder to film in 1968 and '69, *Zabriskie Point* was roundly reviled when it premiered in 1970, not so much for its screenplay by Sam Shepard or its soundtrack, which contained stellar tracks from Pink Floyd, Kaleidoscope, and the Grateful Dead, but because of the inept performances by the relative unknowns playing the lead lovers—rank unknown Mark Frechette and Daria Halprin (who'd only appeared in the documentary *Revolution*)—as a hippie Romeo and Juliet stoned in the desert.

During the filming, in March of '69, Frechette staged a six-day walkout, returning east to the loving arms of his newly adopted family, the selfsame Mel Lyman's Fort Hill Community that housed Geoff and Maria Muldaur (albeit briefly), Gaslight folksinging regular David Gude, and Jim Kweskin (who became its business manager), among others. "I got tired of getting up every morning to go and work in what was essentially a lie," Frechette told writer David Dalton in his epic book-length article that first appeared in *Rolling Stone* in 1971. "So I just took off."

The communal godhead, Mel Lyman, who was hoping to place a few songs in the soundtrack, wasn't pleased by this news. He advised his new, suddenly rich and well-connected devotee to suck it up and finish the film, which he did, "but only after Antonioni promised to spend ten days re-shooting dialogue Mark thought too political and to visit Fort Hill as soon as the movie was done. He kept the first promise," Dalton reported, "although the new dialogue was never used in the film, but not the second. Urgent business suddenly forced him to return to Europe."

Drawn together on the set, Mark and Daria returned to Fort Hill as a couple after the filming was complete, but Daria was never as fully taken in by Mel's mind-controlling methods as Mark had been. Briefly, she and Mark returned to the Bay Area, but Mark eventually chose the family over their relationship. In 1973, Frechette was involved in a bank robbery and sent to prison, where he died under mysterious circumstances two years later. In 1976, Daria and her mother founded the Tamalpa Institute, where they practiced their own form of psychological voodoo called "Movement-based Expressive Arts Therapy."

Although music had always been important to Lyman, apart from Jim Kweskin's dreary *America,*which came out in 1971, only one other commercial album seems to have been put out by the Fort Hill gang, nominally by big-voiced folk singer Lisa Kindred, reduced to background vocals in the mix of 1969's *Love Comes Rolling Down,* also known as *American Avatar*. Released in January of 1970, and attributed to the Lyman Family with Lisa Kindred, it's also been released as a Lisa Kindred solo album. In 2002, a CD called *Birth* came out on Transparency Records, containing what appeared to be more songs from the same sessions.

Lisa Kindred recorded the album with Mel and his friends back in 1964, entitling it *Kindred Spirits*. But she hated the mix and abandoned the project. Ten years later she discovered it released on Warner Brothers as *American Avatar*. She told Dalton, "I said to myself, 'I know Mel is an Aries with a God complex, but this is too much! I mean, I ended up being a sideman on my own album."

Author of the essential '60s tomes *Famous Long Ago* and *Total Loss Farm* Ray Mungo commented,

> I knew Mel Lyman quite well. His community in Boston preceded the one we started in Vermont. We were aware of the Mel Lyman group and we didn't like it at all. The commune I started, Total Loss Farm, didn't have that religious component. I was the leader

but I was never revered as any kind of extraterrestrial being. We didn't have any authority figures. There were no rules on who was going to pay for what. I was writing all the time in 1968 and 1969 and I published two books in 1970, *Famous Long Ago* at the beginning of the year and *Total Loss Farm* at the end. They got great reviews and pretty soon I was sitting on a lot of money. My ideology at that time was anti-financial. I was happy to have the money, but I was not interested in using it for my own personal aggrandizement. So I just gave it away. For example, I owned the farm outright, but I turned it over for one dollar to a nonprofit corporation created, in perpetuity, so that the farm for all time would not be owned by anyone and would only be for the purpose of supporting the arts; artists and musicians and writers would have a free place to live, like the MacDowell Colony.

We did our best to be cut off from the mainstream media. We didn't have a TV set; you couldn't get a newspaper way the hell out in the woods, and we did not have a telephone. But we had a turntable in the living room and thousands of LPs, everybody's record collection from college pooled together in the giant living room, and the big news was when someone had just come from town and would walk in the door with a copy of *Nashville Skyline* by Bob Dylan or the latest record by the Beatles or Joni Mitchell and then we would just listen to that record until we wore the grooves off it. That was one case where we were still in touch with the mainstream culture.

In an effort to stave off not only loneliness, not only adulthood, but also the high cost of living anywhere other than on the bug-infested Lower East Side of

Manhattan, many post-college or college dropout musicians and avid supporters of the arts banded together in commune-like settings, some headed by a guru type, some headed by a sultan type, some headed by a rock star manqué, some just a loose conglomeration of friends yearning like Dylan for an idyllic escape.

Ray Mungo definitely puts his group in the latter category.

The Total Loss Farm was derived directly from the Liberation News Service, which we started in Washington and New York in 1967. By 1969 it had split into two warring factions, the hippie faction, which was my faction, and the serious Marxist politico faction that stayed rooted in New York City and spent the next twenty years grinding out propaganda. Meanwhile, me and my group drifted up to Vermont, where we started chanting and taking acid all the time, playing music and living on the land.

Marshall Bloom was the head of the U.S. Student Press Association, based in Washington, D.C. Although he was politically radical, he'd been elected president of this organization and hired me to be the editor in chief. The only problem was, a couple of months into the job they fired Bloom for being way too far out and I resigned in protest. So did a bunch of other radicals, leaving five or six of us in this house we had rented as a group. We had to do something with our time, so that's how we started the Liberation News Service.

At that time the nation was exploding with underground papers, the *Avatar* in Boston, featuring Mel Lyman, the *Oracle* in San Francisco, the *Berkeley Barb*, the *East Village Other*; Washington had the *Free Press*. Every major city had an underground paper and even the average little one-horse town had an underground paper. William Randolph Hearst said, "Freedom of the press is for those who own one." Suddenly, from 1966 to 1969, any kid of fourteen or fifteen could put out a little mimeographed thing and call it an underground paper. These papers had no money but they would send us fifteen dollars a month and we would send them, two or three times a week, a thick package of news stories and photographs that they could print in their paper. Some of these papers existed because of us. In one year the subscriptions went from a couple of papers to about 400. We allied ourselves with Jerry Rubin and Abbie Hoffman and Paul Krassner in the Youth International Party. We ran around taking lots of drugs and staging crazy demonstrations.

By the summer of '68 we were basically exhausted from years and years of fighting the establishment, but there was still a presidential election going on. In August was the famous convention in Chicago. And in November, when Dick Nixon got elected, it was the bloody end. We were just completely toast. In 1969 it was kind of like the storm had passed, and in the aftermath we were this band of brave or foolish former young radicals hanging on in a remote farmhouse homestead way the hell out in the woods trying to start a new planet, separate and distinct from the United States.

Through 1969, we continued to put out the news service from both locations, one coming from the original group out of a barn in Montague, Massachusetts, and the second one coming from the new group out of the office in the basement in New York City near Columbia. But we gradually got sick and tired of it and more interested in living in the country, being independent of the city, independent of the whole system. The end came on November 1, 1969, when Marshall Bloom committed suicide.

There are people today who will tell you that Marshall Bloom was killed by the CIA or FBI. It was on page one of the *New York Times*: "Founder of radical news service found dead in Massachusetts." David Eisenhower, son-in-law of Richard Nixon, married to Tricia, who went to school at Amherst with Bloom, wrote this long Op-Ed piece about how Bloom's suicide showed the futility of the movement and the moral bankruptcy of the hippie. The suicide was discussed in every major media and it crushed us.

I was driving my old jalopy down to Montague to see him the morning he died. At the same time as he started the Montague Farm, I had started the Total Loss Farm, about twenty minutes away. So we used to see each other five, six times a week. Since we didn't have a phone in Vermont, I pulled over at a pay phone in some little town in Massachusetts and called those guys to let them know I was on my way and they told me Bloom had killed himself the night before. I was absolutely stunned.

All kinds of theories arose, published in the underground press. There was never an autopsy. He was found dead in his car with the tailpipe connected to the window, the classic carbon monoxide poisoning suicide. He was always manic-depressive. And he had threatened to commit suicide on a number of occasions. My suspicion is he probably did commit suicide, but there are still people who think otherwise. I don't think he would have known anything that would cause people to want to have him bumped off, although we know for a fact the FBI did infiltrate our group. That came out with Freedom of Information

Act. But when they released the documents they put black ink over the names, so we never did find out who exactly amongst these groups was working for the government. The ultraradical, violent Marxist people in New York had several FBI infiltrators, who tended to be the most radical, the most incendiary of the group. That was probably their task, assigned to them by J. Edgar Hoover himself, to make the group appear more off the wall than it was, to goad people on to more and more drastic actions that would cause them to lose support.

We didn't have any money or power to speak of, but we did have millions of readers, including people at the State Department, the *Washington Post*, the *New York Times*, and *Time* magazine, who leaked us information. I guess they were terrified of us.

In such a draining year of exalted hopes and crushing disappointments, colliding eras and polarizing priorities, it should come as no surprise that the group of musicians making the most money in New York City at the turning of the decade were the closeted studio types midtown (near the Brill Building) who lent their voices to a succession of simplistic AM radio ditties squarely aimed at the neglected, not-as-yet radicalized pre-pubescent market. The Archies (the voice of Ron Dante) led the way with "Sugar Sugar" occupying the top of the pops for four weeks, making it the fourth most popular song of the year, one slot ahead of the Stones' "Honky Tonk Women," which it displaced at No. 1 on September 20.

Songwriter Paul Leka put together the year's next-biggest bubblegum hit, the future stadium anthem "Na Na Hey Hey Kiss Him Goodbye," which entered the charts while "Sugar Sugar" was still in the Top 5. It could have been Joey Levine singing lead on the 1910 Fruitgum Company's 1969 hit "Indian Giver"; he'd performed that chore for their Buddah labelmates, the Ohio Express, for 1968's epic "Yummy Yummy Yummy" and was probably around, having just sung backup on Crazy Elephant's "Gimme Gimme Good Lovin'" and lead in the Ohio Express's lone Top 40 hit of 1969, "Mercy."

Ron Dante struck again as the Cuff Links with "Tracy," a little further down the Top 10. Future superstar Tony Orlando was still a Brill Building–area session man when he recorded "Make Believe" under the name of Wind. Another Paul Leka group, Peppermint Rainbow, appealed more to the lonesome housewife side of the bubblegum spectrum, with "Will You Be Staying After Sunday" and "Don't Wake Me Up in the Morning, Michael" before calling it quits. Not to be outdone were famed studio mavens Bob Feldman and Jerry Goldstein (two-thirds of the Strangeloves, authors of "My Boyfriend's Back"), who concocted the Rock and Roll Dubble Bubble Trading Card Company of Philadelphia 19141 for their one and only hit, the anthemic "Bubble Gum Music."

The best that can be said of these assorted guilty pleasures of 1969 is that they provided the atmosphere for veteran Brill Building scribes Jerry Leiber and Mike Stoller, destined for the Rock and Roll Hall of Fame, to have another run in the singles arena with "Is That All There Is?" sung by no less a legend than Peggy Lee.

Holding onto his own office at the Brill Building in 1969, Paul Simon wrote "The Boxer" and "Bridge over Troubled Water." His banner year was made bitter only by the knowledge that Simon and Garfunkel were coming to an end—yet it was made sweet by the knowledge that he'd once again stuck it to the folks down in Greenwich Village who'd rejected them at the beginning of their career. "I was keenly aware that we hadn't been accepted by the folk crowd," he once told me. "Suddenly we were very desirable to the folkies, but I resented them."

Simon chose to live in an entirely different neighborhood, the furthest thing from bohemia, on the Upper East Side of Manhattan, in the shadow of the groovy 59th Street Bridge in "a neighborhood largely unaffected by the youth culture."

Even further uptown, as the open wounds of the '60s once again started pulsing, unsettling new sounds could be heard rattling in the wind, more ominous than the recently announced draft lottery. In poet-novelist Gil Scott Heron's fierce *Small Talk at 125th and Lenox*, released in 1970, which included "The Revolution Will Not Be Televised," and the Last Poets' self-titled release, featuring "Niggers Are Scared of Revolution," the authentic voice of black rage was as riveting as it was eloquent. It would take most of the next decade, but soon the entire culture would be immersed in it.

CHAPTER SIX

Don't Forget the Motor City

★ ★ ★ ★ ★ ★ ★ ★ ★ ★ ★ ★

O N JANUARY 1, 1969, *Rolling Stone* put the MC5 on the cover of the magazine, with a gushing tribute by Miami of Ohio student Eric Ehrmann, columnist for the *Miami Student*, anointing the locally popular but nationally unknown political firebrands as the next rock 'n' roll superheroes and symbolically passing the torch of revolution from San Francisco to Detroit. And although this would do relatively little to prevent San Francisco and its bands from suffering their share of the year's steady diet of drug busts, police interference, and other assorted bits of cosmic backlash—retribution for the unparalleled seasons of freedom that preceded it—none of it concerned the MC5, standing on the brink of world domination after toiling for so long in the shadows of Motown.

If Berry Gordy's upstart, uppity label had put Detroit on the map as a potent entity in 1960, by 1969 its cultural (if not musical) influence was drawing to a close. Having been despoiled by the embarrassment of race riots during the Summer of Love in 1967, Berry's Sound of Young America was being challenged by another louder, angrier sound in the street. Not dancing, not close courtyard/barbershop harmony, not giggling girl group, post-doo-wop chattering, this was a much more violent and violence-prone cacophony of free-form noise, with a provocative, antagonistic message.

An astute businessman, Gordy was already thinking about leaving town, following the path of New York City music magnate Don Kirshner, who had uprooted his publishing empire and his top songwriters and moved to L.A. to write custom hits for the Monkees on TV. True, Gordy was still embroiled in legal battles with his own top songwriting outfit, Holland-Dozier-Holland, whom he sued in 1968 for failing to fulfill their contracts and who countersued for insufficient royalties, among other things. But in 1969, he bought a house in L.A. (and one down the block for his paramour, Diana Ross), where, a short time later, the emergent Jackson 5 would become his roommates, led by the twelve-year old Michael. Their tunes were written by an entity known as the Corporation (among them Berry Gordy, Zeke Richards, Fonce Mizell, Freddie Perren, Hal Davis, Willie Hutch, and Bob West). Starting in 1969, the Jackson 5's first four releases would go to No. 1.

In Detroit, songwriter/producers Norman Whitfield and Barrett Strong were perhaps the most in touch with the zeitgeist of 1969, as evidenced by their work for the Temptations, including "Cloud Nine," "Run Away Child, Running Wild," and "Ball of Confusion." In 1970 they'd write the anthemic "War" for Edwin Starr, followed up by the even more explicit "Stop the War Now." Ross had become socially conscious, too, with 1968's Holland-

Dozier-Holland-influenced "Love Child" and 1969's "I'm Livin' in Shame." By the end of '69 she'd be singing "Someday We'll Be Together" as her farewell to the Supremes before launching her solo career in Hollywood with "Reach Out and Touch (Somebody's Hand)," written especially for her by the gifted team of Nicholas Ashford and Valerie Simpson. Ashford and Simpson had scored the plum of all plum Motown staff assignments, to write and produce an entire album for the magisterial Diana, after Gordy rejected the work of the previous producer, the accomplished L.A. vet Bones Howe.

"It was a coup for us," said Valerie, "because most people only got to contribute a song or two to an album, so for him to give us a whole important project was one of the biggest things we did as a production team. Creatively, he left it all in our hands. Once he gave you power he let you do it. He didn't hear it until it was all done." At which point the professor had a minor quibble with their slow-building, Isaac Hayes–influenced, extended version of the 1967 Marvin and Tammi hit "Ain't No Mountain High Enough," which Diana introduced with a sexy monologue. "Berry thought we had gotten it wrong with all that talking in the front," Valerie said. "He thought the build was too slow and he encouraged us to change it around, put the big part in the front. We told him no, we wouldn't do it. Then he told us he wouldn't release it as a single."

But after "Reach Out and Touch (Somebody's Hand)" peaked at No. 20, disc jockeys started playing "Ain't No Mountain High Enough" from the album. Having little choice, Berry revisited his previous decision, with a nod to his producer's original wisdom. The song reached No. 1 six weeks later. "That was kind of nice," Valerie admirably understated.

Meanwhile, Smokey Robinson was still legging it out with the Miracles, whose "Baby, Baby Don't Cry" hit the Top 10 in January of '69. Perhaps distracted by his other function as Motown VP, Smokey took six failed singles and twenty-one months to repeat that success with "Tears of a Clown," which was originally released on a 1967 album.

The MC5 were glad enough to hoist the chalice of working-class rock 'n' roll for themselves, their city, their manager, and their cause, which increasingly had become one and the same. Formed back in the Mitch Ryder and the Detroit Wheels dark ages of 1964, with the simple notion of ramping up their amps to twelve and "kicking out the jams," they intimidated any other bands who passed through Detroit with their anti-authority spiel and their gang war attitude.

But somehow, in the new repressive era foretold by 1969, that taste would rapidly turn to dust. By the time the defining *Rolling Stone* cover arrived they'd already recorded their debut album, live at the Grande Ballroom, on Halloween night, 1968, following up their stint as rock's lone representative band at the bloody festivities outside the Democratic National Convention in Chicago in August. Fueled with the righteous rage provided in part by their experience and in part by their notorious larger-than-life, political activist, ex- and future con manager John Sinclair, they'd just returned from spending December antagonizing the two top promoters on the East Coast, Don Law in Boston and Bill Graham in New York (also of no little San Francisco clout) by demanding excessive courtesy and free tickets for disruptive fellow travelers, among them the radical theatrical troupe the Motherfuckers.

Graham called the MFs a "sociopolitical street gang." In actual practice they appeared to be closer to sociopaths. Already in the building when Graham took over the Fillmore, they demanded one regular night a week to espouse their radical worldview. But this was doomed from the get-go. "The first night it became like an overnight shelter for the homeless," he told Robert Greenfield in *Bill Graham Presents: My Life Inside Rock and Out.* "It went on for two months. It was utter chaos."

No strangers to utter chaos or the appearance of the police "in full riot gear," the 5 brushed off these incidents, having long since declared, through the words of their manager, a "total assault on the culture by any means necessary." A little harder to brush off was the review of their debut record that appeared in the April 5 issue of the selfsame *Rolling Stone*, the first one published by a brash newcomer on the thriving rock criticism scene, Lester Bangs, at the time still a neurotic, cough syrup–addicted shoe salesman in El Cajon, California.

After snidely declaring their main influence to be the recent teen exploitation movie *Wild in the Streets*, Lester went on to trash the band as a lame amalgam of the Kingsmen, the Who, and the Troggs, "a British group who came on with a similar sex-and-raw sound image a couple of years ago (remember 'Wild Thing') and promptly disappeared into oblivion, where I imagine they are laughing at the MC5."

Reportedly taken to heart by the MC5, the review soon drew an irate letter from someone with a more than passing interest in defending the band, a self-described White Panther named Art Johnson, who had lived near the 5 in Detroit: "The power structure—including the rock establishment—is vitally interested in suppressing the MC5. What other group would have the balls to run a full-page ad reading 'Kick out the Jams, Motherfucker, and if the store won't sell you the MC5, kick the doors down.'"

But it was precisely this ad, taken out by the 5 in the Ann Arbor underground paper the *Argus* in response to Elektra's release of a "clean" version of the album without their knowledge, with the lyric of the song changed to "Kick out the jams, brothers and sisters," that led to the group being thrown off the label, even as the album was selling over 100,000 copies. "Back in Michigan, several record retailers had been busted on obscenity charges for selling *Kick Out the Jams*," Fred Goodman reported in his book *Mansion on the Hill.* "Hudson's, Detroit's biggest downtown retailer, wouldn't stock the record." Implicitly advising their fans to bust up Hudson's, the band put the Elektra logo on the ad along with their own. Subsequently, Hudson's returned to the label every Elektra album it had in stock in its store.

According to Goodman, an enraged Jac Holzman, president of Elektra Records, called the 5's manager, John Sinclair, who was also the leader of the radical White Panthers. "John, what are you doing?" he asked. "You cannot put our logo in an ad that we do not support."

"Well, Jac," said Sinclair, "you gotta support the revolution."

The marriage of rock and revolution, of course, was always even more uneasy than the relationship between rock and business or rock and art. By the time the divorce proceedings were concluded, however, the MC5's role in the whole misguided mess would be looked upon with a good deal more nostalgia, especially by Lester Bangs. "Go to the Peoples' Party House in Ann Arbor and they'll toke you down and show you that three-minute film of the Five in everybody's Golden Era," he wrote in an article for *Phonograph Record.* "They probably wouldn't speak to the MC5 now, but the flick is a nice reminder of a time when so many feets were ready to move to get down with it and blast the continent out of space to neon . . . one of the best punk fantasies of the decade."

Before any talk of infiltrating the newspapers and the radio stations, marching in the street, overturning the system, or even releasing their first album, there was the music, the physical act of it, more demanding and magical than anything. "The first tune I ever wrote was called 'Long-Haired Angels Screaming,'" Tyner told the interviewer for the *Warren-Forest Sun*, one John Sinclair, in 1967. "And ever since then I've known that that's my vocation. I have to do it. When Sun Ra talks about leaving the planet, he means when he goes from this planet to the others as our ambassador, who will state the mental and physiological condition of the people of earth. I sincerely believe in that. And I want to play on the show with him."

Two years later, in the big time wake of the piece in *Rolling Stone*, Sinclair, by then the band's manager, did most of the talking. "I guess you could say our thing is a condemnation of everything that is false and deceitful in our society."

A commanding figure who in later years would be blamed by the members of the MC5 for corrupting their heads with his crazy talk of drugs, jazz, energy, and revolution, Sinclair was like the shaggy, hip college philosophy or drama or creative writing teacher who defies the administration by taking his students out into the woods on weekends to feed them LSD. A student himself,

Ehrmann was obviously charmed. Writing of Sinclair's impending arraignment on drug charges, he noted: "If Sinclair gets sent up the river Detroit will burn. There are more politicized hippies in Detroit and its surrounding areas who have helmets, guns, masks, tear gas and homemade mace, along with other ordnance paraphernalia than any other city currently in insurrection."

And yet, after Sinclair was given a nine-and-a-half-year sentence for the possession of two joints, nothing went up in flames, except perhaps the career of the MC5 and the Max Frostian notion of a violent revolution through rock 'n' roll. "Wherever we play we walk through the crowds and rap with the people on the way to the stage," the guitarist Wayne Kramer managed to put in for the benefit of *Rolling Stone's* readers. "We tell 'em to kick out the jams and get down on it. Everybody's got to get down." Adding a cherry on top of the insulting imbecility of the quote, the writer—and by inference the editorial staff of *Rolling Stone*—spelled the guitarist's last name with a C instead of a K.

The MC5's next album, *Back in the USA*, was produced by none other than *Rolling Stone's* record review editor Jon Landau and released early in 1970. It was decidedly less adventurous, musically and politically. "Because of Landau's lack of experience as a rock producer and the MC5's lack of experience in the studio," their drummer, Dennis Thompson, told author David A. Carson in *Grit, Noise, and Revolution: The Birth of Detroit Rock 'n' Roll*, "the album came out balls-less, thin-sounding, sterile and too fast." Although it did contain, according to *Rough Guide* reviewer Steve Knopper, "'50s style Chuck Berry rock 'n' roll and compact guitar solos that inspired Television, Richard Hell, the Sex Pistols, X and Black Flag."

Nevertheless, the mantle of outrageous if not particu-larly revolutionary behavior was passed to the 5's onetime Ann Arbor opening act, signed to Elektra the same day, for $15,000 less, the Psychedelic Stooges, soon to be known simply as the Stooges. Typifying the duck-and-cover mentality of the year, "The world of the Stooges revolves around boredom," Lenny Kaye wrote in *Fusion*. "Not only a mere lack of something to do, but rather a total nega-tion of *anything* to do. . . . This is 1969 now . . . when the hope that came out of Haight Street is nearly dead, when the protest has been neatly swept up and glossified by the mass media. In consequence, the only stance that seems to be left is that of Iggy Stooge."

Dubbed as "the freak to watch" by the *New York Times*, the former James Osterberg, former honor student at Ann Arbor High, former ace drummer for the Iguanas, who grew up at the Carpenter Trailer Park near Ann Arbor, had been profoundly influenced by the provocative style of the Doors' Jim Morrison as seen at a University of Michigan concert. Soon Iggy would be arrested in Romeo, Michigan, for exposing himself (the charges were later reduced to disorderly conduct) a full year be-fore Morrison tried a similar stunt in Miami.

With the Stooges, Iggy Osterberg (later Iggy Pop) combined performance art, self-mutilation, and acro-batic stage diving, alternately courting and sneering at the audience as the rest of the band pounded out their glo-riously trashy songs at as high a volume as could be sustained. (A year later, back in the pages of *Rolling Stone*, Ehrmann extolled Iggy as "a true expression of Sin-clair's irrepressible visionary nihilist in the flesh, who ter-rorizes his audience and relaxes after the show watching the tube.") His mates, hardly masters of their instruments in the first place, often found their lead singer distracting. "I'd just be watching him and cracking up," Ron Ashton told interviewer Jason Gross.

But, as Anne Moore reported in her review of an L.A. performance for Detroit's own homegrown rock magazine, *Creem*: "Who listens to the flutist when the cobra dances?"

Originally fashioned as a newspaper designed to celebrate the local music community, *Creem*'s first issue was published out of head shop clerk Tony Reay's basement on March 1, 1969. Within a few issues, the head shop's owner, Barry Kramer, had taken over as publisher and taken the vision nationwide. Like most rock 'n' roll organizations in those days, from the Jefferson Airplane to Frank Zappa to John Sinclair's artistic political gathering place on Fraternity Row in Ann Arbor, Trans-Love Energies, *Creem* put the commune in community, housing most of the staff on the premises, including local boy Dave Marsh, who launched his prolific career from 3729 Cass Avenue.

As on the coasts, the fledgling rock magazine formed a comfortable alliance with the local righteous underground FM radio stations, in tandem solidifying the base and adding to it with their incessant pronouncements, backed up by the actual product, the fevered white noise proffered either by the editors, the deejays, the politicos, or the bands. In Detroit, this meant the antiwar, pro-marijuana WABX, whose trailblazing status had been golden since October 21, 1968, when they previewed ten songs from the Beatles' White Album a full two weeks before its official release.

By mid-1969 the Detroit scene was flourishing. "Across the metropolitan area there were stores catering specifically to the new youth culture, selling records, black lights, posters, strobe candles, incense, pipes, denim and paisley bell bottoms," Carson reported in *Grit, Noise, and Revolution.* "Groove Shop on Mack Avenue, Other Place on Lahser Road, Head Shop on Grand River, Poster Pit in Lincoln Park, Plum Pit in East Detroit, Paper Lion in Mt. Clemens, Paraphernalia in Birmingham and Bell, Book and Candle in Westland were some of the most popular stores. As for the music, it was everywhere."

Indeed it was. WABX staged two free concerts on the Wayne State campus in the spring, leading off an incredible festival season. On April 7 there was the Detroit Pop Festival, on the eighth the Grand Rapids Pop Festival, and on the ninth the Saginaw Pop Festival, all featuring essentially the same mix of the MC5, Bob Seger, the Amboy Dukes (with Ted Nugent), and the Stooges. On Memorial Day weekend, the First Annual Detroit Rock and Roll Revival at the Michigan State Fairgrounds added Chuck Berry, Doctor John, Johnny Winter, and Sun Ra to the mix, along with the first Detroit appearance of Grand Funk Railroad, in from Flint, who were roundly reviled by the parochial locals for their impending national success. Then there was the Kalamazoo Rock Festival on June 8, the Second Annual Detroit Rock and Roll Revival on July 4, the Second Annual Saugatuck Pop Festival the same weekend, and the Petosky Rock Concert and Jive Festival on August 1. The Mt. Clemens Pop Festival on August 3 featured Country Joe and the Fish, the Stooges, Frijid Pink, and Alice Cooper, etc., etc.

The season peaked on Halloween night, 1969, at the Black Magic and Rock 'n' Roll Festival staged at Olympia Stadium, with a lineup slated to include, along with the regulars, Arthur Brown and Pink Floyd, as well as the obligatory Dr. Timothy Leary. But when 14,000 people arrived to find that Arthur Brown, Pink Floyd, and Dr. Timothy Leary would not be appearing as advertised, and neither would Bob Seger or the MC5, the bad vibes started flowing, enhanced by the liquid and leafy enhancers passing hand to hand through the crowds. It was hardly an Altamont moment, but a harbinger nonetheless, as the abbreviated concert was shut down by the Detroit police—although not until Ted Nugent thrilled the crowd (if not the police) when he grabbed "a hanging stage rope and swung out over the cheering audience," as reported in the article "A Fiasco of the Black Arts," by Barry Kramer and Dave Marsh, that later appeared in an issue of *Creem.*

In an ironic sidelight, the next event scheduled at Olympia Stadium was A Day of Peace, on November 11, featuring the MC5, the Frost, the Parliaments (with Funkadelic), Mitch Ryder and the Detroit Wheels, the Stooges, the Amboy Dukes, and the Magic Veil Light Show. It was canceled in response to what was viewed to be the previous concert's "riot." Three days later 300,000 antiwar demonstrators marched on Washington, D.C., and 150,000 more participated in a two-day moratorium in San Francisco to the tune of "Give Peace a Chance" by the Plastic Ono Band.

With the MC5's second album a bomb and the Stooges' first album already off the charts after an eleven-week run, Bob Seger continuing to struggle, the Amboy Dukes devolving into little more than an exhausted Ted Nugent's exhausted backup band, and John Sinclair still in jail, a new decade welcomed a new local hero, Vincent Furnier, who had relocated to Arizona at the age of ten and then to Los Angeles, where his namesake psychedelic hard rock band, Alice Cooper, was discovered, signed, and recorded by Frank Zappa.

Fashion-coordinated by Zappa's female tenants, the GTOs, Alice's stage wardrobe, as he described it in his memoir, *Alice Cooper, Golf Monster*, "became a pair of black leather pants worn underneath a torn black lace slip with some GTO lingerie, smeared Bette Davis makeup, unusually long hair, and black lace gloves . . . .stylistically a cross between an out-of-control freight train and a horrible car crash." Naturally, the band was a perfect fit for Frank's label roster that included the GTOs, Captain Beefheart, Wild Man Fischer, and Tim Buckley during his freak-out period. But Alice was never at one with the Flower Child philosophy that prevailed among L.A. musicians, at least until the end of 1969. "At that time, no one would ever say, 'I'm in a rock 'n' roll band for the glamour, the outrage, the art, to write great hit songs, to buy Ferraris, to snag blondes and wield switchblades,'" he wrote.

Alongside the uninhibited nihilism of the Stooges, the blatant theatricality developed by Alice Cooper's plucky troupe fit Detroit like an Al Kaline model baseball glove. "We were now one of the local bands who could draw as many fans as some of the visiting headliners," Alice recalled. "It got to where we didn't need headliners anymore; the local Detroit talent was that red hot. If you were a West Coast band on acid, beware. We're talking a no-frills shot of reality, Detroit style."

No frills, that is, except for the costumes, the props, the stuffed animals, the feathers, and, of course, once it was introduced into the act by their manager, Shep Gordon, during their legendary set at the Toronto Rock Revival in September of '69, the chicken. "There were lots of photos circulated of me throwing the chicken," Alice confessed in his book. "Of course no one could tell that I honestly thought it would fly away. The press blew the incident way out of proportion."

By 1969, the rule book of decorum was basically out the window in polite society, let alone impolite rock society. About the only place it was still posted on the wall of the cafeteria for all the employees to read was at the Motown commissary.

"The manner of grooming a group certainly helped prepare them for what they were going to encounter in the outside world; Motown was strong about that," said Valerie Simpson from her vantage point as a staffer based in New York City. "But nobody has control over anybody when they close the door. It really comes down to the values you're raised on and how crazy fame makes you. Some succumbed to demons and that's going to happen in all genres of music. The tremendous exhilaration an audience can give you can push you into places that are not real and it's like, can you come back to reality and find your footing?"

That year Motown scored a total of fourteen Top 10 singles and the label showed no outward signs of losing its mojo. "We were such an insulated world," Valerie recalled. "Motown had its own scene, its own clubs. Everybody was doing well, at the height of their popularity. Everywhere people went they were treated like royalty. So you were part of a very special inner circle. The average person in Detroit, working for Ford, might have been going through a very different thing."

Like the town's resident automakers, however, Berry maintained an assembly-line approach. "Everyone had a cubicle, so you could almost literally hear the music coming out of everyone else's room," said Valerie. "We all worked with an ear to the door, listening for what every-body else was doing, just to make sure your stuff sounded stronger. You were always amidst creativity; it was like going to college." And Berry Gordy was the cool but demanding professor whose class was always filled to capacity, even if he was stingy with the As.

"We were really lucky because in the first batch of songs we sent in was 'Ain't No Mountain High Enough,' which was recorded by Marvin Gaye and Tammi Terrell," said Valerie. "So we got music on the street right away. After 'Your Precious Love,' when it came time for the third single, we kind of realized we had sent them great demos and they were pretty much following them, so maybe we should produce as well. So that's when we asked for a production deal."

But Berry always believed his writers should be well schooled in the fine art of competition. Said Valerie, "He decided we should cut 'Ain't Nothing Like the Real Thing,' and Johnny Bristol and Harvey Fuqua should cut it as well, and whichever version came out the strongest would be released. So we were lucky again that ours turned out stronger. And that's how we started off as producers, thanks to the indulgence of Marvin and Tammi, since they had to pay for both songs."

Adding to the pressure during that particular pro-duction were a couple of unannounced visitors to the stu-dio, Smokey Robinson and Norman Whitfield. "They were standing in the control room watching us," said Valerie, "so it made us a little nervous, but it was also re-assuring, like whoa, this must be important here. We gotta get this right." That they did. "Once it was determined you could write a good song and produce it well, we had total creative freedom."

Marvin and Tammi remained their biggest clients until Tammi's death in 1970 from a brain tumor. "When she got sick, I was always doing the demos anyway," said Valerie. "I would sing with Marvin and then we'd bring her in and we'd kind of put together a vocal and doctor it up a bit. That's been perceived as I did the singing, but basically it was her singing and it was just doctored."

Marvin Gaye was a particular favorite of Valerie's. "The studio was a place where he was totally free of whatever demons he might have been dealing with on the outside. So we got to see him at his happiest," she recalled. "He was always my favorite artist, because his gift was so tremendous, his sensibility as to how to bring out a lyric. In duets, he excelled on making a singer better. He didn't have a lot of ego, where he tried to outshine anyone."

In 1970, reeling from Terrell's death, Gaye was on the brink of retirement. Shortly after the murders at Kent State, he went into the studio with a heartfelt message song he helped Al Cleveland and the Four Tops' Renaldo Benson write, called "What's Going On." He thought he might give it to the Originals, the group he was producing, whose "The Bells" had just peaked on the pop charts at No. 12. Then he decided he wanted to do it himself. Just one thing stood in his way: Berry Gordy, who didn't think the track's antiwar sentiments conformed to Marvin's sexy image. Marvin threatened to leave the label if Gordy didn't let him release it. Gordy threatened to let him. A legendary impasse ensued.

"He was the most charming man," Valerie said of Berry. "He could talk you into anything. Even if you didn't agree with him, he was still charming."

But Marvin Gaye was equally staunch in defending his passions no matter how charming his antagonist; he eventually prevailed in his standoff with Gordy, releasing "What's Going On" eight months after it was finished. On the *Detroit Metro Times* list of the 100 Greatest Detroit Songs, it ranks No. 1.

If Gaye, Ross, the Jackson 5, and Stevie Wonder represented Motown's present and future, as Motown relocated to Los Angeles in the early '70s, some of its stalwart veterans of the past were fading into the mists of '60s history. Soon Smokey Robinson would leave the Miracles; soon Gladys Knight would leave the label entirely for Buddah Records, taking the Pips with her. With Gladys Horton having already left the Marvelettes by 1968, their subsequent album releases, *In Full Bloom* and the misleading *Return of the Marvelettes*, went nowhere. Neither did 1969's *Sugar and Spice* or 1970's *Natural Resources* restore Martha Reeves and the Vandellas to their 1964–67 peak. And the Four Tops had been searching for a Top 10 hit since "Bernadette" paid a call in the spring of 1967, something which neither *Soul Spin* in 1969 nor *Still Waters* in 1970 provided them.

Like most of their other hits, "Bernadette" had been written by the team of Holland, Dozier, and Holland, who had left Motown under a cloud of suits and counter-suits and set up shop on the other side of town under the rubric of twin labels Hot Wax and Invictus. "While You're Out Looking for Sugar" by the Honey Cone came out in June. It was followed in September by "Mind, Body and Soul" by the white R&B group the Flaming Ember, which cracked the Top 40. 100 Proof (Aged in Soul) was next, reaching the charts in December with "Somebody's Been Sleeping," which must have aroused particularly mixed feelings in the Four Tops' Levi Stubbs, whose brother Joe was a member of the group.

Interviewed in the magazine *Beat Instrumental* in 1970, Stubbs was determinedly optimistic in the face of loss: "There's a limit to how often you can keep coming up with the old hits, so you can say that we're very much in an experimental stage. You should hear our new album, *Still Waters Run Deep,* because there's a storyline running through it and we think it's very unusual and also puts the accent on love and peace throughout the world." In fact, the album would produce the near hit "Still Water (Love)," written by Smokey Robinson and Frank Wilson. But even Levi knew his musical life would never be the same without H-D-H. "Losing them was like ending a marriage," he said. "But who knows what could happen in the future."

In this respect, like many in the business in 1970, Stubbs was looking to one particular entity for guidance. "So often the Beatles will trigger a whole new thing which alters the course of the whole recording industry," he confessed.

If that was the case, Stubbs couldn't have been too pleased to hear of Paul McCartney's temporary break from the Beatles, announced in April 1970—bookended by the release of "Let It Be" in March and "The Long and Winding Road" in May—and made permanent in December, by which time *Melody Maker* would have already declared Led Zeppelin to be the most popular band in England.

He'd have been better off taking his cues from a former Motown staff writer and producer and part-time Plainfield, New Jersey, barber, George Clinton, whose band of barbershop brothers had attempted no less than Nolan Strong and the Diablo's 1954 Detroit doo-wop classic "The Wind" (No. 11 in the *Metro News* Survey) in their first session in a New Jersey railway station record-yourself-at-a-quarter-a-tune booth in 1956. Reinvented as Parliament, they hung around the outskirts of Motown from 1963 to 1966, only achieving a bit of success after they left with "(I Wanna) Testify" in 1967.

By then the mood of the music had changed, nowhere more profoundly than in Detroit, with its radical mix of drugs, politics, and free-form rock 'n' roll noise, typified by the White Panthers, *Creem*, Iggy Pop, and the MC5. As the writer Lloyd Bradley put it in *Mojo*, "It was into this seething cauldron of the most aggressive, demented acid rock and uncompromising Black nationalism, that Funkadelic was born, kicking out the jams with big boots on."

"Back then white people was going totally black with Cream," Clinton told Bradley. "They were doing the blues in a way black people weren't. We wanted to get some of it back, our version of the blues."

Their first Funkadelic album, entitled *Funkadelic*, was released in 1969. George told Peter Murphy in *Hot Press*,

> That was the beginning of our psychedelic era. Jimi Hendrix at that time was the king of it. I knew him as Jimmy James and he wasn't playing like that with King Curtis. As far as I was concerned, we was already doing it slightly ourselves anyway. And then Sly came along. And so we did *Funkadelic* and *Free Your Mind and Your Ass Will Follow* was the next one. That was blatantly psychedelic, we just said, "Let's just go all the way crazy."

Commercially, the music of Funkadelic was less than an immediate success. "It was too black for white folks," Clinton said in the Bradley interview. "It was even too black for some black folks."

Nowhere is the acid influence more prominent than on the *Osmium* album, released in 1969 under the Parliament name, but definitely containing the Funkadelic attitude. Reviewer Ned Ragget wrote for *All Music Guide*,

> After a stripped-down start, things explode into a full-on funk strut with heavy-duty guitar and slamming drums setting the way, while the singers sound like they're tripping without losing the soul. Sudden music dropouts, vocal cut-ins, volume level tweaks and more add to the off-kilter feeling. *Osmium*'s sound progresses from there—it's funk's fire combined with a studio freedom that feels like a blueprint for the future. Bernie Worrell's keyboard abilities are already clear, whether he's trying for hotel lounge jams or full freakiness; similarly, Eddie Hazel is clearly finding his own epic stoned zone to peel out some amazing solos at the drop of a hat. As for the subject matter and end results—who else but this crew could have come up with the trash-talking, yodeling twang of "Little Ol' Country Boy" in 1970 and still made it funky with all the steel guitar?

Clinton then admirably summed it all up—the album, the era, the band's philosophy of life—with a statement to Bradley that will ring especially true to anyone who played music or listened to music during the late '60s. "At the time, I didn't realize we were doing what we were doing because we were doing so much acid," he said.

CHAPTER SEVEN

The Long and Winding Road to Altamont

★ ★ ★ ★ ★ ★ ★ ★ ★ ★ ★ ★ ★

FROM THE TIME THEY FIRST FACED OFF against each other in the British rock scene of the early '60s, the Beatles and the Rolling Stones have been cast as mortal opposites, brothers under the skin perhaps, nurtured by the same Queen mother, but miles apart in their inborn personalities. Briefly: Beatles good, Stones evil. The Beatles were into Little Richard; the Stones were into Little Walter. The Beatles cleaned up nicely; the Stones had pimples. The Beatles were pop; the Stones were punk. Artistically, the Beatles were all about love and peace, while the Stones couldn't get any satisfaction. Beatles: *Let It Be*; Stones: *Let It Bleed*. As their careers progressed, the Beatles made it all happen in the studio; the Stones made it all happen on stage.

For all that, they were perhaps more similar than people thought. In 1969, both were dealing with the loss of a critical Brian. Both were having drug troubles beyond the usual for a rock band in the '60s; both were beset by women troubles that threatened the bonds of the brotherhood. By 1969, both bands were under the financial thumb of the swaggering New Yorker Allen Klein, and both bands were getting antsy from having been off the road, the Beatles for three years, the Stones for two. Still, they were the top two rock 'n' roll bands in America as far as the singles chart. In that domain, through 1970, the Beatles whipped the Stones, thirty-two to twelve; after 1970 the situation was reversed, with the still active Stones smashing the broken-up Beatles, eleven to two.

In 1969, however, it was less about the Beatles versus the Stones than it was about the Beatles versus each other. "The differences between John and Paul were always greater than between Mick and myself," Keith Richards once told me. So there was John versus Paul, the long-simmering brotherly jousting born of intense togetherness and intense success over so many years, so competitive they even got married within two weeks of each other. But there was also George versus Paul, the little brother struggling under the thumb of his artistically superior older sibling, caught so eloquently on the *Let It Be* documentary. And there was John versus George, probably over George's susceptibility to the mystic manipulations of the Maharishi and his success at sucking the rest of the group in with him. There was a little bit of John and George versus Paul and Ringo over that scene as well, with the latter two bugging out of India soon after the Maharishi was accused of coming on to Mia Farrow, leaving the former two to contemplate the ironies. On the return to Abbey Road in the spring of 1968 to begin work on the White Album, which came out in November, this may have been the leading cause of the tension in John's voice on "Revolution," the first track they worked on that night.

But with their manager and father figure Brian Epstein dead of an overdose, they were now all suddenly unmoored, set free to flounder in the real world grappling with a host of other tensions. Not least of these was Paul, George, and Ringo versus Yoko Ono, who made her first tentative steps into the studio in 1968 as John's shadow, love interest, and creative partner, the other woman in every sense of the word. By 1969 she was a constant whispering voice in his ear, urging him further and further from the blood-brother orbit of the other three.

Another in-house feud was Allan Klein versus John Eastman, battling over who would represent the Beatles' financial interests in 1969 with Papa Brian gone and the new Apple Records venture hemorrhaging cash. "Apple was like playing Monopoly, only with real money," John has been often quoted as saying. Originally started as a clever tax shelter, Apple sported offices complete with antique desks and genuine pieces of art on the wall, and a private dining room with two chefs, in which executives could enjoy eight-course lunches. There was a record division, a movie division, a TV division, an electronics division, a charitable wing, perhaps a concession stand. There were rumors that a line of Beatles greeting cards was imminent. James Taylor debuted on the label in 1968. Mary Hopkin had a No. 1 hit with Gene Raskin's updated Russian folk tune "Those Were the Days," introduced in San Francisco in 1962 by the Limelighters. But they also put out David Peel's inflammatory *The Pope Smokes Dope*. John Lennon's custom imprint, Zapple (an homage to Frank Zappa's Bizarre?), on which he planned to record spoken word albums by Allen Ginsberg, Lawrence Ferlinghetti, and Lenny Bruce, never got off the ground, other than to put out Beatles vanity projects. "We owned a house no one could remember buying," George recalled. Naturally, Paul wanted his fiancée Linda Eastman's cultured father and brother to handle their affairs. Just as naturally, John and the others stood by his choice of the streetwise Klein, who worked for the Rolling Stones.

But neither one of these financial gurus could prevent the fiasco of bogus "Head Engineer" John Alexis Mardas, a.k.a. Magic Alex, versus Abbey Road Studios that drained another $500,000 off the top through Alex's ill-informed attempts to design Apple's recording studio. Or to stop Brian Epstein's brother, Clive, from selling off their beloved Northern Songs publishing company to a huge conglomerate. Or to keep John and Yoko from posing in the nude on the cover of the album they were doing, *Two Virgins*, released late in '68. No wonder Ringo was slipping out early to work on *Sentimental Journey*, a group of aged pop songs only his mother could love. No wonder George was spending so much time with his Moog, releasing his initial noodlings on *Electronic Music* in 1969. No wonder Paul had decided to play all the instruments himself on his own moonlight project, to be entitled *Paul McCartney*.

In light of all these mounting irreconcilable differences, it only stood to reason that Paul should decide it would be a cool idea to bring in a film crew to capture them at work on *Get Back* (eventually re-titled more appropriately *Let It Be*) at Twittenham Studios, a cold, drafty movie soundstage seemingly heated solely by the intense emotions flaring. No wonder someone suggested they bring it all outside, up to the roof, for a pleasant little spontaneous outdoor concert, interrupted only by the whistling birds and the sirens of the police, who shut it down after forty minutes. Talk about your reality TV.

As early as January 4, 1969, the third day of the *Get Back* sessions, the Beatles were talking amongst themselves of breaking up. Or else playing a live gig at the Coliseum in Rome—or, as John lightheartedly suggested, at an insane asylum. This is where George walked out, lured back only by the promise that they'd give up the idea of playing live and they'd finish the album at Apple Studios. He might also have suggested they not film the whole agonizing process, but that was vetoed. They wound up playing live, their first such excursion into the open spaces since San Francisco, 1966, offering "Get Back," "Don't Let Me Down," "Dig a Pony," "I've Got a Feeling," and "One After 909" to a largely quizzical audience of neighboring office workers.

By the time the acrimonious *Get Back* sessions—abandoned in February, remixed in March, and completed under the auspices of Glyn Johns in May—were shelved in September, Paul had married Linda, George and Patti had gotten busted, and John had married Yoko, the latter couple by far receiving the most publicity, starting with staging their honeymoon week at the Amsterdam Hilton as a "Bed-In," two parts performance art, one part political protest. Very quickly, the couple released two more albums, more like documents of their consuming love affair: *Unfinished Music No. 2: Life with the Lions* and *Wedding Album.* This was the era of Andy Warhol–inspired experimental minimalist art. This was also the era of the Shaggs. Nonetheless, the Lennon-Ono releases sound as if they were in fact recorded at an insane asylum, with the inmates doing the vocalizing, except for *Wedding Album's* fourteen-minute "John and Yoko," a perhaps accidental homage to satirist Stan Freberg's magnificent "John and Marsha," which needed only 2:33 to make its point.

To paraphrase Dave Van Ronk paraphrasing Lenin's comment about the works of a certain poet, "Doesn't he know there's a paper shortage? He should have printed two copies, one for himself and one for his wife."

John and Yoko made much more of an impact, musically and politically, with "Give Peace a Chance," recorded at their hotel suite in Montreal and released in July, credited to John Lennon and the Plastic Ono Band, with backing vocals by Yoko Ono, Tom Smothers, Derek Taylor, and Rabbi Feinberg. In Ottawa they attended a peace seminar. They staged "Bed-Ins" in the Bahamas and in Montreal, where they met with the prime minister. They lent their support and their names to an extravagant peace festival slated for the following summer in Mosport, Ontario, in which the headliners were projected to be the Beatles and Elvis Presley.

On September 13, they jetted to Toronto to participate in the Toronto Rock 'n' Roll Revival, headlined by the Doors and featuring Chuck Berry, Bo Diddley, Little Richard, and, inexplicably, Alice Cooper. It was this performance, backed by an impromptu pickup band consisting of Eric Clapton on guitar, Alan White, and Klaus Voorman, as well as the keening Yoko, that many say led directly to John confronting Paul a few days later with the inevitable news that he wanted out for good. By September 20 a radio station in Iowa was reporting that Paul was dead. They had it wrong, actually; it was the entity known as the Beatles.

A similar confrontation had taken place within the ranks of the Rolling Stones in May, when Mick and Charlie and Keith found it their unpleasant duty to inform founding lead guitarist Brian Jones that his services with the group were no longer needed. He'd been distant from the band for quite a while, a situation compounded no doubt by his girlfriend of two years, actress and Andy Warhol socialite Anita Pallenberg, shifting her allegiance to Keith in 1967. Now she was due to give birth to Keith's baby in August. Jones's penchant for booze and drugs was severely limiting his ability and his desire to play his guitar or any of the multitude of other instruments he knew. On the *Let It Bleed* album he'd thus far only made two contributions, neither on guitar, playing autoharp on "You've Got the Silver" and percussion on "Midnight Rambler."

Brian sensed what was coming in advance of the meeting and invited various musicians to his house to tell them his plans to form a supergroup, not unlike Eric Clapton's Blind Faith, whose free concert in Hyde Park that month drew 150,000 people, among them Mick Jagger. Having been off the road for more than two years and in the midst of setting up an American and a European tour, Jagger immediately made plans for the Stones to participate in a similar free concert in the park in July, along with King Crimson and several other acts. With rehearsals for the gig about to commence at Apple studios, officially ousting Jones and finding a speedy replacement was thus made even more pressing. With no time to hold proper auditions, Jagger turned to Clapton's mentor in the blues, John Mayall. "I've got this guitar player you can have," Mayall said, naming Mick Taylor, "and he can come down right away."

Reportedly happier than he'd ever been, though looking physically worse than he ever had, Brian Jones appeared to take the news of his dismissal in stride. On July 2 he retired to his mansion at Cotchford Farm to party with friends, including his new Swedish girlfriend, who discovered him floating in his swimming pool around midnight. Whether his death was due to an accidental overdose or foul play or suicide, the coroner's designation of "misadventure" still stands.

At the Hyde Park concert two days later, Mick Jagger admonished the audience into silence before reading a couple of long, agonizing verses (XXXIX and LII) of Shelley's "Adonais," written in 1821 to memorialize fellow poet John Keats. (In my opinion, Jagger could have made his life and that of the audience a whole lot simpler by instead just reciting the last two lines of the very first verse: "Forget the past, his fate and fame shall be/ An echo and a light unto eternity.")

After the poem, 3500 butterflies were let loose, and the band launched into a Brian favorite, Johnny Winter's "I'm Yours and I'm Hers," the leadoff track from the first of the Texas bluesman's two Columbia albums of 1969. They closed with "Sympathy for the Devil," backed by George Johnson's African Drummers.

The next day the single "Honky Tonk Women," with "You Can't Always Get What You Want" on the B-side, was released. It would reach the top of the American charts a week after Woodstock. By this time Keith's son Marlon had been born and Mick had completed filming his starring role in Ned Kelly in Australia, his follow-up to his 1968-but-not-released-until-1970 role in Performance (on which his best song, "Memo from Turner," appears).

On the first day of filming, Mick's girlfriend Marianne Faithfull overdosed on sleeping pills and wound up in a coma in a Sydney hospital. Mick nearly joined her when a prop gun he was holding in his left hand exploded, requiring sixteen stitches.

No wonder the Stones were looking forward to the road, twenty-four shows in twenty-nine days, starting at a college date in Fort Collins, Colorado, with a lavish base camp set up in Peter Tork's big spread in the Hollywood Hills, now occupied by Stephen Stills.

John and Yoko spent some time recuperating in the hospital in 1969 as well, after a car wreck in Scotland prevented them from joining the sessions for the Beatles' next album, *Abbey Road*, until they were already underway that summer.

Not surprisingly, the first few days at the old Abbey Road studios without them were free from the kind of tension that marked the White Album of '68 and the *Get Back* sessions earlier that year, with Paul sliding down the banister, Ringo blowing bubbles, and George playing his slide guitar and his Moog. Paul laid down "Her Majesty" on the second day. When tape editor John Kurlander accidentally cut the song off one beat too early, Paul was, according to Beatle's engineer Geoff Emerick's memoir, *Here, There and Everywhere*, uncharacteristically mellow, saying, "Never mind, it's only a rough mix."

This would lead to an important error in Beatles mythology when "Her Majesty" wound up on the record with the last note still clipped. "I guess he figured that since 'Her Majesty' was starting with the last note of 'Mean Mr. Mustard,' she might as well not have a last note of her own," Emerick surmised of producer George Martin's intentions.

In a different book of Beatles history Martin is reported to have been unaware of clipping off the last note, replying to the questioner, "Oh, did we?"

To which the interviewer said: "What do you mean, did we? There's a million guys in America right now who were high on LSD during the sixties reading the meaning of life into your leaving that note off and you didn't even know you did it?"

Mike McGear, Paul McCartney's brother, added a further illuminating insight. "That's exactly what the whole Beatle thing was," he said, "doing it in complete innocence. Sometimes I suppose they used to tease the listeners a bit. Particularly John, I think, would love to fool around with people's heads."

Safe to say, John and Yoko immediately got inside the other Beatles' heads upon their return to Abbey Road in July. First there was general dismay that Yoko was there at all, looking wan and disoriented in a flimsy nightgown; next the dismay was upped to fuming if unexpressed rage when deliverymen arrived to install a bed in a corner of the studio, on which she obtrusively reclined, snacked, and took visitors. One such snack was a biscuit extracted from a stash belonging to George Harrison. Famously protective of his food supplies, as were all the other Beatles, George was reported by Emerick to have exploded, "That bitch!"

Further alienation, as if any were needed, was supplied by John's decision to play all the instruments and sing all the vocal parts on the thus ironically entitled "Come Together," a song he'd originally started writing for Dr. Timothy Leary during his losing California gubernatorial campaign against Ronald Reagan.

Despite some high points, like Ringo's first recorded drum solo at the end of "The Medley," the three live-in-one-take guitar solos from Paul, George, and John on "The End," George's emergence as a songwriter on "Something," and the album's eventual run of eleven straight weeks at No. 1 (until it was replaced for a week just before Christmas by *Let It Bleed*), it was pretty much a foregone conclusion that they'd never record together as the Beatles again. Later it was revealed that John had been on heroin during the entirety of the sessions. Subsequently, he wrote the confessional "Cold Turkey," which was released by the Plastic Ono Band, peaking at No. 30 in January, with Eric Clapton on guitar.

When the other shoe finally fell, after John got back from Toronto (but not announced for six months), George, for one, was relieved. "I realize the Beatles did fill a big space in the '60s," he told Geoffrey Giuliani in *The Beatles: A Celebration*, "but all the people they really meant something to are all grown up. Anything that people grow up with, they get attached to. I can understand that the Beatles, in many ways, did some nice things, and it's very much appreciated that people still like them. But the problem comes when they want to live in the past."

Like many of the musicians of the era in many less prominent bands, he washed his hands of his group's impact on the culture, especially the Alternate Culture. "All this thing about the Beatles being able to save the world is rubbish," said George. "It was just people trying to put that responsibility on our shoulders. The thing about the Beatles is they saved the world from boredom. We didn't really create any great change; we just heralded that change of consciousness that happened in the '60s. We went along with it, that's all."

To which Paul added in the press release for his early 1970 solo album, "My plan is to grow up."

Despite what has been said and written about the gruesome symbolism and symmetry surrounding the last stop on the Stones tour, the violence-ridden free December concert at the Altamont Speedway in Livermore, California (especially as compared to the milder vibes in August at Woodstock, its eternal companion in history), the real message of the event can be summed up in Paul McCartney's flip yet profound statement—it was time to stop behaving as out-of-control children.

As a generational loss of innocence the Altamont Festival was hardly on a par with the Kennedy assassinations, the Martin Luther King assassination, the bloodbath at Grant Park in Chicago, the bloodbath at People's Park in Berkeley, the bloodbath in Benedict Canyon that Charles Manson and his cronies had just been accused of creating, or the ongoing bloodbath in Viet Nam that had prompted the reinstatement of the draft lottery. Governor Reagan was quoted in California early the next year as saying in response to the quelling of student riots, "If it takes a bloodbath, let's get it over with." Nineteen-sixty-nine, let's face it, was a year of bloodbaths.

As Frank Zappa in the Mothers of Invention noticed in "Trouble Comin' Every Day," and Stephen Stills of the Buffalo Springfield predicted in "For What It's Worth," and John Fogerty in Creedence Clearwater Revival raged in "Bad Moon Rising," and the Stones foretold in "Street Fighting Man," and the Beatles forewarned in "Revolution," and Roger McGuinn lamented in "Ballad of Easy Rider" by the Byrds, and the Jefferson Airplane profanely suggested in "We Can Be Together," an unequal but opposite reaction was heading toward the collective festival audience on the Santa Ana winds.

In the controversial hiring of the Hell's Angels to serve as crowd control at Altamont, class and race and rock 'n' roll, 1969, collided. Not merely a throwback to the music's earlier image and audience, the Angels were idolized by the elite of the counterculture, from Ken Kesey to Jerry Garcia. Despite their own outsized outlaw proclivities, they obviously saw themselves on the same side of the law and order issue as Nixon and Agnew, who a mere two days before, in a scene straight out of *Reefer Madness*, had, according to *Rolling Stone*, locked themselves in a room (in an undisclosed location) with the governors of forty states to "embark on a magical mystery fact-finding mission to discover the causes of the generation gap. They viewed films of simulated acid trips and listened to hours of antiestablishment rock music." With the full weight of Nixon's law-and-order mandate behind them, the Angels felt as free as ever to knock the heads of any head at will, or anyone else who looked or acted in a manner they deemed insufficiently patriotic.

(Probably in a similar state of delusion, Elvis Presley, who was performing in Las Vegas at the height of the festival season, spent the rest of 1969 feverishly jotting down notes for his eventual letter to Nixon, offering to become the president's "Federal Agent-at-Large" in the Bureau of Narcotics and Dangerous Drugs, a position for which he had already done an enormous amount of personal research. As a gift at that December 1970 Oval Office meeting, Elvis gave Nixon a Colt 45 pistol; Nixon may have given Elvis a pen.)

Staring at the roughs of the murder in the Maysles Brothers documentary *Gimme Shelter*, back home in London, Mick and Keith had little comment on seeing a white Angel stabbing a black man with a gun while the Stones, at the burnt-out end of a brutal day, were segueing from "Under My Thumb" to "Sympathy for the Devil," except to point out that the youth of Great Britain were by and large a much friendlier crowd than their American counterparts, as were the Hell's Angels.

"Mick wrote 'Sympathy for the Devil' almost as a Dylan song, but then it ended up a rock 'n' roll samba," Keith once explained to me, going on to describe the band's general attitude toward their provocative, some might say irresponsible lyrics. "To a certain extent you play on your image," he said. "Oh, that's the general perception? And you just come up with a line or a song and lean on it, push it, go for it. Nobody writes a song to put it in a back drawer."

Journalist and future Patti Smith guitarist Lenny Kaye, writing about the Stones' U.S. tour in the January 1970 issue of *Fusion*, was not graced with the benefit of hindsight. In fact, he was saddled with a deadline that made actually attending Altamont impossible. Nonetheless, he was only wrong about its dénouement in his chilling assessment:

> It's fitting that the last great musical moment of the six-
> ties should belong to the Rolling Stones. It seems pe-
> culiarly a time for the Stones, more suited to them than
> any of the others from whom we've expected leadership
> in the past. Only the Stones seem on top of things, get-
> ting stronger and more vital as time goes on. In Amer-
> ica and appearing for the first time in three years,
> their presence seemed to signify that in a way they,

rather than any of the others, were there to lead the way into whatever the seventies would bring.

As Altamont brought the decade to a close, the generational cohort that had defined the music since 1965, changing rock 'n' roll to folk rock, acid rock, blues rock, jazz rock, and progressive rock, creating the album market, and populating the Alternate Culture—a middle-class, college-educated, elitist brigade—seemed to crash all at once, coming down from a five-year psychedelic high. Some would move to Canada to avoid the draft. Some would follow the Weather Underground to the next violent confrontation. Some would struggle on to the McGovern campaign. But the music would never mean the same thing to them once the next Baby Boom wave, born after 1953, a carefree, draft-free, working-class bunch, took over. With numbers even bigger than the first wave, these Boomers would bring the music to new levels of popularity, as the album market thrived, the touring industry prospered, and FM radio settled into a profitable corporate groove.

Still a dreamer at heart, John Lennon released *Live Peace in Toronto* in December of 1969, while plotting the Mosport Peace Festival at the home of Ronnie Hawkins, the rockabilly legend who was the Band's first employer. But in February he had to pull the plug, mainly for reasons having to do with the intricacies of Canadian politics. "The peace festival went bankrupt and I was left with a $16,000 phone bill," Hawkins recalled. Lennon's single "Instant Karma" came out at the end of February 1970, with George Harrison on guitar, produced by Phil Spector, beating to the marketplace by three weeks the Beatles' next-to-last No. 1, "Let It Be," written by Paul the previous January. The Phil Spector–produced version of the song appeared on the *Let It Be* album over Paul's protests when it came out in May. By then, *McCartney* would be out, beating Ringo's *Sentimental Journey* to the marketplace by four days.

So when McCartney announced the breakup of the Beatles in April, it was a mere formality. Similarly, when Nixon sent the National Guard in to Kent State the next month to perpetrate another bloodbath, it was also a formality.

As Jagger quoted Shelley at the Brian Jones tribute concert, a generation can now look to William Wordsworth for the final say.

Though nothing can bring back the hour
Of splendor in the grass, of glory in the flower;
We will grieve not, rather find
Strength in what remains behind.

PART TWO

Opiates for the People

★ ★ ★ ★ ★ ★ ★ ★ ★ ★ ★ ★ ★ ★

CHAPTER EIGHT

Three Minutes of Heaven

★ ★ ★ ★ ★ ★ ★ ★ ★ ★ ★ ★ ★

OF ALL THE CULTURAL AND POLITICAL wars going on in 1969—between hawk and dove, moderate and radical, hippie and square, gay and straight, man and woman, parent and child, veteran and peace marcher, cop and protester, Nixon and his enemies—the battle between old guard singles fans of commercial AM radio and the new breed of album cut aficionados who preferred the mellow tones of progressive FM radio was nowhere near the most deadly. But it was nonetheless a surefire argument starter and social divider, the latest wrinkle in the age-old music fan caste system—epitomized in the past by Elvis vs. Pat Boone, the Shangri-las vs. Brenda Lee, Buddy Holly and the Crickets vs. Bobby Vee and the Shadows, and Bob Dylan vs. Peter, Paul and Mary (Dylan vs. the Beatles was a big one at first, the Beatles vs. the Stones was eventually a non-issue, Muddy Waters vs. the Stones was a red herring, Lesley Gore vs. Connie Francis was a fight none of us wanted to see, and the Four

Seasons vs. the Beach Boys was strictly an East Coast–West Coast thing).

Launched in the summer of 1966, in less than three years the underground stations of the FM band had risen to become an instinctual if not street poetic force for all relevant music and propaganda, the voice of the counterculture, resulting in a concurrent surge of album sales, while the entrenched AM stations relied more and more heavily on market research, catchy slogans, canned bells and whistles, and the same twelve songs repeated every hour between Clearasil commercials.

At least, that was the format over WABC in New York City. Elsewhere, in the mythical secondary markets beyond the Hudson, great singles were born, played, and died unheard by sheltered Manhattanites and their brethren in the boroughs. But that was the price you paid for living in "the greatest city in the world," on its way in the 1969 through May 1970 period to championships in professional football, baseball, and basketball. But even these secondary markets had a formula for what was playable, not at all based on artistry or the personal vision or taste of the deejay or program director. It had more to do with what the station up the road or across the river was playing: Buffalo looked at Cleveland, St. Louis looked at Chicago, Houston looked at Denver, San Jose looked at San Diego. Of course, a record had to start somewhere and somehow, usually in the even more mythical tertiary markets, their identities hidden from the average listener like the reporting bookstores on the *New York Times* best-seller list.

We all knew payola was still involved, chart numbers bought and sold, favors traded like Topps bubblegum cards, but exactly what the price of admission was, how much it paid for, and how much was earned was another mystery. As Berry Gordy implied in Motown's inaugural hit in 1960, "Money" was what he both wanted and needed. But as the Beatles said in 1964, money alone "Can't Buy Me Love." For those remaining diehard transistor listeners with a strong antenna who could haul in some of those stations from their rooftop on a good night, the payola question was always rendered moot by the music. But by 1969 the limitless new world provided by progressive FM stations had all but eliminated the need to keep tabs on the weekly drama of the singles chart, unless, of course, you were a true believing fan of a form in danger of becoming a dying art.

Like John Sebastian, author of "Summer in the City" and "Do You Believe in Magic" for the Lovin' Spoonful, reduced in 1969 to writing show tunes. "If anything I was pooh-poohing people who were trying to put art into rock," he said. "At the time I was going, that's really bullshit. A forty-five is special; it's three minutes of heaven. It's got to be an opiate. An awful lot of good chemistry has to happen in the studio. Moments—you have to get a series of them, magic moments that you did not plan, that you couldn't train for . . . that just happen."

"There's something in me that's singles-oriented," Paul Simon told me. "You start to make a track and all of a sudden it's got a great feel to it. A kind of magic happens that you couldn't have predicted. 'Let's pull out all the stops and make an AM record.' That sentence comes up a lot in the studio."

"I once met John Lennon at a BMI dinner," Doc Pomus said. "In fact, we spent the whole dinner together. And he was telling me originally all they wanted to do was reach a point, like Morty [Shuman] and myself, or like Carole King and Gerry Goffin, where they could make enough money to survive writing songs."

Gerry Goffin attempted to explain.

> There's a certain magic that some records have and that some records don't have. It's not a quality you can capture unless everything is going right. I'm talking about even at a record session. There are so many personalities involved, so many variables. It has to go through a lot of different ears, different people have to decide if it's something people want to hear. I could always tell if a song was going to be a hit or not, or how big a hit it would be, by listening to it on the radio. I never listened at home; I used to always listen in the car. It was just something about the resonance of the car radio. Usually with the good records you caught the sound of a hit single.

While the hit single never did die out entirely, by the end of the 1960s AM radio was a severely wounded white buffalo staggering through the hinterlands, its whole oeuvre called into question by critics cramming for term papers in league with record executives looking for a bigger slice of the profits to be derived from album sales. As a longtime singles diehard, owner at the time of a life-threatening stack of *Cashbox* magazines, whose first attempt to get published was an enraged essay submitted to *Seventeen* magazine about the emotional veracity of the single "Judy's Turn to Cry" by Lesley Gore, my bias is as pronounced now as it was obsessive then. However, 670 singles made the *Billboard* chart in 1969 for at least a week, and while that was down from 1966's peak of 743, the next decade would barely average 500. With FM stations continuing to siphon off the album market of sophisticated college students, more and more the single was regarded as the lowest of common denominators, the gateway drug, as it were, for lusty adolescents fiddling with their first radio.

Nonetheless, a careful study of the singles charting during this tumultuous period of social and political change reveals that many of them addressed the issues of the day with more directness (and a better beat) than the so-called artistically superior album cuts on the FM dial.

To get a better understanding of what transpired on the singles charts of 1969, we first need to revisit the final four months of 1968, when the counterculture started its inevitable descent just after the battle for Chicago at the Democratic National Convention. At the very top on September 7 was the idealistic, imploring "People Got to Be Free" by the Rascals. Written by Felix Cavaliere in response to the second Kennedy assassination, it was spending its second week at No. 1, replacing treacle like "Hello I Love You" by the Doors and Herb Alpert's "This Guy's in Love with You," which had dominated the summer. But entering the chart that week were three singles that would begin to set the challenging and disturbing tone for the next eighteen months.

James Brown's "Say It Loud—I'm Black and I'm Proud" was released just a few weeks after it was written in response to the Martin Luther King assassination, in the aftermath of which Brown had become a de facto spokesman for the middle ground in race relations, an openly patriotic supporter of Hubert Humphrey. Despite its ameliorating motive and uplifting message, the song would become much more of a rallying cry for extremists than Brown had bargained for. Similarly, "Street Fighting Man" by the Rolling Stones, on the surface a dig at rootless youths in "sleepy London town," would be taken more literally on campuses across America and, infamously, at a Stones concert a year later in California. "The Shape of Things to Come" by Max Frost and the Troopers was even more insidious. Written on assignment by the former Brill Building team of Barry Mann and Cynthia Weil for the brainless teen exploitation movie *Wild in the Streets* and produced by noted conservative pop impresario Mike Curb, who concocted the group in the studio, the tune might be dismissed as typical soundtrack product for the bubblegum set. Except the product they were selling was a mass teenage revolution in the streets, a notion the MC5, who had played at Grant Park in Chicago, were peddling for real.

The following week the Beatles tried to have it both ways, releasing the hopeful "Hey Jude" on one side and the more cantankerous "Revolution" on the other, both songs taking a step back from the whirlwind they'd been busy stirring by advising restraint. In October, Andy Williams's "The Battle Hymn of the Republic," which he sang at RFK's funeral, hit the charts, followed by Jose Feliciano, who drew a lot of flack for his interpretation of The Star-Spangled Banner." While Jimi Hendrix ("All Along the Watchtower") and Eric Clapton in Cream ("White Room") offered the hope of release or at least escape, elsewhere a tepid nostalgia reigned in "San Francisco Girls" by Fever Tree and "Those Were the Days" by Mary Hopkin. In her version of Joni Mitchell's "Both Sides Now," Judy Collins assigned the troubling discrepancies to the aging process alone.

At the end of October, Dion's earnest "Abraham, Martin and John" was hardly a call to arms. It was even matched on the country charts a month later by "Ballad of Two Brothers" by Autry Inman. Closer to the basic country music attitude that would make significant inroads in 1969 were "Stand by Your Man" by Tammy Wynette and "The Straight Life" by Bobby Goldsboro, which entered the charts within a month of each other. Soon a generation would don Stetsons and try to follow, to the tune of "Going Up the Country" by Canned Heat.

If the voice of Young Black America was still being channeled by Motown, that voice was getting exceedingly desperate. In "Cloud Nine" the Temptations tapped into the depressed, angry reality of the inner city. A week later, Marvin Gaye's sinister version of "I Heard It Through the Grapevine," actually recorded before the Gladys Knight and the Pips 1967 hit, was prodded into release by a thousand kids in Chicago reacting to its tribal tom-tom. Diana Ross and the Supremes may have reported themselves children of poverty in their October release, "Love Child," which became their eleventh No. 1, but the 1969 follow-up, "I'm Livin' in Shame," was more believable, portraying Diana as a successful social climber denying her roots. A few months later she'd be comfortably in character celebrating her mentor and lover, Berry Gordy, in "The Composer," and a few months after that, she'd be out of the Supremes entirely.

In October, when Carla Thomas brought the first cover of a song from the tribal rock musical *Hair!* to the charts, she was drawn not to one of its more celebratory anthems but to the soulful existential lament "Where Do I Go," symbolizing the crossroads where a lot of less privileged folks stood arm in arm (though few were arm in arm on the line to buy tickets to a Broadway musical). For the Impressions' second release on Curtis Mayfield's Curtom label he chose "This Is My Country," an impassioned call for racial justice, only a month after the election of Richard Nixon. By the end of the year James Carr was riding the "Freedom Train" and the Esquires were singing "You've Got the Power," both of which were heard only on R&B stations at the far left of the dial.

It took a couple of months into 1969 before the message of the street was converted into singles crafty enough to make the charts, even the lower rungs of which connoted some kind of acknowledgement that the songs were at least worth ponying up for. With a smoother road to that peak than most, the Temptations made use of the Motown machine in "Run Away Child, Running Wild," their social commentary starting to become formulaic. Former Impression Jerry Butler was more committed to the task ahead in "Only the Strong Survive." Written with the Philadelphia producing team of Kenny Gamble and Leon Huff, its laid-back soul propelled it into the Top 5. The songs that followed wouldn't be as forgiving.

As if to head off the impending stampede, James Brown got to the gate next, with the relatively empowering "I Don't Want Nobody to Give Me Nothing" before lapsing into a year mainly spent doing the Popcorn, including "The Popcorn," "Mother Popcorn (Part 1)," "Lowdown Popcorn," "Let a Man Come In and Do the Popcorn (Part 1)," and, to finish up the year, "Let a Man Come In and Do the Popcorn (Part 2)." By then so much had changed that Brown had to title his first release of 1970 "It's a New Day," although the title doesn't even appear in the lyric of that song, which seems to be more of a reaction against Women's Lib than anything else.

Following Curtis Mayfield and Jerry Butler to the podium abandoned by Brown were Sly and the Family

Stone, with the philosophical "Stand," and Nina Simone, with the self-penned "Revolution," both arriving the same week in April, Simone's composition spending only two weeks on the R&B chart. A jazz singer of incredible power and substance, she'd fared no better in the U.S. with the *Hair!* cover "I Ain't Got No/I Got Life" a couple of months earlier. By the end of 1969 she'd more than make up for it with the definitive "To Be Young, Gifted and Black," a Top 10 R&B hit cowritten with Weldon Irving in honor of the Lorraine Hansberry play.

Mad but visionary producer Phil Spector, who made his original name as the genius behind inner-city girl groups like the Crystals and the Ronettes, had his last hurrah with "Black Pearl," a stirring citified romance by the interracial Sonny Charles and the Checkmates. The controversial "Israelites" by Desmond Dekker came next, the first reggae record to hit the charts, rising as high as the Top 10. The Winstons' "Color Him Father" was a softer but even more hopeful slice of black life, depicting the growing middle class. The Detroit-based Parliament, brainchild of the mad but visionary producer George Clinton, was six months ahead of James Brown in declaring "A New Day Begins." By the end of the year Clinton would expand his operations and his consciousness to include the outrageously costumed and more musically compelling Funkadelic, which started out in fairly tame fashion with "I'll Bet You" and "Song for My Mother." They were still miles away from the epiphany of "Free Your Mind and Your Ass Will Follow."

The summer of the moon landing featured the return of Curtis Mayfield's rational take on race relations, "Choice of Colors," coming out the same week as Edwin Starr's "I'm Still a Struggling Man." The Miracles covered

"Abraham, Martin and John" in July, a week after racy comic Moms Mabley's version. In defiance of the prevailing Motown picture of black family disintegration, the Chi-Lites fell into the positive, "Color Him Father" mode with their second release, "Let Me Be the Man My Daddy Was," while Johnny Taylor was considerably more militant in "I Could Never Be President."

The approaching holiday season offered some hope of conciliation, with "Friendship Train" by Gladys Knight and the Pips coming in November. On December 6 radio programmers welcomed reggae singer Jimmy Cliff into the fold with his first hit, "Wonderful World, Beautiful People," and welcomed back Wilbert Harrison, whose "Let's Work Together" was his first chart record since "Kansas City" in 1959. Worlds away, in Altamont, California, a black Rolling Stones fan was stabbed to death by Hell's Angels. A week later, as if in response, Syl Johnson asked the rhetorical question "Is It Because I'm Black?" His two follow-up singles of 1970, "Concrete Reservation" and "One Way Ticket to Nowhere," charted only R&B. These days he's better remembered as the father of current R&B songstress Syleena Johnson.

The year ended with blues singer Little Junior Parker, famous for providing Elvis Presley with his "Mystery Train," having a cup of coffee on the R&B charts with "Worried Life Blues."

The early part of 1970 offered more uneasy listening, with Thelma Houston's version of Laura Nyro's stark "Save the Country," Curtis Mayfield keyboard player Donnie Hathaway's "The Ghetto," and the Temptations' "Psychedelic Shack," followed in February by the Smokey Robinson–influenced Whatnauts' "Message from a Black Man," whose message was, in brief: You can't stop us now.

But saner heads seemed to prevail in the personas of the previously blissful but now chastened 5th Dimension, with the poetic "Declaration" followed by the medley of "A Change Is Gonna Come/People Got to Be Free." Even the Chambers Brothers of ominous "Time Has Come Today" fame were now opting for "Love, Peace, Happiness." It was thus up to two ancient acts from the earliest days of rock 'n' roll to cap the period, with doo-wop stalwarts the Flamingos praising their black heritage in "Buffalo Soldier" and the former right Reverend Little Richard laying into "Freedom Blues," which would appear on the chart two weeks after the shootings at Kent State and remain there for nine weeks, by which time Crosby, Stills, Nash and Young's "Ohio," speaking for an entirely different constituency, would be ensconced.

Christened in the blood of Grant Park in Chicago, 1968, to the riotous chords of the MC5, with the lyrics to Joe Cocker's jaunty Beatles cover "With a Little Help from My Friends" stuffed back down their throats, a bleary-eyed bunch of true believers might have awakened on the Ides of March, 1969, if they were listening to AM radio, to the delicious irony of "Kick Out the Jams" (minus the "motherfuckers" rallying cry) battling it out on the bottom 10 of the charts with "The Pledge of Allegiance" by sentimental comedian Red Skelton. This alone would have been enough to lead them to convene shouting matches in ivy-covered meeting rooms for the next couple of months, at which point John Fogerty gave them what for in "Bad Moon Rising," while the Beatles advised a strategic retreat in "Get Back." Only Sly and the Family Stone held to the program in "I Want to Take You Higher."

By the summer of Woodstock, the Youngbloods' version of "Get Together" was a public service announcement waiting to be a hit record a couple of years too late. Rehearsing for the epic outdoor concert at home in Los Angeles, Crosby, Stills and Nash released what I believe is their most authentic and revealing song, also their first hit, "Marrakesh Express," charting the great European summer hitchhiking exodus of America's affluent rebel culture that CSN (and sometimes Y) would come to embody so well.

In the 1980s, Graham Nash told me:

> With songs like "Chicago" and "Ohio," CSN began to reflect the environment in which we were totally immersed. For instance, in "Chicago," when I saw them bind and chain Bobby Seale to a chair and put a gag in his mouth [at the ludicrous trial of the Chicago Eight before it became the Chicago Seven] and put him in the witness box and try to call that a fair trial, every fiber of my Englishness said, "Wait a second, that's just not fair." Songs as news means people want to hear songs that mean more to them than "Carrie Ann." In fact, the Hollies recorded "Marrakesh Express." I haven't heard the tape for fifteen years, so I'm not quite sure how it came out.

The Hollies did, however, reflect the generally exhausted yearning for relief that came with the turn of the decade, in "He Ain't Heavy, He's My Brother," which hit the charts the same week Judy Collins revived the Pete Seeger chestnut "Turn Turn Turn," a hit for the Byrds in 1965. A few weeks into 1970 a Detroit rock band, Frijid Pink, took a stab at "House of the Rising Sun," another of the defining landmarks of folk rock as done in 1964 by the Animals, as if such revivals were all that was needed to restore the faith of the faithless.

Although the Frijid Pink take on the New Orleans chestnut was almost as big a hit as the Animals' version, folk rock II failed to take hold. Instead, 1969 was a year that began with no less a lounge singer than Tommy Leonetti attempting to co-opt the folkies' campfire rallying cry of "Kum Ba Yah," rendering it a running joke for the next forty years. A few months later, the Vogues attempted to revive the Brothers Four classic "Greenfields," to nil effect, Rick Nelson covered Dylan's "She Belongs to Me" without success, and Peter, Paul and Mary, six months after declaring "Day Is Done," were "Leaving on a Jet Plane," their only No. 1 song, courtesy of John Denver (from whose 1969 album, *Rhymes and Reasons*, it was plucked). The Dylanesque folksinger Donovan was looking for the lost city of "Atlantis" and the born-again folksinger Dion was wandering around in a "Purple Haze" after his ill-advised Jimi Hendrix cover stiffed, while Zager and Evans preferred the sci-fi lite vision of "In the Year 2525," turning it into an unaccountable monster hit. Foretelling the religious revival just around the corner more than another folk revival, Jim Pepper's chant-like "Witchi Tai To" by the very 1969-sounding duo of Everything Is Everything stalled at No. 69 early in the year, although it did wind up a staple in the repertoire of Brewer and Shipley.

By far folk music's best commentary on the entire Summer of Love/Love Is All You Need zeitgeist it had wrought came from the pen of Bob Dylan, the man who was arguably responsible for all the tumult and the nestling and who was even now declaiming in a strange countrified voice, "I Threw It All Away," and from the lips of his former lover, Joan Baez, who released as a single the scathing "Love Is Just a Four-Letter Word."

And so when John Lennon shouted, "Give Peace a Chance," there was no chance. When Tim Hardin pined for a "Simple Song of Freedom," the issue was anything but simple. When Thunderclap Newman said there was "Something in the Air," there was nothing in the air. When John Lennon (again) called for a generation to "Come Together," there was no generation left and there were no Beatles left. On November 1, this became even clearer with the release of "The Ballad of John and Yoko."

Also entering the chart that week was Creedence Clearwater Revival's blistering diatribe on class and privilege as reflected by the draft, "Fortunate Son," written by John Fogerty when his own tour of military service had come to its honorary conclusion. It was joined in perpetuity by one of the saddest songs ever recorded, "We Love You, Call Collect" by Art Linkletter and his twenty-year old daughter, Diane.

A companion if not an answer song to Walter Lundberg's "An Open Letter to My Teenage Son" from 1967, in which the Michigan newscaster tells his hippie offspring, "If you burn your draft card you may as well burn your birth certificate" (and which was itself answered that year by Every Father's Teenage Son in "A Letter to Dad"), the popular entertainer Linkletter's response is a good deal less ponderous and more forgiving than Lundberg's. On record, in her letter to Mom and Dad, the daughter reveals herself a child of the age, a sixteen-year old runaway who has found respite from her family in the loving arms of a commune of like-minded rebels. "I met a lot of weirdos," she says, "but I've learned how to tell the beautiful people from the phonies." On October 4, shortly after the recording was finished, Diane Linkletter jumped to her death from the kitchen window of her apartment in West Hollywood. Art Linkletter attributed this tragedy to LSD and worked diligently for drug reform ever after. But more likely it was suicide.

Released on November 1, the record sold 250,000 copies in eight weeks, inspiring filmmaker John Waters to use the event as the basis of his fledgling effort, a ten-minute docudrama called *The Diane Linkletter Story*, shot the day after the suicide, starring his favorite transvestite, Divine, as Diane. Later, Waters, disavowing any exploitative intent, said he was just trying out a new camera.

As the tune wended its way up to an eventual No. 42 by the end of November, this stark lament was joined on the charts by several other wounded participant observers of the unraveling dream. Coming the week of November 8, Janis Joplin's first solo effort, "Kozmic Blues," was probably as pure a distillation of her harried mindset as she ever put to vinyl. She told writer David Dalton,

> Kosmic blues just means that no matter what you do, man, you get shot down anyway. You know, I'm a middle-class white chick from a family that would love to send me to college and I didn't wanna go. I had a job. I didn't dig it. I had a car. I didn't dig it. I had it real easy . . . and then one day I realized in a flash . . . it was your whole life. You'd never touch that fucking carrot, man, and that's what the Kozmic Blues are, cause you know you ain't never going to get it.

It was joined the same week and peaked on the charts the same week in December as Joplin's San Francisco Jefferson Airplane soul sister Grace Slick's by now outdated call to revolution in the streets, "Volunteers," which resurrected the word "motherfuckers" in tribute to the MC5's bowdlerized "Kick Out the Jams." A week later John Lennon joined them with his anguished confessional, "Cold Turkey." The year ended with one man's good-humored draft day odyssey, "Alice's Restaurant," which was easier to endure as a movie when it appeared in the summer but impossible to endure when the draft lottery of December 1 coughed up your number.

In the encroaching anxiety surrounding that event, as the war raged on and students, fearful of losing their deferments among other things, staged protests at the University of California at Berkeley, the University of Wisconsin at Madison, the University of Massachusetts, Howard University, Penn State, Harvard, and CCNY, many took refuge in music for comfort and salvation. In this context, country music represented a fitting escape for a Baby Boom generation of college age and just past it, looking, like their former savior Bob Dylan, to grow into and finally accept their parents' world and worldview.

In the conservative bastion of the country charts, rebel whispers were few and far between. In Jim Webb's "Galveston," as sung by Glen Campbell, released in March, the narrator seems radical merely by confessing his fear of dying overseas. "I'll never forget the first thing Glen Campbell said when he met me," Webb recalled. "He said, 'Why don't you get a haircut?' We were sort of philosophically on opposite sides of the line, at least politically, but what started out as kind of shaky developed into a wonderful friendship."

On April 4, former rock icon Wanda Jackson almost certainly had nothing subversive in mind when she revived Pete Seeger's folk classic "If I Had a Hammer." In May, Elvis's "In the Ghetto," written by Mac Davis, reached the chart, but only stayed a couple of weeks. It picked up support from the always feisty Dolly Parton, whose rendition was much more convincing, undoubtedly based on her own childhood struggles with poverty.

In general, Elvis's singles output for the year found him in a nervous, melancholy, and especially prescient state, reflecting Martin Luther King–like on the present in "If I Can Dream," released in November 1968, pondering the past in "Memories" in March, confronting a jealous wife (Priscilla) in "Suspicious Minds" in September, and leaving his beloved baby daughter (Lisa Marie) in "Don't Cry Daddy" in November. Elvis's other release of the year, in July, came from his twenty-second and last movie, *The Trouble with Girls*. But even in "Clean Up Your Own Backyard" he sounded somewhat irritated as he railed against the "back porch preachers," "drugstore cowboys," and "armchair quarterbacks" he knew and loved.

A much more typically retrograde country attitude was presented by the brilliant Joe South, who, in the earlier "Games People Play," found fault with people who meditated, were into astrology, and said "to hell with hate." In September, Freddy Weller had a hit with South's "These Are Not My People," which depicted the country cousin of the girl in Dylan's "Like a Rolling Stone" and contains one of the best put-down verses in country music history.

Dylan himself missed the country charts with his three single releases, "I Threw It All Away" in May, "Lay Lady Lay" in July, and "Tonight I'll Be Staying Here with You" in November, although "Lay Lady Lay" went Top 10 on the pop charts. Neither did Dylan's cohorts in the Band fare any better with their version of Americana, including "The Weight" and "Cripple Creek." The songwriter in the rock sphere who most warranted country attention in 1969 was John Fogerty. "Proud Mary" was covered by Anthony Armstrong Jones in August and "Lodi" was covered by Buddy Alan in December, the same month George Hamilton IV covered James Taylor's "Carolina in My Mind." But IV's affinity for great rock songwriting dated at least as far back as 1967, when he brought Joni Mitchell's breathtaking "Urge for Going" to the country Top 10, the first song of hers to chart anywhere.

The country corridor had its own great songwriters to care for and feed, the most promising of whom was Kris Kristofferson, whose "Me and Bobby McGee" debuted (sung by Roger Miller) the week of August 30. The similarly inclined Ray Stevens appeared with the dour "Sunday Morning Coming Down" in October (a few months later he'd totally recovered in the blissful "Everything Is Beautiful"). Johnny Cash's version of "Sunday Morning Coming Down" appeared in 1970. In 1969, Cash was helping the songwriter Shel Silverstein establish a beachhead in Nashville similar to the one he maintained at the Playboy Mansion as a chrome-domed cartoonist for the house magazine. This he did with "A Boy Named Sue," the biggest hit of his career, recorded live at San Quentin.

Perhaps country music's finest minutes on the charts of 1969 occurred near the end of the year, when Merle Haggard released "Okie from Muskogee" in November, a song that signaled its anti-hippie intents right from the get-go. This was followed up a month later by one of the great patriotic anthems of the century, "God Bless America Again," by Bobby Bare.

Often invoked in song lyrics, God would play a prominent role in the pop sphere in 1969, with the Baptist hymn "Oh Happy Day" by the Edwin Hawkins Singers the first gospel track to ever hit the Top 40, let alone the Top 5. The record business being the copycat animal it is, this development didn't create the kind of groundswell you might expect. Billy Preston's "That's the Way God Planned It" didn't arrive on the charts until the end of August and never made it to the Top 40. Lawrence Reynolds had a semi-hit with "Jesus Is a Soul Man" (the Billy Grammer cover version made the country charts). The Brooklyn Bridge's version of "You'll Never Walk Alone" failed to evoke much fervor in October. Harry Nilsson had slightly better success with "I Guess the Lord Must Be in New York City" in November, but he definitely brought a secular frame of mind to his message, having originally written the song for the movie *Midnight Cowboy*.

The real impact of pop's spiritual drift began in 1970 with the arrival of "Superstar" by Murray Head on the charts in January. The show for which it was composed, *Jesus Christ Superstar*, hadn't yet opened or, for that matter, even been written. Said *Superstar*'s lyricist, Tim Rice,

> For economic reasons, we were forced to try to get somebody to back a record first, when we really wanted to write a show. After being turned down by several people, we got MCA in London interested, but they said it would be too expensive to do the whole LP. They said they'd just put out a single and "if that goes it will prove there's a market for an album."
>
> This was late summer of '69. We just had an outline, the framework, which was a lot of work, but there were only a few tunes and a few ideas. We hadn't thought in terms of a single, but we went away and polished "Superstar" and took it back to them. As soon as the single was finished, even though we

didn't know whether it was going to be a hit or not, we began writing the rest of the album. This was around Christmas, '69. Meanwhile, the single by Murray Head began taking off. It was a small hit in the U.S. and a big hit in Brazil and Belgium and Australia. By February of 1970 MCA gave us the go ahead for the album and we had the colossal job of actually getting people to sing on it.

In October it was released in England and America and it sank in England. It was an immediate total flop. We'd already been booked to come to the States, so we thought at least we'll get one trip out of it. But when we got here, at the airport we were met by a great army of people, press and everything, and we suddenly realized it was going to be a big hit here.

Like Lou Reed and so many others during the '60s, Rice realized there were "a lot of us." Only in this case, it was a new interest in all kinds of religious experience that was attracting the leading heads of the generation in the wake of the success of the "Superstar" single. Among them, not surprisingly, were the recently countrified Byrds, whose "Jesus Is Just Alright" charted for a week in February 1970. They were still led by Roger McGuinn, a convert to Subud in 1967, who had recently lost faith in his new faith.

Said McGuinn, "I said, 'Oh God, how can I keep from feeling like this?' And I got this sort of . . . not a loud voice or anything, 'Well, you could accept Jesus.' So I said okay, and I felt good again."

The last week of February found "Spirit in the Sky" by Norman Greenbaum and "Instant Karma" by the man now known as John Ono Lennon entering the charts, both bound for a Top 3 slot later in the year. Given that Greenbaum was best known as the author of the 1966 jug band novelty 'The Eggplant That Ate Chicago,' many may have doubted the profundity of his religious feelings. But Ono Lennon definitely had a vision about "Instant Karma," writing it and recording it on the same day and releasing it ten days later. This vision may or may not have been shared by his producer, Phil Spector, but it was definitely embraced by his guitarist, George Harrison, whose own "My Sweet Lord" would hit the charts by the end of the year, reportedly influenced by 1969's "Oh Happy Day" if not Paul Kelly's July hit, "Stealing in the Name of the Lord," but deemed so melodically similar to "He's So Fine," the 1963 hit by the Chiffons, that he was successfully sued for plagiarism.

The Who's Peter Townshend came out with "The Seeker" in April of 1970. Lennon and Harrison didn't influence him; he wrote the song for his own guru, Meher Baba, who had died in January 1969.

"I liked a lot of the Beatles' stuff," Townshend admitted, "but I was never influenced that much by it. I mean musically they just seemed to have such a peculiar method of working. A lot of it was melodic in a way—although it sounded great when they did it—when you tried to find out what it was that made it tick and react to it musically, it was very sort of Italian love songs sort of stuff. How can you be influenced by that?" He didn't mind hanging out with them, however:

> John Lennon was incredibly funny and Paul was always a little bit embarrassing, because he was never very sure of himself. He used to start off conversations with . . . "Don't treat me like somebody big or

anything. I know you think I'm great . . . and I know you're good, and you know I'm good . . ." And this would go on for about five minutes and then John would come in and say "Hello, want a sandwich?"

In May of 1970, Aretha Franklin charted with "Spirit in the Dark," but the spirit invoked in that song had little to do with the Lord and more to do with the religious experience of sex, always a staple of the pop, rock, and soul formula. But in 1969, even sex had become politicized, with the pendulum swinging decidedly against the Revolution, which had proven to be a boon primarily to the male gender. Now women were beginning to have their say, in the bedroom (if not the boardroom) and on the charts.

Guided through adolescence by the black girl groups of the early '60s like the Chantels, the Crystals, the Shirelles, and the Marvelettes, once again young girls— as well as some older ones, hardened by bitter experience—were looking to black women for emotional education (having for the most part rejected Janis Joplin and Grace Slick as too loopy to be role models). And the women were more than happy to oblige. On her way to anthems like "Wedlock Is a Padlock" and "Women's Love Rights," Laura Lee offered "Hang It Up" in January 1969. On her way to "I Feel Like Breaking Up Somebody's Home," Ann Peebles revealed her frustrations in 1969, first with "Walk Away" and six months later with "Give Me Some Credit." Onetime Motown golden girl Mary Wells, on her own since 1963, came up with "Never Give a Man the World" in 1969. Aretha herself was looking for love in her cover of Bobby Bland's "Share Your Love with Me" and acknowledging how hard it was to find in this day and age, a sentiment ratified in October by Honey Cone in "Girls It Ain't Easy," their first R&B hit for Hot Wax, the new Holland-Dozier-Holland imprint. In November the Supremes may have been reacting to the loss of their aforementioned favorite songwriting team, or else playing it safe by pining for an unavailable lover, in "Someday We'll Be Together."

Not surprisingly, the soul men in attendance were at first confused by these developments. Whereas in December of '68 Sam and Dave were celebrating "Soul Sister, Brown Sugar," less than two months later, a neglectful William Bell was singing "I Forgot to Be Your Lover." In February, Tyrone Davis was halfway out the door when he asked, "Can I Change My Mind." In March, Clarence Carter got fed up with his on-again, off-again lady in "Snatchin' It Back." In April, the observant folks at Chess/Cadet put out blues singer Howling Wolf's truly scarifying vision of the female sex, "Evil," which resulted in his first chart record in thirteen years. In May, Joe Simon just managed to keep his rage in check in "The Chokin' Kind." In Memphis in August Isaac Hayes, coauthor of the above Sam and Dave hit, took his sweet time but eventually decided to bolt with his elaborately rendered "By the Time I Get to Phoenix." However, on the B-side he was regretting it in "Walk On By." In September, Marilyn McCoo, singing lead for the 5th Dimension on a tune by fledgling feminist songwriter Laura Nyro, was getting antsy about her man in "Wedding Bell Blues." By the end of the year, even the blissfully patient B. B. King had seemingly lost it, releasing "Get Off My Back Woman" in August and "Just a Little Love" in October. After spending much of the fall learning about love from the Rolling Stones on their fateful American tour of 1969 (and along the way providing half the San Francisco psychedelic guitarists with their sound) he had every reason to come out with "The Thrill Is Gone" in December, for which he was rewarded with his biggest crossover hit.

Over at the Motown House of Hits the situation wasn't any better. Marvin Gaye and Tammi Terrell led off February with "Good Lovin' Ain't Easy to Come By." It was followed later in the month by David Ruffin's "My Whole World Ended (the Moment You Left Me)," which may have been equally inspired by his leaving his beloved Temptations, whose August release was "I Can't Get Next to You." In May Junior Walker put out "What Does It Take (to Win Your Love)." The only Motown regulars who seemed to be getting it regular were the obsessive Marvin Gaye in "Too Busy Thinking about My Baby" and the blind prodigy Stevie Wonder in "My Cherie Amour." Even the Jackson 5, prepubescent heirs to the Frankie Lymon and the Teenagers/Nolan Strong (cousin of Motown's Barrett Strong) and the Diablos mantle of ethereal teenage innocence redeemed were feeling the pull in the tug of war, debuting with "I Want You Back" in November.

In Chicago, veteran blues singer Little Milton, in his remake of the Little Willie John classic "Grits Ain't Groceries (All around the World)," vowed to dig a ditch with a toothpick and fight off lions with a switch to prove his love. In Memphis, even critically coddled white boys like the Box Tops swore in "Soul Deep" to work themselves to death for love. In New Orleans Lee Dorsey came up with a less strenuous solution via songwriter Allen Toussaint, "Everything I Do Gonh Be Funky (from Now On)." But in San Francisco, the members of Quicksilver Messenger Service were walking across forty-seven miles of barbed wire to prove themselves worthy in their remake of Bo Diddley's "Who Do You Love." And in Crow's "Evil Woman (Don't Play Your Games with Me)" the line in the sand was drawn at accepting responsibility for someone else's baby (much as Michael Jackson would do years later in "Billie Jean").

Which only makes the appearance of "Je T'aime . . . Moi Non Plus" by Serge Gainsbourg and Jane Birkin on the bottom rungs of the chart on the morning of November 29 that much more of a triumph. A No. 1 hit in England but banned throughout much of the rest of the world, this salacious taste of pre-disco foreplay by a man who was known to have fooled around with Brigitte Bardot might have single-handedly restored the sexual equilibrium so sorely missed throughout 1969. But two factors prevented it from breaking into the Top 60. One was that Serge and Jane were married at the time of the recording, thus taking a lot of the forbidden edge off it. (Although Jane had already achieved notoriety for having appeared in the nude in the 1966 film *Blow-Up*, she only did the record because Bardot refused to approve the release of her own original version). The other of course was that Serge was French and the last song with French lyrics to become an American hit had probably been "Dominique" by the Singing Nun (who was from Belgium), and we all know what happened to her (big pop hit, followed by steep decline, followed by suicide).

Two years later almost to the day, Helen Reddy hit the top of the American charts with "I Am Woman," and the rest was history.

In the face of this history, most American men retreated under their headphones for the better part of a decade, finding solace in the blast of a loud guitar. Fortunately, the album market of 1969 had enough spillover to provide even the weak-kneed Top 100 with a bevy of brilliant noisy singles to get them started.

"Crosstown Traffic" was hardly Jimi Hendrix at his best, but it was enough to get the juices flowing as 1968 ended. If you lived in Detroit, you also might have heard Bob Seger's invigorating "Ramblin' Gamblin' Man" around that time. If not, you'd have to wait for eight years and seven more failed singles for "Night Moves" to come along. In the meantime, January provided Eric Clapton in Cream with a showcase in "Crossroads" and Ritchie Blackmore a platform in Deep Purple's version of "River Deep, Mountain High." But it wasn't until March that nirvana and Valhalla arrived at once in the persons of Jimmy Page and Robert Plant in Led Zeppelin's "Good Times, Bad Times." "Badge" came in April, with Eric Clapton singing lead and George Harrison on rhythm guitar. Clapton had left Cream by then, to form Derek and the Dominoes, whose transcendent "Layla" would not arrive for a couple more years. In the meantime, arriving on April 5, "Tommy," the title song from the Who's rock opera, would suffice.

Schooled in the old blues records of Jimmy Reed, Townshend probably thought he was the last person on Earth who'd wind up associated with that stodgy term evoking medieval tenors and busty contraltos. But his manager Kit Lambert always knew his man was destined for greater things. "About a year after I started writing, Kit started announcing to everyone that he thought I was a genius," Townshend told me. "He often used to fantasize about me doing something on a grand scale even then. I mean, it was his idea to do a mini opera on the *Happy Jack* album."

Although no *Hair!* on the record charts, *Tommy* did produce a second single, "I'm Free," in July, the same month Mick Jagger supplied "Honky Tonk Women" to his hungry male audience, marking the debut of new guitarist Mick Taylor. In September Grand Funk Railroad began their legendarily loud crusade with "Time Machine." This was followed by Carlos Santana's "Jingo," the instant classic new single from Led Zeppelin "Whole Lotta Love," and, to bring in the New Year, albino Texas bluesman Johnny Winter's frantic take on Chuck Berry's essential "Johnny B. Goode."

But man could not live on guitar solos alone, even the highly selective men bred in the '60s who could drop the needle on their record machines exactly on the spot where a certain mammoth run of notes went from the sublime to the ridiculous. Sated by a diet of nothing but the blues-derived bombast of heavy metal, in time these fans developed a tolerance for a bit of jazz, accepting into their record collections, if not their hearts, the new horn-laden version of the once bluesy Blood, Sweat and Tears with "You've Made Me So Very Happy" and "Spinning Wheel," if only to appease their girlfriends, who might have liked the looks of new lead singer David Clayton Thomas. A few months later, the horny Chicago broke through with "Questions 67 and 68." The Joe Jeffreys Group was nicely slick in "My Pledge of Love" in June. And Italian conductor Piero Umiliani filled an unspoken need in September with "Mah-Na-Mah-Na" from the notorious sex documentary *Sweden Heaven and Hell*, which doubled as the theme for *The Benny Hill Show*. Blood, Sweat and Tears were back in October with a spiffy version of a Laura Nyro tune, "And When I Die." Keyboard great Les McCann did a fine job of vocalizing on the Gene McDaniels song "Compared to What," with Eddie Harris on sax, to start the new decade.

For better or worse, it would be a decade that defined if not deified virtuosity, often for its own sake, as heavy metal morphed into arena-sized clouds of sound. Santana came back in January with "Evil Ways," followed by Buddy Miles with the drum-soaked "Them Changes" and the torrential "Mississippi Queen" by Mountain. But the more exciting future lay in the relatively complex progressions of progressive rock, exemplified by King Crimson, who actually hit the singles chart on January 31, 1970 with "In the Court of the Crimson King (Part 1)," featuring the inspired noodling of Robert Fripp.

Although Jimi Hendrix had a club in the Village called Generation, where he frequently jammed, New York City veered much more toward the music it did best—singles—through 1969, with the legendary Brill Building staging a literal and figurative comeback. Paul Simon, who had taken over the entire top floor with his publishing enterprise, crafted one of his best hits, "The Boxer," and followed it up with his biggest hit, "Bridge over Troubled Water." His probable neighbors, Jerry Leiber and Mike Stoller, capped their career writing a single for Miss Peggy Lee, "Is That All There Is?" Down the street, John Sebastian was extracting "She's a Lady" from the musical *Jimmy Shine* and turning it into his first single as a solo artist. Across the street, at her Tuna Fish publishing outfit, Laura Nyro added Three Dog Night's cover of "Eli's Coming" to her already blistering resume. Around the corner, Paul Anka gained the biggest honor of his career when Frank Sinatra covered his "My Way." Frank also covered George Harrison's 1969 hit, "Something," but did so thinking it was a Lennon and McCartney song. He never released it as a single. The April-Blackwood offices handling the publishing for *Hair!* did a land office business in 1969, with "Aquarius" by the 5th Dimension, "Hair" by the Cowsills, "Good Morning Starshine" by Oliver, and "Easy to Be Hard" by Three Dog Night. Operating out of Morris Levy's dimly lit offices at Roulette, Tommy James paid the rent with "Crimson and Clover," "Crystal Blue Persuasion," and "Sweet Cherry Wine." Operating out of nearby Philadelphia, Todd Rundgren started his wizardly career with "Hello It's Me," by his group Nazz (obviously a tribute to the Beatles' favorite hipster comic, Lord Buckley, who died in New York City in 1960).

Studio mavens Ron Dante, Paul Leka, and the team of Kazenetz and Katz kept the cash cow of bubblegum music alive with "Sugar Sugar," attributed to the Archies, "Na Na Hey Hey Kiss Him Goodbye," nominally by Steam, and "Indian Giver," the final hit for the ersatz 1910 Fruitgum Company. Neil Diamond, a 1650 Broadway expatriate now adapting to life in L.A. without good bagels, displayed his admirable chops with "Sweet Caroline," a song written about Caroline Kennedy. L.A. returned the favor to Coconut Grove's honorary Greenwich Village hipster, Fred Neil, by putting Harry Nilsson's version of his composition "Everybody's Talkin'" in the movie *Midnight Cowboy*, the leverage from which gained it a Top 10 showing. Three Dog Night returned the favor to Harry Nilsson by covering "One" and sending it into the Top 10.

New York City was even responsible for two of the three best songs about Woodstock, the culture's signal event of the year (even though it was staged by the city's poor upstate cousins): "For Yasgur's Farm," an album track by Mountain, and "Lay Down (Candles in the Rain)," by the West Side's own flower child, Melanie.

"When I recorded 'Lay Down,' I said, 'Oh, I hope I just die. This is just the greatest thing. I don't want to have to do anything else,'" Melanie told me. Although she was speaking about the recording of the song, she could have been speaking of her rainy night performance. "I was sure it was the greatest thing I ever did, but I wasn't sure people were going to like it . . . and I didn't care."

Joni Mitchell, author of the other notable song about Woodstock, was safe and dry and watching news of the concert on television in her hotel room, having opted to fulfill a previous commitment to appear on *The Dick Cavett Show* instead, where she played "Chelsea Hotel" for the first time and gave a stunning a cappella performance of the antiwar "The Fiddle and the Drum." She debuted "Woodstock" at the Big Sur Festival in September on a bill that included Woodstock survivors John Sebastian, Joan Baez, and Crosby, Stills and Nash (with Young); as well as the Flying Burrito Brothers; Baez's sister, Mimi Fariña; Ruthann Friedman, the author of the Association's hit "Windy"; and Dorothy Morrison and the Edwin Hawkins Singers, who had so ably backed Melanie on "Lay Down."

Mitchell was enjoying a hot streak of her own at the time, sparked by Judy Collins's hit version of "Both Sides Now," which peaked on the Top 10 Christmas week of 1968. Now Judy had just returned to the charts with "Chelsea Morning," the song Joni had written at New York City's famed bohemian dive, the Chelsea Hotel. In October, Crosby, Stills and Nash would pay tribute to Collins in Stephen Stills's "Suite: Judy Blue Eyes."

But many of the other icons of the Southern California scene, who'd been surfing on the crest of the good vibes spawned by the Monterey Pop Festival of 1967, were finding the waters of 1969 a bit choppier. Jim Morrison of the Doors opened the year with "Touch Me" sailing to a respectable No. 3. But it would be the band's last Top 10 hit. The follow-up, "Wishful Sinful," arrived in March, a few weeks after Morrison was busted in Miami for exposing himself. The record stiffed and the group's U.S. concerts for the rest of 1969 were canceled. Said guitarist Robbie Krieger,

> The Doors were living theater. Jim really lived the life you saw on stage. He was like that all the time. He created this kind of image and then we got so big that he couldn't live up to it. We didn't go on the road that much because, frankly, Jim got too wild to stay out too long. The longer we stayed out, the crazier he'd get. After Miami we couldn't play anywhere anyway. That's why Jim decided to go to Paris, where he died.

After Dennis Wilson's disastrous run-in with Charles Manson and his flock, the houseguests from hell, the Beach Boys put out "I Can Hear Music," "Break Away," and "Add Some Music to Your Day" through 1969. No one, however, was listening, except for the studio group Sagittarius—including Terry Melcher, alleged to be Manson's intended target, who covered "In My Room" (where he undoubtedly stayed until the Manson gang was put away toward the end of the year).

With their TV show canceled, the Monkees' perpetual wounded cry of "Listen to the Band" was especially poignant. It was the second of three singles of 1969, including the earlier "Tear Drop City" and the later "Good

Clean Fun," all of which flopped. "The series left the air early in 1968," Tork recounted. "We toured the Far East, made the movie, *Head*, and a TV special. We didn't go into the public eye in America at all. That's one of the reasons the movie didn't go, the special didn't go, and nothing ever happened to the Monkees again."

After the Mamas and the Papas imploded, Mama Cass was the only one to sustain a solo career, even if that career seemed terminally mid-list. One of the few hits emanating from Laurel Canyon came wafting out of Jackie DeShannon's house a few blocks away. Having amassed a resume that included hits for Marianne Faithfull, the Searchers, and Brenda Lee; songs for Ricky Nelson written with Eddie Cochran's girlfriend Sharon Sheeley; a tour of soccer stadiums at sixteen with the Platters; and six weeks of basically one-nighters on the Beatles' first American tour (and with it the opportunity to witness the writing of John Lennon's "I'm a Loser" and to show George Harrison the guitar riff to "When You Walk in the Room"), Jackie's career was lacking only one thing. "I had never written and recorded my own million-selling song," she said. Neither was she considered an album artist. But that was hopefully going to change.

"*Laurel Canyon* was really the first album for which I had control of the material and the direction of the album," she said of that late 1968 release. "I had the chance to bring my vision into reality. Barry White sang background, Russ Titelman played guitar, and Dr. John was on keyboards. It was an amazing group."

And so, when "Put a Little Love in Your Heart" came flying off the keyboard in the spring of '69, she wasn't about to peddle it to the highest bidder.

I had been showing songs to other people for a long time, and I wanted to record this one myself. The original demo session and the final recording were very much the same, with the exception of the strings and the horns. The final record took nine hours to get the exact rhythm, tempo, and feel of the demo. I thought I had recorded my best vocals. But when I heard the playback, they had somehow lost the original vocals. I remember calling up my mother, hysterical, saying I had just done the best singing of my life and it was erased. I finally did nail the vocal again, and it became my favorite record.

A seasoned veteran of the songwriting wars, Jackie knew she had a hit "when WABC radio in New York put it on their playlist when it was only Top 30 in *Billboard*. Back in the day, they would add a new record only when it reached the Top 5 with a bullet. So when they started playing 'Put a Little Love in Your Heart' when it was only Top 30, radio stations across the country dropped their socks and I just knew we had a chance at having a big record."

So why wasn't Jackie the next Joni Mitchell, or at least the next Carole King, the former Brill Building conscript who was laboring in the neighborhood on the work that would result in *Tapestry* a couple of years later? "When I was recording for Liberty I was never encouraged to tour. They were interested in building their publishing company and they wanted me to concentrate on songwriting," DeShannon said. "The record company was not into promoting concept albums. I had a blues/jazz/gospel background and I had a difficult time finding producers who were attuned to the direction I wanted to go. I think

John Hammond at Columbia would have been the perfect producer for me, and I always wondered where that might have taken my career."

By the time Crosby, Stills, Nash and Young's version of Mitchell's "Woodstock" hit the charts in March of 1970, the world depicted by the song had changed completely. A stirring portrait of togetherness and revolution now sounded like irreversible nostalgia. More immediate and telling was the Byrds' melancholy November release, "Ballad of Easy Rider," from the movie where the entire counterculture was shot in the back. Or CSNY's follow up to "Teach Your Children" that starts with "Tin soldiers and Nixon's coming" and ends with "Four dead in Ohio."

Nowhere was this change more deeply felt than in San Francisco, which had pretty much had it as a commercial scene. Politically, the atmosphere was too charged for anything as trivial as a listening to singles. Janis Joplin was between bands. Grace Slick was between husbands. The Quick and the Dead would never be singles bands. Although Santana would hit the Top 10 twice in 1970, with "Evil Ways" and "Black Magic Woman," the two most viable bands from the area were Creedence Clearwater Revival and Sly and the Family Stone. Creedence seemingly scored at will, with five hits in twelve months: "Proud Mary," "Bad Moon Rising," "Green River," "Down on the Corner," and "Travelin' Band." Like Elvis and the Beatles (and the Monkees), even their B-sides were good enough to make the charts, including "Lodi," "Commotion," "Fortunate Son," and "Who'll Stop the Rain." Only "Proud Mary"'s B-side, "Born on the Bayou," failed to make the charts. Sly was a little more erratic, but still strong in the paint, cashing in No. 1 hits "Everyday People" at the end of '68 and

"Thank You (Falettinme Be Mice Elf Agin)" at the beginning of 1970, with "Hot Fun in the Summertime" in the middle, peaking at No. 2.

Hence, it would be tempting to sum up the entire year in America by citing three songs recorded in England, two at Abbey Road Studios; but the Zombies' "Time of the Season" was written in 1967, and, as with "Get Together," the season for love was long gone by the time the Top 40 nodded its approval. And the Beatles' "Let It Be," although released in March 1970, was written in January of 1969, when its seeming farewell to the golden age (farewell to the Beatles) would have been slightly premature. Only the Stones' "You Can't Always Get What You Want," recorded at Olympic Studios in London in the summer of '69, has the required time frame to make it relevant. "Much has been made of the lyrics reflecting the end of the overlong party that was the 1960s, as a snapshot of Swinging London burning out," critic Richie Unterberger observed. "That's a valid interpretation, but it should also be pointed out that there's an uplifting and reassuring quality to the melody and performance. This is particularly true of the key lyrical hook, when we are reminded that we can't always get what we want, but we'll get what we need."

For the clearest expression of what we needed, as a weary generation approaching the end of a long strange trip that had begun with Elvis overthrowing the establishment in Memphis and Nashville, New York City and Hollywood; continued with Timothy Leary turning on in a lab in Stanford and Lyndon Johnson dropping out in Washington, D.C.; and culminated on a pig farm in Woodstock, one need only revisit the morning of the last day of that fabled get-together, just before Jimi Hendrix

summoned the crowd to attention with "The Star-Spangled Banner," when a smart-aleck group of greased-up
showboats in gold suits from Columbia University
named Sha Na Na presented a set consisting of "Yakety
Yak," "Teen Angel," "Jailhouse Rock," "Wipe Out," "Book
of Love," "Duke of Earl," and "At the Hop."

I'm talking, of course, about the oldies revival that en-
gulfed the airwaves of 1969, more powerful than the folk
revival for the same wounded soldiers who'd expected so
much of their music, their country and themselves.
Barely two months after Woodstock, the boys from Columbia U. were to be found on the stage of Madison Square
Garden's Felt Forum, performing with the likes of
Chuck Berry, the Platters, the Shirelles, and headliner Bill
Haley and the Comets, in the first of what would be many
Rock 'n' Roll Revival concerts presented by Richard
Nader. It was, to paraphrase astronaut Neil Armstrong,
one step forward for a group of men, a giant leap back-
wards for music.

In retrospect it was as inevitable as the heavy nostalgia binge for the '50s that was to follow in film (*American
Graffiti*), theater (*Grease*), and TV (*Happy Days*) as an embarrassed and harassed generation began to realize that
no matter how many of "us" there were, there would always be more of "them," and therefore effected a retreat
back to a simpler past.

It would be comfortable to blame it all on Tiny Tim.
But his version of "Great Balls of Fire" barely dented the
charts in February 1969. In March, Otis Redding revived
Clyde McPhatter's now suddenly relevant "A Lover's
Question," Righteous Brother Bobby Hatfield took on
the Platters' "Only You," and Paul Anka went up against
the Five Satins' monumental "In the Still of the Night." In

April, Chubby Checker was probably being facetious when he recorded the Beatles' facetious rewrite of Chuck Berry's "Back in the U.S.S.R." But Jay and the Americans and the Vogues were totally serious in their homage to doo-wop classics "When You Dance" and "Earth Angel," respectively. If we'd doubted his motives in March, Paul Anka was back in May with the Moonglows' "Sincerely." Ray Stevens nearly had a hit in June with the Coasters classic "Along Came Jones," which appeared on the chart the same week as Cat Mother and the All Night News Boys' "Good Old Rock and Roll," a medley of "Sweet Little Sixteen," "Long Tall Sally," "Chantilly Lace," and "Whole Lotta Shakin' Goin' On" that nearly cracked the Top 20. It was produced by Jimi Hendrix, the man for whom Sha Na Na served as opening act at Woodstock.

The biggest oldie revived that year belonged to an L.A. group called Smith, who brought the Bacharach-David hit for the Shirelles, "Baby It's You," back to the Top 10. But the most heartwarming oldie of the year, far surpassing Harlem scufflers turned Vegas stalwarts Little Anthony and the Imperials' version of "The Ten Commandments of Love" (with Galt MacDermot's personal favorite version of "Aquarius" on the B-side, titled here "Let the Sunshine In") had to be "Oh What a Night" by the Dells, a remake of their very first R&B hit, from 1956. "People say we came from the doo-wop era and we did," Dells original bass singer Chuck Barskdale said in Adam White and Fred Bronson's book *Number One Rhythm and Blues Hits*. "But we grew—we grew as men as well as musically and we were singing a lot of very hip jazz things, just trying to keep food on the table." The song not only hit No. 1 R&B, but was a Top 10 pop crossover, entering both charts the very week of August 16 that

Sha Na Na served notice to the elders of the Baby Boom generation that it was time to shed the love beads, the long hair, and the rustic trappings of the counterculture and come home.

"As evidence I give you 'Summertime, Summertime,'" I wrote in the liner notes to the 1986 reissue of the live Sha Na Na album *From the Streets of New York*:

> They understood the one-shot miraculousness of the Jamies. They knew the tone poem of summer release and relief, the boardwalk, the roof, the submarine races. And then they made a one-act play out of all these rock and roll verities, complete with Max Factor's hair and pre-slacker patter down to the taps on their dancing pumps. They even named themselves after a line in "Get a Job." After hearing that song Smokey Robinson wrote "Got a Job," but it was Sha Na Na who got the job and not as a ten-headed bicycle messenger either, but as messengers and scavengers and impresarios of rock and roll itself.

Of course, being listed as a coproducer of that reissue, I may have had a slight conflict of interest in the writing of those notes. But, as we will see in the next section on the albums of 1969, it was surely not enough to stop a true believer from preaching to the choir.

CHAPTER NINE

The Joy of Segues

★ ★ ★ ★ ★ ★ ★ ★ ★ ★ ★ ★ ★

IN 1969 YOU COULD STILL LISTEN to both AM and FM radio; that is, singles and album cuts, the best of all possible worlds for an Elvis-bred connoisseur. Unfortunately, with WMGM having gone the way of Beautiful Music in 1962 and WINS tragically driven to all-news one dark day in April 1965, only "the Good Guys" on WMCA stood between the diehard and the dreaded WABC, which basically played the same twelve well-established monsters over and over again every day, whereas WMCA had room for the occasional sleeper, the odd stiff, an album cut or two. But even by 1968, the Good Guys, waging a losing battle against the soul stations on one side of the dial and the FM underground on the other, were edging into the all-talk format that would take them over in 1970.

The AM experience was a simple one, hit based, like a daily newspaper, filled with headlines, ads, and little else. FM was more like a literary magazine. You got poems, elaborate essays, funky short stories, excerpts from novels in progress. You could appreciate AM for the familiarity it offered, the chance to hear your favorite single during any given half-hour stretch. On FM the object was just the opposite, to hear something totally unexpected. If AM was order personified, adhering to a dictum passed down from the home office, FM made order out of chaos. If the role of the deejay on AM radio was strictly entertainment, on FM it was creative, educational, and, epitomizing the buzzword of the era, mind-expanding. The primary tool of the AM deejay in fulfilling his mission was the bell or the whistle; the FM deejay was instead schooled in the art of the segue.

A lost art on free radio, to be sure, segues can still be heard here and there, on public and/or listener-supported stations of 5000 watts or less, situated between two mountain ranges and broadcast only during daylight hours in months that end in Y. Satellite radio has become fairly popular of late by offering the kind of segues developed during the heady heyday of so-called "free form," "progressive," or "underground" radio in the late '60s, but minus the creative dimension, the element of surprise, and hence the magic. If you're listening to a station called Garage Rock, most of your questions have already been answered.

But, luckily, over the course of the last ten years technology has enabled everyone to become a music programmer, indulging a personal segue philosophy on mixed tapes for all occasions, from breakup to make-up to the eternal vernal equinox. Unluckily, this development has mainly served to reveal the paucity of the average person's imagination, to say nothing of the average person's record collection (let alone the aching and perhaps irreparable gaps in the record collections digitally stored in cyberspace).

Going hand in hand to make a good segue, or, ideally, a good series of segues, leading to a lengthy, satisfying set of music, an extensive imagination and an unlimited record collection can never in and of themselves substitute for the kind of emotional commitment to the music and to the art that some generational bigots tend to think are beyond the grasp of anyone who didn't come up in the era of "Radio Unnamable," circa 1966 to 1970. (It was after 1970 that the segue started to go the way of the hula hoop and the hippie, as consultants were already out in force, looking to "monetize" the FM experience, eventually transforming it into, lo and behold, the New AM.)

Hence 1969 was one of the last plush years in the life span of the album artist, the album, the album cut, and the album cut aficionado. Previously the province of players in fringe genres like jazz, folk music, and the blues, who supposedly never craved and certainly never expected but anyway never got significant sales or airplay, the album market had been exponentially altered in 1965 by the second coming of the Beatles. As their first coming in 1964 consisted mainly of hit singles, the AM band and the AM market of Baby Boom adolescents had no problem dealing with the arrival of the Mop Tops. Raised on Elvis, mania was their bag; deejays were dispatched, with every town claiming its own "fifth Beatle." No fewer than thirty-one Beatles singles occupied the charts in 1964, including several reissues of older material on competing labels, a bunch of two-sided hits, a four-track EP, and "Sie Leibt Dich," the German version of "She Loves You." This number dropped to ten in 1965, six in 1966, six in 1967, four in 1968, five in 1969, and three in 1970.

Did the Beatles suddenly suffer a dramatic creative drop-off? Quite the contrary. Fame, and its attendant horrors of instant and utter vindication, untold celebrity, unlimited riches, and constant ego gratification, was surprisingly all the impetus they needed to produce four albums in 1965, accounting for approximately forty tracks, depending on which side of the pond you called home and whether you cared to count instrumentals by musical director Ken Thorne as Beatles songs. But they couldn't keep up that ferocious pace forever. From 1966 through the remainder of the decade they reduced their output to about an album a year, but those albums were *Revolver, Sergeant Pepper's Lonely Hearts Club Band* (which contained no AM singles), *The Beatles* (the White Album) and *Abbey Road*, with the soundtracks to *Magical Mystery Tour, Yellow Submarine*, and *Let It Be* (released in 1970) thrown in for good measure.

Coincidentally, 1967 was the year FM radio came along to handle the spillover of quality material produced by the Beatles and every other musician who came under their spell or influence, which would be approximately eighty-eight percent of all rock 'n' roll musicians under the age of thirty on several continents (and probably fifty percent of those over thirty). Not properly trained to accept the scraps considered banquets by the genre musicians of the past, these rock 'n' rollers of the 1965–70 era, many of them expectant, privileged, educated, entitled Baby Boomers themselves, needed—demanded—adequate recompense for their labors, which the record labels, flush from expanding album sales, and the FM stations, flush from commercials directed at this vast new market of Alternate Culture consumers, were more than happy to provide.

Unfettered by professional or artistic restraints and with lots of product in the marketplace to choose from,

FM radio presented its fans with an embarrassment of riches in the form of album cuts, starting in mid-1966, with the wheat and the chaff separated only by the segue. But, as reported in an early 1970 issue of *Rolling Stone* under the headline "FM Underground Radio: Love for Sale," the new decade brought trouble in (the music fan's) paradise. According to our man on the scene Ben Fong-Torres, "underground radio is safe stuff nowadays, no more 'progressive' in terms of hard politics, experimentation with music, or communication with the so-called 'alternate culture' than the everyday AM station."

Another victim of Nixon-era repression combined with the pendulum of events catching a generation unaware like a shot in the back, the artistic (as well as personal) freedoms so taken for granted by FM were about to be stripped from the album market as well (and from the underground "rock" press that it supported with its feisty ads). Indeed, to paraphrase one of those antiestablishment ads, the man was busting our music. Soon *Rolling Stone* would be the only '60s rock magazine left standing, having transformed itself in the meantime into a cultural publication, a new-generation *Esquire* with writers like Hunter Thompson and a new home office in New York City, the major leagues. It would take years before the album and the album market disappeared. But the album listening experience, aided and abetted by the album artists and album cuts showcased on FM radio, was already beginning to seem like a quaint predilection favored by certain old radicals at the general store, like dial-up phones and party lines.

According to Pete Fornatale, the beginning of the end for WNEW-FM, or at least for his extended tenure there, didn't arrive until April 1979, when a playlist was enforced at the station for the first time. "The music director looked at my albums," said Pete. "Eric Andersen out, Harry Chapin out, Arlo Guthrie out, Phil Ochs, Gordon Lightfoot, the artists that the station had been built on, the politics the station had been built on, were now getting lopped off."

Only two years before the twin purges of MTV and Ronald Reagan lopped off everything else countercultural in a seismic generational backlash whose aftershocks are still being felt, 1979, I'm guessing, is a good five to ten years after all but the generation's most fervent music fans (most of them making their living in the music business) had drifted from the underground into easy listening and from the barricades into their father's furniture business.

The following albums and album cuts from mid-1968 through mid-1970 are grouped into the kind of extended set lists you might have encountered on FM radio had you possessed, as many dreamed of, an antenna powerful enough to cover the entire U.S. and England (and maybe Jamaica) and the unlimited free time (as many managed to finagle during the period) to spend hour upon hour diddling the knobs in search of creative segues. Ironically, while such possibilities for random sampling now exist on the Internet, along with dozens of sites enabling the listener to construct customized set lists, like MTV, these revolutionary data banks arrived way too late to save the souls of the disheartened, leaving most visitors to ignore their potential treasures in favor of the latest hit by the latest hit-maker. But perhaps this is all for the best, since too much wallowing in nostalgic tunes once deemed the gospel, or at the very least superior to anything written and recorded before or since, is bound to stir the ashes of a dream and a childhood best left buried in the attic for the next family to dispose of with the trash on moving day.

THE DYLAN INFLUENCE

Since his arrival on the scene in 1961, following his own alleged Woody Guthrie influence, Bob Dylan has influenced almost as many musicians as the Beatles. Indeed, the "Great American Folk Scare" of 1963–65 could be directly linked to Peter, Paul and Mary's version of "Blowin' in the Wind," which hit the top of the singles chart in the summer of 1963, leading to a land-office business for Dylan's publisher in the next few years, including a PPM cover of "Don't Think Twice, It's All Right" that brought Dylan back to the Top 10 at the end of 1963. As a visible presence beside the lustrous Joan Baez at all the most fashionable rallies and demonstrations, Dylan presented a far feistier image than the cardigan-wearing folk contingents of the '50s, like the Kingston Trio, who nevertheless populated the same singles charts of '62–'63 with "Where Have All the Flowers Gone," "Greenback Dollar," and "The Reverend Mr. Black." Baez herself experienced her first singles chart appearance with the civil rights hymn "We Shall Overcome," which came and went on the list two weeks before JFK was assassinated in Dallas—a demoralizing event that nonetheless galvanized everyone in the folk movement.

By 1969, having undergone several influential transformations of his own, Dylan moved full bore into country music with *Nashville Skyline*, released in May, either in the attempt to extricate himself from the role of generational leader he'd been handed, or to further insinuate himself into the crumbling zeitgeist as a pilgrim showing the way out of the mess he'd had a hand in creating. Not surprisingly, his two closest clients and associates, the Byrds and the Band, were right there with him.

In the spirit of Dylan's January 1968 release, the Western-tinged *John Wesley Harding*, the Byrds also jumped into country music with *Sweetheart of the Rodeo*, released in the summer, aided and abetted by the presence of the man who arguably invented the country rock genre in the International Submarine Band, guitarist/ songwriter Gram Parsons, whose "Hickory Wind" would soon become a classic. They also covered the Louvin Brothers ("The Christian Life") and Dylan's idol, Woody Guthrie ("Pretty Boy Floyd"), after which Parsons took Hillman with him to start the Flying Burrito Brothers, leaving McGuinn to form a new Byrds. Replacing Parsons with bluegrass guitarist Clarence White guaranteed that *Dr. Byrds & Mr. Hyde*, released in March, shortly after Dylan returned from recording in Nashville, would continue along a country road, at least another mile or two. Included in the album was the White-McGuinn collaboration "Nashville West," the Parsons-McGuinn collaboration "Drugstore Truck Driving Man," which Joan Baez would sing at Woodstock, and a cover of "This Wheel's on Fire," written by Dylan at Big Pink in Woodstock with the Band's Rick Danko and included on the Band's debut album, *Music from Big Pink*, released in the summer of '68.

Hailed as a classic piece of Americana, kicked off by the stirring Dylan–Richard Manuel collaboration "Tears of Rage," *Music from Big Pink* also contained a chilling version of the folk classic "Long Black Veil" and the Robbie Robertson gem "The Weight," as well as Dylan's elegiac closing "I Shall Be Released." While Dylan moved from this eloquent missive straight into ditties like "I Threw It All Away" and "Country Pie," the Band expanded on their vision in *The Band*, released in October 1969, without a single Dylan song. On this album Robbie Robertson stepped up to the songwriting plate in grand fashion with "Across the Great Divide," "Rag Mama Rag," "Up on Cripple Creek," and "The Night They Drove Old Dixie Down," which a year later became Joan Baez's first and only Top 10 single.

In 1969, Joan was steadfastly carrying the torch for Dylan, releasing *Any Day Now* in January. Recorded in Nashville the previous October, it contained sixteen covers, including four songs from *John Wesley Harding* ("Drifter's Escape," "I Pity the Poor Immigrant," "I Dreamed I Saw St. Augustine," and "Dear Landlord") and two from Big Pink ("Tears of Rage" and "I Shall Be Released"), as well an eleven-minute version of "Sad-Eyed Lady of the Lowlands," which Dylan wrote for his then wife Sara Lownds, and "Boots of Spanish Leather," which he wrote about his longtime girlfriend Suze Rotolo—but not "She Belongs to Me" or "Queen Jane Approximately," which were supposedly written about Joan herself. Eschewing gossip and yet inflaming it, her first single from the album was "Love Is Just a Four Letter Word."

Of course, Joan was married at the time to David Harris, who had just been sent to prison for draft evasion. In fact, while in Nashville, she recorded *David's Album*, which would be released in the spring, containing a number of country and bluegrass standards, including "Green, Green Grass of Home," "My Home's Across the Blue Ridge Mountains," and "Will the Circle Be Unbroken," as well as Gram Parsons' "Hickory Wind."

Another famed female Dylan interpreter, who actually beat the Byrds to the charts in 1965 with "All I Really Want to Do," her first single as a solo, Cher came out with three covers from *Nashville Skyline* by August 1969, working on her own *3614 Jackson Highway*, which is the address of Rick Hall's Fame Studios in Muscle Shoals, Alabama, including her incomparable twist on "Lay Baby Lay," which the Byrds beat her to as a single in June (it stiffed). Also notable on this album are her covers of Dr. John's "I Walk on Gilded Splinters" and two stellar Oldham and Penn compositions, "Cry Like a Baby" and "Do Right Woman."

Oldham and Penn's "Do Right Woman" also shows up on the track list for *The Gilded Palace of Sin*, the first album Gram Parsons recorded with the Flying Burrito Brothers after he and Chris Hillman flew the Byrds coop, along with the team's soulful "Dark End of the Street." As the man considered even more responsible for taking the Byrds in a country direction than Dylan himself, Parsons' vision of sin and redemption was quite a long way from Dylan's yokel's-eye view of country music, although it must be said that "Sin City" is about Los Angeles rather than Nashville. As such, the song and the album's appearance in the spring of 1969 heavily influenced a generation of weary L.A. musicians ready to abandon the psychedelic politics of acid rock for the greener pastures of country rock.

Far more Dylan-influenced was Atlanta native Joe South on the early 1969 release *Introspect*, especially on the caustic "These Are Not My People," originally the B-side of "Birds of a Feather," the follow-up to his biggest crossover hit, "Games People Play." Matching Dylan's talent as an unrelenting social observer and devout moralist, he was also no slouch in choosing sidemen, who range on this album from guitarist James Burton to sitarist Ravi Shankar (on "Games People Play"). Beyond that, as the author of the class-conscious anthem "Down in the Boondocks," covered by Billy Joe Royal in 1965, his dour purview in songs like "Rose Garden," later a hit for Lynn Anderson, was far more down to earth than anything Dylan would attempt on *Nashville Skyline*.

Closer in literary spirit to the pre–country squire Dylan was the former English teacher Kris Kristofferson. A reluctant performer, toiling in the shadows of Nashville for years, often as a janitor, Kristofferson had to be persuaded by Johnny Cash to play at the 1969 Newport Folk Festival. But, as it had for Dylan, Newport served as the perfect segue to the rest of Kristofferson's career as an acclaimed singer/songwriter. After Newport, he was signed to record his first album, *Kris Kristofferson*, which appeared in 1970. By then he'd hit the country charts as a writer with "Me and Bobby McGee" for Roger Miller, "Sunday Morning Coming Down" for Ray Stevens, and "Your Time's Coming" for Faron Young. Later, Ray Price ("For the Good Times"), Sammi Smith ("Help Me Make It through the Night"), and Johnny Cash ("Sunday Morning Coming Down") would have No. 1 country songs with tunes from the album. The Kristofferson signature was good enough in 1970 to hoist Jerry Lee Lewis ("Once More with Feeling") and Waylon Jennings ("The Taker") into the Top 5 that year as well.

Cash, enjoying the peak of his popularity in the late '60s, recorded an entire album's worth of duets with Dylan in Nashville in mid-February 1969, after which he immediately left to entertain the convicts at San Quentin prison, following up his similar concert at Folsom Prison the year before. One of the most powerful performances of his career, the album provided him with his biggest hit,

"A Boy Named Sue," written by a boy named Shel Silverstein. The Dylan song on the album, "Wanted Man," seems so appropriate for the occasion you might believe Dylan had custom-written it for Cash in Nashville, perhaps handing it to him on the back of an envelope the night before he left for California. But apparently the song was written for the Everly Brothers, who turned it down (as they had "Lay Lady Lay"), although Cash and Dylan did attempt it as one of their abortive duets.

In England, the mantle of Dylan interpreter was worn most proudly by Fairport Convention (just slightly edging out the worthy Manfred Mann). In 1969's *What We Did on Our Holidays* Sandy Denny picked up on the obscure "I'll Keep It with Mine" (also done hauntingly by Nico), while the follow-up album, *Unhalfbricking*, offered the lengthy "Percy's Song" and the *Basement Tapes*–era "Million Dollar Bash" along with Denny's own poignant "Who Knows Where the Time Goes," which had just appeared as the B-side of the Judy Collins hit single "Both Sides Now," penned by Joni Mitchell.

Once thought of as the English Dylan, much to his chagrin and Dylan's undisguised dismay, Donovan was very careful never to record a Dylan song. Perhaps the closest he came to trifling with his idol or his influences was his cover of Woody Guthrie's "Car Car (Riding in My Car)" on his first album, in 1965. By 1969's *Barabajagal* Donovan was deep into his own mystique, far more the flower child than Dylan ever was. This is not to say that Dylan ever *was* a flower child, although a case could be made that the voice and the lyrics and the cover photo displayed on *Nashville Skyline* were Dylan at his most flowery: happily married, happily creative, happily out of the spotlight, and happily reworking the 1546 axiom "you can have your cake and eat it too." Donovan was equally blissful, exploring "Atlantis," planning a return "To Susan on the West Coast Waiting," and declaring "Happiness Runs" in a circular motion.

Never considered anything close to the Next Dylan, Country Joe McDonald had no qualms about abandoning his prosperous San Francisco agitprop contingent, Country Joe and the Fish, to record an entire album of Woody Guthrie songs, *Thinking of Woody Guthrie*—in Nashville, too—including "Pastures of Plenty," "This Land Is Your Land," "Tom Joad," and "Pretty Boy Floyd," a tune the Byrds covered on *Sweetheart of the Rodeo* and one Dylan himself would choose to sing, twenty years later, on a star-studded Woody Guthrie tribute album that featured Willie Nelson, Bruce Springsteen, Emmylou Harris, and Arlo Guthrie—but no Country Joe McDonald.

Arlo himself, the fifth and youngest of Woody's actual children, had a big 1969, highlighted by the Arthur Penn–directed *Alice's Restaurant* (the movie version of his epic song) and his appearance at the Woodstock Festival, in which he sang his other countercultural anthem, the hippie drug-smuggling tale "Coming into Los Angeles" as well as a Dylan cover, "Walking Down the Line." There are no Dylan songs on *Running Down the Road*, released that fall, but there is a fine Woody Guthrie cover of "Oklahoma Hills."

Although he didn't cover a Dylan song until 1990 ("Blowin' in the Wind"), strictly in terms of nasal yearning, Neil Young was tabbed as one of the first of the next New Dylans upon the release of his first solo album, *Neil Young*, in the winter of 1969. While songs like "The Loner," "The Old Laughing Lady," and "The Last Trip to

Tulsa" were certainly Dylanesque in their droning verbiage, none could compare to Neil's all-time yearning classic, "Expecting to Fly," from his Buffalo Springfield days. A few months later, perhaps on hearing the album for the first time on his own living room turntable, Neil abandoned New Dylan territory for a more optimistic, rocking experience, aided and abetted by his band, Crazy Horse. From the opening guitar riff of "Cinnamon Girl," the opening track on *Everybody Knows This Is Nowhere*, released in June 1969, Neil had found a new voice and a new sound that would inspire a generation behind him nearly as much as Dylan had inspired Neil and his peers. Of course, Neil never had and never could have totally abandoned his yearning side, epitomized by the unremittingly nostalgic "Sugar Mountain," written about a teen club in Canada, which served as the B-side of three of his first four singles, including his first, "Cinnamon Girl."

Similar to Dylan's adroit sidestep into country music as a response to the roiling whirlpool of 1969, his earliest champions, Peter, Paul and Mary, contributed the Grammy-winning children's album *Peter, Paul and Mommy* to the mix, recycling "Puff the Magic Dragon" and Tom Paxton's "The Marvelous Toy." But they'd hardly abandoned Dylan, paying their respects on *Late Again*, which was still on the charts in 1969, featuring "I Shall Be Released" and "Too Much of Nothing."

Dylan's closest acolyte and competitor for relevance in the protest era was always Phil Ochs, who by 1969 had swung as fiercely to the left as Dylan had to the right. In *Rehearsals for Retirement* his journalistic impulse was a strong as his anger as he recalled the 1968 siege of Chicago in "William Butler Yeats Visits Lincoln Park and

Escapes Unscathed" and the election of Nixon in "Another Age," in which he vows to "pledge allegiance against the flag." But running counter to the political winds of 1969 would wreak havoc on Ochs's psyche, to say nothing of his sales and airplay potential. His 1970 release, produced by Van Dyke Parks, was entitled *Greatest Hits*, spoofing the fact that he'd never had one (although Joan Baez's version of "There But for Fortune" cracked the Top 50 in 1965 and Crispian St. Peters' version of "Changes" peaked at No. 57 in 1966). But on another level his last studio album, largely bereft of protest material, suffered from a lack of direction, from his meandering reminiscences ("Jim Dean of Indiana") and regrets ("Chords of Fame") and country songs ("My Kingdom for a Car") to his sadly prophetic finale ("No More Songs"). When he committed suicide in 1976, his friends were not surprised.

"Everyone knew when Phil killed himself that a statement had been made," Dave Van Ronk reflected. "But nobody could agree on what that statement was."

THE GUITAR INVASION

As if to drown out the sound of a generation's anxieties crashing down on their banging heads, fans of rock guitar in all its various and searing interpretations had an unparalleled field day in 1969, with Jimi Hendrix's early-morning Woodstock version of "The Star Spangled Banner" serving as both a belated welcoming blast to the year's festivities and a pentatonic dirge for the generation's walking wounded on the littered battlefield of Yasgur's Farm.

Culminating in Hendrix's performance, the Woodstock Festival was a kind of guitarist's field of dreams, with blistering performances from Carlos Santana, Johnny Winter, Peter Townshend, Lesley West, and Alvin Lee, with only Jerry Garcia falling victim to the external and internal circumstances. Joining Hendrix's *Electric Lady-land* on the shelves of 1969 would be *Johnny Winter* ("Johnny B. Goode") in May, the Grateful Dead's *Aoxomoxoa* ("China Cat Sunflower") in June, Hendrix's *Smash Hits* ("Red House") in August, and *Santana* ("Soul Sacrifice") and Ten Years After's *SsssH* ("Good Morning Little Schoolgirl") in September. Lesley West's New York–based contingent, Mountain, delivered *Mountain Climbing* the next spring, featuring the Woodstock tribute "For Yasgur's Farm" along with the hit single "Mississippi Queen," which, coming hot on the heels of *The Allman Brothers Band* ("Whipping Post"), caused them to be thought of for a time as a Southern rock band.

Although the legendary Paul Butterfield Blues Band also appeared at Woodstock, by this time stellar guitarist Michael Bloomfield was long gone. The best you could hear from him in 1969 was on his own meager solo album *It's Not Killing Me*, in which his singing competed with his playing for weakest link. Even his encouraging performance on 1968's *Super Session* with Al Kooper ("Her Holy Modal Majesty") was ultimately frustrated by an illness, prompting Kooper to bring in Stephen Stills to fill out side two.

Of course the artistic bar had already been raised (or lowered, depending on your opinion) by the arrival to these shores of Jimmy Page's new ersatz, heavily juiced, nominally blues-based outfit, Led Zeppelin ("Dazed and Confused"). Where Page's previous band, the Yardbirds, had been universally revered, the at times adolescent posturing of Led Zeppelin was as troublesome to connoisseurs of the genre as it was liberating to those unimpeded by any critical frame of reference—especially in view of its competition in the stores during its month of release, *Goodbye*, the final album by Eric Clapton in Cream ("Badge," "I'm So Glad"), and Fleetwood Mac's *English Rose* ("The Green Manilishi," "Black Magic Woman"), led by the brilliant Peter Green. By the end of the year all such debates were rendered moot by *Led Zeppelin II* ("Whole Lotta Love"), which ripped to shreds any thoughts that the band might be a one-off in the spirit of Clapton's recent alliance with Ginger Baker and Stevie Winwood in *Blind Faith* ("Can't Find My Way Home"). No, Led Zeppelin were in it for the long haul, and quite a haul it was.

Fans of blues-rock guitar from England would have to be satisfied by *Beck-ola*, the second album from Jeff Beck, Jimmy Page's former sometime partner in the Yardbirds (the band that also spawned Eric Clapton). Something of a letdown from their debut, *Truth* ("I Ain't Superstitious"), which was still on the charts in '69, *Beck-ola* ("Plynth (Water down the Drain)") was the last album Rod Stewart and Ron Wood made with Beck before departing for the Small Faces.

Fans of blues-rock guitar from New York, meanwhile, could cuddle up with *The Best of the Blues Project* and their memories of Danny Kalb's whirling fingers ("I Can't Keep from Crying," "Wake Me, Shake Me"). And fans of psychedelic blues rock from California could take heart from the Grateful Dead's first live album, *Live/Dead* ("Dark Star," "St. Stephen"), released in December, or Frank Zappa's first (almost) completely instrumental album, *Hot Rats* ("Peaches En Regalia," "Willie the Pimp"), released in November. Fans of straight blues guitar could appreciate the success of Albert King in *King of the Blues Guitar* ("Born under a Bad Sign"), released in March, and the continued success of B. B. King, with *Live and Well*, released in June ("Why I Sing the Blues," "Sweet Little Angel"), and *Completely Well* ("The Thrill Is Gone"), released in December.

And for those who preferred not to live on blues rock alone, there was plenty of hot six- and twelve-string electric and acoustic action in 1969, from the return of the surf gods, the Ventures, in *Hawaii Five-O* ("Hawaii Five-O") to the stylish Latin-tinged coverings of Jose Feliciano in *Feliciano 10-23* ("Hey Jude," "She's a Woman") to the more adventurous offerings in Leo Kottke's debut, *6 and 12 String Blues* ("Vaseline Machine Gun"), Bert Jansch's influential *Lucky Thirteen* ("Angi"), and John Fahey's definitive *The Yellow Princess* ("East from the Top of the Riggs Road/B&O Trestle"), culminating in Ry Cooder's eclectic 1970 debut, *Ry Cooder* ("Dark Is the Night").

VIRTUOSOS

Their minds expanded in the late '60s by blues-based guitarists like Bloomfield, Zappa, and Garcia, musicians and fans of differing stripes were totally captivated in 1969 by the unlimited horizons suddenly offered by rock 'n' roll. If folk rock could lead to acid rock, then why couldn't blues rock lead to jazz rock and classical rock? This was the year a rock version of Bach's Fifth Brandenburg Concerto, as played by the Juilliard-trained New York Rock & Roll Ensemble on their second album, *Faithful Friends*, took center stage on TV under the auspices of conductor Leonard Bernstein. In London, Dave Edmunds' frenzied Love Sculpture ripped into Khachaturian's "Sabre Dance" and Bizet's "Farandole" on *Forms and Feelings*.

Just as England in those days featured the four-headed guitar law firm of Hendrix, Beck, Clapton, and Page, the progenitors of progressive rock added a new four-headed monster to the musical firmament, consisting of the Moody Blues, Pink Floyd, Yes, and King Crimson (Genesis, starting then, were a long way from progressive), all with swirling ambitions and talent to match. In their self-titled debut album, Yes displayed their copious instrumental and vocal chops on a couple of masterful interpretations of the Byrds' "I See You" and the Beatles' "Every Little Thing." Pink Floyd's two-disc *Ummagumma* featured a live greatest hits collection on disc one ("Saucer Full of Secrets," "Set the Controls for the Heart of the Sun") and a solo workout on disc two ("Sysyphus," "The Grand Vizier's Garden Party"). In *On the Threshold of a Dream*, the Moody Blues ("Never Comes the Day") solidified their symphonic vision, while King Crimson took off for points unknown, melodically and lyrically, with *In the Court of the Crimson King* ("21st Century Schizoid Man").

In New York City in '68 Al Kooper created Blood, Sweat and Tears, the first (and still the ultimate) "Big Rock Band," with *Child Is the Father to the Man* ("I Can't Quit Her," "I Love You More Than You'll Ever Know"), still on the charts in '69; David Clayton Thomas took over a slicker version of the band that year in *Blood, Sweat & Tears*, which produced three hit singles ("You've Made Me So Very Happy," "Spinning Wheel," and "And When I Die"). The Rascals let tenor sax great David Fathead Newman loose on "Adrian's Birthday" from their expansive *Freedom Suite* ("People Got to Be Free"), which also contained the thirteen-minute Dino Danelli drum solo "Boom" and the fifteen-minute jam "Cute." And Genya

Raven went from girl group Goldie and the Gingerbreads to fronting the full-scale horn band Ten Wheel Drive in *Construction No. 1* ("Tightrope," "Eye of the Needle"). In Chicago, the versatile Chicago Transit Authority mixed jazz and blues on their self-titled debut ("Does Anybody Really Know What Time It Is"), as well as sampling the riots at the Democratic National Convention ("Prologue, August 29, 1968," "Someday (August 29, 1968)").

Inspired by multitalented jazz great Roland Kirk, Ian Anderson brought the flute to rock in Jethro Tull's second album, *Stand Up* ("Bouree," "Fat Man"). Andy Kulberg had done the same in the Blues Project with "Flute Thing," written by Al Kooper; he expanded upon that vision in his next group, Sea Train ("Rondo"). David Lindley's inspiration in Kaleidoscope's *Incredible* came from the Middle East ("Banjo," "Lie to Me") as well as the American Southeast ("Let the Good Love Flow"). And Captain Beefheart's muse was clearly out of control and all over the map on the wonderfully subversive *Trout Mask Replica* ("Dali's Car," "Dachau Blues"). Jack Bruce followed Eric Clapton, his boss in Cream, into a solo career with *Songs for a Tailor*, which featured his melodic epic "Theme for an Imaginary Western," soon covered by producer Felix Pappalardi's next project, Mountain. Buddy Miles displayed his drumming prowess before his future boss, Jimi Hendrix, who produced *Electric Church*, featuring Jimi's trademark wah wah sound on "69 Freedom Special." In Memphis, the ultimate sideman Steve Cropper took a busman's holiday, teaming up with Albert King and Pop Staples on *Jammed Together* ("Knock on Wood"). At the Montreux Jazz Festival, Les McCann recorded his twenty-eighth album, *Swiss Movement*, which included the scintillating chart single "Compared to What."

Back in New York City, as attracted by the merger of rock's energy and audience with the much more venerable but much less popular form of jazz as Dylan had been half a decade earlier when he foresaw the big bucks in rock's union with folk music, Miles Davis began hastily assembling a recording session to capture this sound. For three days in August immediately following the three days of Woodstock, his producer Teo Mateo rolled tapes for Davis, Wayne Shorter, Bennie Maupin, Chick Corea, Larry Young, Harvey Brooks, Dave Holland, Jack DeJohnette, Don Alias, Lennie White, Jumma Santos, and John McLaughlin, advising the musicians to stay in the groove. In *Working Musicians*, Lennie White told me:

> *Bitches Brew* was the very first recording session I ever did. The recording was at ten o'clock. I was at the studio at nine. The cleaning lady let me in. I was setting up my stuff and kind of practicing and Miles comes in and he says to Jack DeJohnette, "Hey Jack, tell that young drummer to shut up." So I was intimidated right off the bat. I had been playing funky type music, James Brown stuff for a long time. Of all the guys who were on that session, I was the one guy who knew how to play all that stuff. So there was this tune that Miles wanted a funky beat on and he runs through it. I'm playing with Miles Davis now, so I'm trying to play all this slick stuff. He comes over to me and he says, "You ain't getting the chicken." I wound up playing percussion on the tune. Don Alias came up with a real hip beat and I just played percussion. I was bummed out. When the day was over I said to myself, "Well, I had my opportunity to play with Miles Davis, and that's going to

be it." And then he came over to me and said, "Be here ten o'clock tomorrow morning." So I was vindicated.

As was Davis; the album peaked at No. 35 and remained the biggest hit of his career until a 1997 reissue of *Kind of Blue.*

"I wanted to change course," he told Gene Santoro in the book *Highway 61 Revisited.* "I had to change course for me to continue to believe in and love what I was playing."

With the release of *Bitches Brew* in April of 1970, Fusion was born, although Miles, with the time-honored modesty of all visionary musicians, denied having anything to do with it. "After we did it, someone named it and said it was this or that," he said. "But we didn't do that. It's like jazz; I don't know what that means." Fusion would hardly become the new folk rock, but Davis would nevertheless headline shows at the Fillmores, East and West, in San Francisco and New York, passing his gospel and his genius to whichever acolytes had the ears to hear.

At the Fillmore West this meant opening for Stone the Crows and the Grateful Dead in April 1970. "Miles was very reluctant," Bill Graham told Robert Greenfield in *My Life Inside Rock and Out.* "Going to visit him was like going to see the Dalai Lama. What got me was that a good portion of Dead fans really got into Miles. Some of them even danced to his music."

At the Fillmore East, Davis opened for San Francisco cats Steve Miller and Neil Young and Crazy Horse on March 6 and 7 in a pair of performances that were captured on the album *Live at the Fillmore East*, which in its original release was fairly disappointing. "The problem is that although the music is compelling, it's schizophrenic because there are no full performances on the final release," Thom Jurek wrote in a review. "Just as a composition starts to gel, it segues into another rather abruptly." Eventually a different, more satisfying version of the album emerged, taken from just the March 7 performance, and featuring a lot of tunes that would appear on *Bitches Brew*, including former Tony Williams' Lifetime guitarist John McLaughlin's much lauded solo on "Miles Runs the Voodoo Down."

Remembering all of these influences and possibilities floating in a sea of uncharted waters, Buffalo Symphony Orchestra bassist Paul Schmid, in 1969 a short-haired teenager growing up in the wilds of Buffalo, New York—a youth unaware of Woodstock, who had to wear a tie to his strict Catholic high school—thought long and hard before naming his first musical hero. "I loved Iron Butterfly's bass player Lee Dorman," he said without shame.

> I loved the way Atco engineered the sound of his Rickenbacker bass. I loved that punchy sound. The second time I saw him he had a Dan Armstrong clear Lucite bass that you could see through, and very soon after that I got one. Before that I had a knock-off Hofner, which I did not get because of Paul McCartney. I wasn't trying to emulate him; they were just popular. When I went to pick up the kind of bass Lee Dorman had, I did not like it and I called up the Ampeg people to try to figure out why. For a whole academic year I had a conversation with this one guy there almost once a week. Now as an adult I know exactly what the problem was. I had gone from flat strings to the early round wounds and I'd just lost that punch that a flat string has on a bass. A flat string starts out with an explosion and it's over quicker, whereas the round wounds that John Entwistle was

into have a longer profile. They won't have quite the punch in the beginning but they sustain longer.

Schmid's professional journey started out about that time in the legion halls of Buffalo, playing oom-pah music to old folks.

> After playing all that Rhinelander stuff, when you get to learn a tune really well your mind starts to wander and you start looking around the room and you're thinking, for one thing, I want to play for younger people. That spring I ran into these guys at school; we all loved BS&T and Chicago, so we put a band together—horns, trumpet, trombone, bass, guitars, lead singer, and a beautiful B-3 organ with a spinning Leslie that we had to herniate ourselves to carry around but it was worth it. We did stuff from the Kooper and Bloomfield at Fillmore East album. We did a darn good job figuring out the horn arrangement for Blood, Sweat and Tears' "You've Made Me So Very Happy." That's tough stuff for a high school kid to not only figure out but then transpose and get written properly. That took a bit of musicology.
>
> We were an original two-car garage band. My house had this big wooden garage door that the bass frequencies would just rattle it. On Friday nights we'd rehearse until ten o'clock, when the police would come and stop us.

Schmid has sustained a career as a player, teacher, and author longer than anyone else from his original high school band, many of whom went on to become captains of Buffalo industry. "My greatest musical moment from that time was one Sunday in early 1970, when I saw *Hair!* at the Royal Alexandria Theater in Toronto," he said. "I remember the stage was raked—tilted toward the audience—so the back of the stage was higher than the front of the stage and there was this dirty old bus actually on stage where the band played and they were so good. They played it exactly like the record. To me the nudity was minor. I had my eye on something much bigger."

WHAT?

For an equal and opposite reaction to the rampant virtuosity in the air and on the airwaves of 1969, you hardly had to wait for the Punk Revolution of 1974–77. There were plenty of bands and artists either consciously or subconsciously or just as likely accidentally operating at the other end of the spectrum.

Some called their wounded yelps Art; for example, Yoko Ono, under whose bewitching spell no less a streetwise survivor than John Lennon paraded physically and mentally naked before the world in such homemade travesties as *Unfinished Music: Two Virgins*, *Unfinished Music No. 2: Life with the Lions* ("John and Yoko"), and *Wedding Album* ("Two Minutes of Silence"). Some called them Politics, for example, the MC5, who delivered the otherwise strictly headbanging *Kick Out the Jams* ("Kick Out the Jams") while under the bewitching spell of John Sinclair's program for violent revolution. Or David Peel, who proselytized tunelessly on *Have a Marijuana* ("Show Me the Way to Get Stoned"), under the bewitching spell of which his career was mistaken by many for something other than a witless attempt to maintain his own supply of dope forever. And some called them Sexual Liberation, for instance Jane Birkin, who gave us *Je T'aime (Beautiful Love)*, from which came the heavy-breathing although somewhat melodic "Je T'aime . . . Moi Non Plus," under the bewitching spell of Serge Gainsbourg, her notoriously dirty-minded lover (it's surprising the song was never covered by John and Yoko). Or the GTOs (Girls Together Outrageously), who turned their all-around "girls with the band" ethos of fashion, choreography, and sexual servicing into *Permanent Damage* ("Captain's Fat Theresa Shoes") under the bewitching spell of the Wizard of Odd, Frank Zappa.

Some let others do the talking; for instance, the Godz, whose third release, delivered under the bewitching spell of their new amplifiers, *The Third Testament* ("Quack, I'm a Quack"), actually managed to find critics who could differentiate between the tuneless noise on this album and the tuneless noise on the two that preceded it. Or the unfortunate Wiggins sisters from New Hampshire, recording as the Shaggs, obviously and sadly under the truly bewitching spell of their father, whose *Philosophy of the World* has had several generations of music and arts critics falling all over themselves in an effort to explain how compelling as a car wreck it is (on the other hand, the drum solo on "My Pal Foot Foot" has to be heard, at least once). Or Moby Grape's sad acid casualty Skip Spence, whose *Oar* ("War in Peace") was recorded directly under the bewitching spell of a stay at Bellevue, a fact that only added to the veracity of the demented fragments found within it.

But if you're talking about bewitching spells, there is nothing that compares to the crackly cackle of Peter Stamfel in the Holy Modal Rounders, a chattering Mad Hatter of a bluegrass throwback to a simpler time of moonshine, crinolines, wigs, and windmills, before women were allowed to vote, let alone run a land-office business in nostalgia on the Internet forty years after singing for their father.

"A lot of the more mainstream guys like the Kingston Trio were theatrical types who considered the traditional folk people impostors, sloppy and untalented," Stamfel told me, "because to them the stage was a sacred, holy thing, and our stagecraft attitudes were heretical and not sufficiently dedicated; whereas the traditional people thought that the music was the sacred holy thing. So both groups felt the other was doing things for the worst possible reasons and there was a lot of mutual hatred."

At their most typical, the Holy Modal Rounders offered a slice of backwoods life far more authentically weird than anything the Band or Bob Dylan ever dreamed of in their limited philosophies. Unfortunately, the excessively loopy *The Moray Eels Eat the Holy Modal Rounders* ("Bird Song," "Werewolf," "Mobile Line") is for the most part even more of a train wreck than the Shaggs album (and trains hadn't even been invented yet).

As far as combining stagecraft with an appropriately extreme reaction to the events, let alone the music, of the day, could there ever be a more perfect expression of the era than that evinced by Sha Na Na? Originally formed at Columbia University during the hectic maelstrom of the same 1968 student takeover that inspired the book *The Strawberry Statement*, by James Simon Kunen (made into a movie in 1970 that featured not a single Sha Na Na appearance on the soundtrack), these guys parlayed a one-shot frat boy joke (in an era when fraternities themselves were as belittled on campus as the ROTC, team sports, business majors—anyone seeking a degree, in fact) into a stint at Woodstock, where they literally brought down the house with their letter-perfect yet loving parodies—in fact, adequate covers—of early rock 'n' roll classics like "Rock and Roll Is Here to Stay," "Book of Love," and "Teen Angel," all found on their 1969 debut album, *Rock and Roll Is Here to Stay*. The fact that the house was already down thanks to the weekend deluge and lack of food, sleep, shelter, or basic plumbing is unimportant. Many drenched, sleepless, hungry, constipated people went straight from Woodstock into the Oldies Revival, eschewing the upcoming Hendrix wake-up call to arms. Sha Na Na went straight from Woodstock into a successful performing career and a long-running TV show that can still be seen (according to my liner notes for one of their albums) in the hills of Buenos Aires.

The only remotely rock 'n' roll group in the same comedic league with Sha Na Na—other than the Three Stooges—was the Bonzo Dog Doo Dah Band, previously known as the Bonzo Dog Dada Band, soon to be known as the Bonzo Dog Band, whose "I'm the Urban Spaceman," produced by Paul McCartney, topped the British charts in 1969. Comprised of Viv Stanshall, whose song "Death Cab for Cutie" appeared in the Beatles movie *Magical Mystery Tour*, and Neil Innes, who later teamed with Eric Idle of Monty Python to create the great Beatle parody group and documentary *The Rutles*, the Bonzos were pressed into releasing three albums in 1969, only the first of which lived up to their Monty Pythonesque potential, *Urban Spaceman* ("Trouser Press," "We Are Normal," "Can Blue Men Sing the Whites"), also known as *The Doughnut in Granny's Greenhouse*.

But getting back to my thesis of 1969 being a year of bewitching spells, hardly anything in music (or horror movies) is more bewitching than the sound of a Theremin, in rock 'n' roll the exclusive domain of Lothar and the Hand People, Lothar being the pet name bestowed on the instrument by the Hand People, especially its primary keeper, John Emelin. Unfortunately, no hits emerged from *Presenting . . . Lothar & the Hand People*, but "Machines" did get a televised spin on what would have to be considered a priceless episode of Dick Clark's *American Bandstand*, and the literally hypnotic "Space Hymn" from the follow-up album of the same name, inspired by the moon walk, was a big FM radio favorite, especially in psychiatrists' offices.

A bewitching spell was also what Tom Rapp's outfit, vision, and overall predicament, Pearls Before Swine, was all about. One of those late '60s albums that may have initially sold on the basis of its cover, like Dr. John's *Gris Gris*, the first Pearls Before Swine album, *One Nation Underground*, had no immediate precedent and called for no other immediate reaction than a stunned ". . . *What?*" By the time of his third album, *These Things Too*, much had changed; for one thing, aside from Rapp, only the banjo player Wayne Harley remained from the original lineup. For another thing, the album was being paid for and released on a major label, always a troublesome sign for artists whose intention it is to inspire comments like ". . . *What?*" But a close listen to *These Things Too* ("Frog in the Window") and especially the follow-up, *The Use of Ashes*, written in 1969 in the Netherlands and recorded in Nashville, reveals no lack of bewitching spells ("The Jeweler"), although by this time even Wayne Harley had departed.

More on the order of ". . . *Why?*" than ". . . *What?*," the Zagar and Evans ultimate one-shot "In the Year 2525 (Exordium and Terminus)," from the album of the same name, soared to prominence in the summer of 1969, epitomizing perhaps the most bewitching spell of all, the one that overcame radio programmers en masse during the four-week stretch it took for Rick Evans's 1964 ditty to vault from a motel lounge in Lincoln, Nebraska by way of a recording studio in Odessa, Texas, abetted by an article in *Time* magazine, to the No. 1 slot in America for six weeks (and three weeks in England). Though Zager and Evans as a duo quickly broke up, Evans as a songwriter benefited from the five million units the single attained, as well as the thirty weeks the album filled with his original compositions spent on the charts. He lives today, and still sings, in Lake Tahoe, California.

VOICES

Such was the freedom available in 1969 that to be an interpreter rather than a writer of songs was not as yet a pejorative description. Some of the best songs and songwriters of the era came to the attention of the masses after being introduced in often-definitive performances by some of the greatest voices of the era. If these singers operated as one-man or one-woman quality magazines, curating the literature of rock music, Tom Rush was the *New Yorker* and Judy Collins was the *Paris Review*.

Although the folk singers of the '50s and '60s routinely covered the material of other writers (in fact, Dylan was considered revolutionary—and, beyond that, hopelessly gauche—for writing his own songs) the songs they covered were usually written in the 1930s and '40s, if not the 1830s and '40s. In his 1968 release, *The Circle Game*, Tom Rush, already an established, Harvard-bred folk singer, was one of the first to alert his discerning, upscale audience to this new breed of folk- and country-, Elvis- and Dylan-educated writers of rock songs, with important new work from Joni Mitchell ("The Circle Game," "Tin Angel," "Urge for Going"), Jackson Browne ("Shadow Dream Song"), and James Taylor ("Something in the Way She Moves"). A year before that the German chanteuse Nico provided much the same service for the downtown bohemian crowd by debuting Browne's "These Days," "Somewhere There's a Feather," and "The Fairest of the Seasons" and Lou Reed's "It Was a Pleasure Then" and "Wrap Your Troubles in Dreams" in the landmark *Chelsea Girl*—but she was living with Browne at the time, and about to be employed by Reed in the Velvet Underground. Rush had no such ulterior incentives as he followed up *The Circle Game* with *Tom Rush* in 1970, including another Taylor ("Rainy Day Man") and more Browne ("These Days," "Colors of the Sun") as well as Canadian writers David Whiffen ("Drivin' Wheel") and Murray McLaughlin ("Child's Song").

Judy Collins had been partial to another Canadian writer, Leonard Cohen, since introducing "Suzanne" and "Dress Rehearsal Rag" to her plentiful folk audience on her 1966 album, *In My Life*, and providing Cohen himself the same opportunity in the flesh with an opening slot at one of her concerts soon after, an experience Cohen once described to me. "Performing is definitely like [being thrown in a vat of] boiling oil," he said. "You can't really develop an intellectual perspective on it. I mean, you're in it. You realize the next moment could bring total humiliation—or you could actually be lifted up into the emotion that began the song. But you're already in the boiling oil by the time you've gotten that far."

Cohen is represented on Collins's late 1968 release, *Who Knows Where the Time Goes*, by "The Story of Isaac" and "Bird on a Wire." But the signature spot was reserved for the title song, by Fairport Convention's Sandy Denny, which would appear on the British folk group's upcoming *Unhalfbricking*. Collins also pays tribute to veteran folk songwriter Ian Tyson's "Someday Soon" and "First Boy I Loved," her version of "First Girl I Loved" by Robin Williamson of the Incredible String Band.

Judy's folk movement sister, Joan Baez, remained captivated a lot longer by the echoes of antiquity for which her soaring voice was so supremely suited, only occasionally interspersing her repertoire with a union organizing hymn or a song (or sixteen) by Bob Dylan. But late in 1968 she began recording with Nashville musicians and on the subsequent *David's Album* displayed a penchant for quality country material, including the Gram Parsons future standard "Hickory Wind" and the Utah Phillips gem "Rock Salt and Nails," which has also been covered by the cream of country and country-influenced singers, including Dylan, Levon Helm, Buddy Miller, Joe Ely, Waylon Jennings, and Steve Young. The album also includes a great reading of the traditional "Poor Wayfaring Stranger" and leads off with a fine new topical song, "If I Knew," written by Nina Dusheck ("Saigon Bride") and Pauline Marsden ("Pack Up Your Sorrows").

Also visiting Nashville was the rock group Mother Earth, led by emotionally devastating lead singer Tracy Nelson. In 1969 they came to record their second album, *Make a Joyful Noise*, and Tracy stayed on after the sessions were over to make her own country album, *Tracy Nelson Country*. As an escape from the sex, drugs, and violence of San Francisco, Nashville was a tonic for Nelson, as were sidemen like Scotty Moore, who accompanied her on "That's All Right," the Arthur Crudup tune that made his old boss Elvis Presley's career. Tracy's poignant, winning, and nuanced interpretations of material like "I Fall to Pieces" and "Stand by Your Man" was as much of a revelation to her as Nashville's laid-back approach to music and musicians. She's been living in Tennessee ever since.

Like Nashville, Memphis was a place where singers were singers and songwriters were songwriters and never the twain shall meet except in the recording studio, surrounded by the best of sidemen. During a particularly fruitful four-month period, from the end of September 1968 through the end of January 1969, American Studios, featuring Tommy Cogbill on bass, Gene Christman on drums, Bobby Wood on piano, and Reggie Young on guitar, played host to two of the world's most commanding and cherished voices, Dusty Springfield and Elvis Presley. *Dusty in Memphis*, released on the same day in January that Elvis reported for his own album's first sessions, sported the hit single "Son of a Preacher Man," originally rejected but quickly covered by Aretha Franklin as the B-side of "Call Me," her first hit of 1970. But in addition to marking Dusty's peak as a soul stylist, the album's true tribute was to the Brill Building craftsmen of the early '60s, among them Barry Mann and Cynthia Weil ("Just a Little Lovin'"), Hal David and Burt Bacharach ("In the Land of Make Believe"), and especially Gerry Goffin and Carole King ("No Easy Way Down," "I Can't Make It Alone," "So Much Love," and "Don't Forget About Me").

On *From Elvis in Memphis*, Presley also chose a Bacharach song ("Any Day Now") but primarily stuck to the soul and country repertoire that was his bread and butter, covering Gamble and Huff ("Only the Strong Survive") and John Hartford ("Gentle on My Mind") as well as the Dallas Frazier, Doodle Owens collaboration "True Love Travels on a Gravel Road," a song that also found its way into repertoires by artists as varied as Percy Sledge, Nick Lowe, the Afghan Whigs, and the country supergroup known as the Highwaymen, consisting of Johnny Cash, Willie Nelson, Waylon Jennings, and Kris Kristofferson.

Working out of nearby Fame Studios in Muscle Shoals, Alabama, just 119 miles East on U.S. 72, Aretha Franklin released *Soul '69* in February, exhibiting a knowledge, taste, and instinct for the best of the genre, from bluesman Percy Mayfield's "River's Invitation" to crooner Sam Cooke's "Bring It on Home to Me" to James Ray's 1961 hit, "If You Gotta Make a Fool of Somebody." A few months later *Aretha's Gold* came out, collecting her Atlantic output of the past few years, including "I Never Loved a Man (the Way I Love You)," her first Top 10 hit, written especially for her by Ronnie Shannon, the final take of which was described by writer Peter Guralnick as "one of the most momentous takes in the history of rhythm and blues, in fact in the history of American vernacular music."

More known for writing her own songs, Buffy Sainte-Marie offers the scintillating music for Leonard Cohen's lyric in "God Is Alive, Magic Is Afoot" on her controversial 1969 album, *Illuminations*, on which her already quavery voice is seemingly run through a Grand Canyon's worth of synthesizers, especially on the album's emotional highlights, "The Angel," written by Ed Freeman, and "Adam," written by Richie Havens.

More known for his interpretations of Dylan songs and Beatles songs, by 1969 Greenwich Village troubadour Richie Havens was drifting with the mood of the neighborhood into trying his hand at writing his own material, with largely inconsequential results. Luckily, the double disc *Richard P. Havens, 1983*, featuring his indelible takes on Cohen's "Priests," Donovan's "Wear Your Love Like Heaven," Lennon and McCartney's "Strawberry Fields Forever" and Dylan's "I Pity the Poor Immigrant," showed he hadn't forgotten the great natural resource and wonder that was his voice—though he did admit to taking it for granted. "I'm not a singer in the show business sense of the word," he once told me, "so I don't consider it something I'm ever going to lose. I never practice before I sing on the stage. I just sing."

Leonard Cohen's "Suzanne" makes an appearance on the incomparable folk/blues/jazz singer Nina Simone's 1969 album, *To Love Somebody*, along with the title song by the Bee Gees (which went Top 5 in England) and Dylan's "Just Like Tom Thumb's Blues," but the standout performance is of her own two-part "Revolution," written with Weldon Irvine, with whom she also wrote "To Be Young, Gifted and Black." Her pop/blues/jazz counterpart, Peggy Lee, was making a Top 40 comeback in 1969 by virtue of her Leiber and Stoller–penned and Randy Newman–arranged "Is That All There Is," from the album of the same name, which also contained Randy Newman's "Love Story," George Harrison's "Something," and a remake of her 1963 hit, "I'm a Woman," by Leiber and Stoller.

"To Love Somebody" is also one of the highlights of Janis Joplin's first solo album, *I Got Dem Ol' Kozmic Blues Again Mama!*, which also includes the Jerry Ragovoy/Chip

Taylor R&B weeper "Try (Just a Little Bit Harder)" and Richard Barrett's doo-wop classic for the Chantels "Maybe." From the same doo-wop era, Dion (DiMucci) had moved from soulful pop into folk rock, steaming into 1969 with *Dion* on the engine of his success with Dick Holler's "Abraham, Martin and John." In addition to that Top 5 single, the always evocative Dion picked up on Joni Mitchell ("Both Sides Now"), Leonard Cohen ("Sisters of Mercy"), and Fred Neil ("The Dolphins," "Everybody's Talkin'").

Echoing Joplin's throaty rasp, Joe Cocker took on the Beatles and Bob Dylan in *With a Little Help from My Friends* ("I Shall Be Released," "Just Like a Woman," "With a Little Help from My Friends") as well as a couple of more inspired choices, the Animals hit "Please Don't Let Me Be Misunderstood" and the poignant "Do I Still Figure in Your Life," written by British blues contemporary Pete Dallo. In his follow-up album, *Cocker!*, released in November, Joe even borrowed Joplin's exclamation point, while resorting to covering the usual songwriting suspects, Dylan ("Dear Landlord"), the Beatles ("Something," "She Came in through the Bathroom Window"), and Leonard Cohen ("Bird on a Wire"). In December, Joe's throaty counterpart Rod Stewart delivered his first solo album, *The Rod Stewart Album*, with its refreshing lack of the big three, although "Man of Constant Sorrow" was also covered by Dylan on his first album in 1961. Here Rod lays the groundwork for future unique interpretations with Mike D'Abo's "Handbags and Gladrags," Ewan MacColl's "Dirty Old Town," and "Street Fighting Man" by Mick Jagger and Keith Richards.

Celebrating one of the biggest years of his legendary career, Frank Sinatra came out with three new albums in

1969, including *My Way* in May—featuring the Paul Anka title song as well as Paul Simon's "Mrs. Robinson," Jim Webb's "Didn't We," and the much-covered Lennon and McCartney tune "Yesterday"—and *A Man Alone*, a tribute to Rod McKuen, in September ("Love's Been Good to Me").

Celebrating the first year of what would be an all too brief career, Karen Carpenter debuted with her accompanist brother Richard as the Carpenters in *Offering* in October 1969, later re-titled *Ticket to Ride* after the single's Top 60 showing in 1970. Containing covers of Neil Young's "Nowadays Clancy Can't Even Sing" and Dino Valenti's "Get Together," it's the downbeat, downcast version of "Ticket to Ride" that draws the most attention, foreshadowing a career of moody, lost love ballads for Carpenter, who died of an eating disorder in 1983 at the age of thirty-two.

SINGER/SONGWRITERS

In 1969, the definition of the singer/songwriter as any solitary troubadour with a guitar or behind a piano who wrote "album cuts," that is, material publishers deemed not fit for Top 40 unless performed by the artist in question, was not yet written in stone. The 1969 definition of a practicing singer/songwriter was a singer whose songs had been or had the potential to be covered by enough other artists to generate significant outside royalties, or a songwriter who, having racked up a number of successful covers, was urged, often by his or her publisher, to put out an album, even if the object of that album was not to advance the songwriter's career as a singer, but rather to have a convenient way to peddle the writer's latest twelve songs to other artists.

In that context, Van Morrison had been lunching off "Gloria" since 1965, when he wrote it for his group Them, with covers from the Blues Magoos, the Hombres, the Outsiders, the 13th Floor Elevators, and Jimi Hendrix. Although *Astral Weeks*, released late in 1968, is regarded as one of the finest rock albums ever made ("Cypress Avenue," "Madame George"), only Johnny Rivers picked up on "Slim Slow Slider," and Rita Coolidge covered "Crazy Love." A year later *Moondance* solidified Van's claim on history ("Moondance," "And It Stoned Me," "Caravan") but only gained a cover from his major client, Rivers, who took "Into the Mystic" into the Top 50.

After appearing together in Tom Rush's *The Circle Game*, Joni Mitchell and James Taylor needed no more help from anyone in launching their careers as singer/songwriters (and launching the genre). On "Both Sides Now" alone Mitchell probably could have retired, with covers from Dion, Judy Collins (the hit), Frank Sinatra, Chet Atkins, Neil Diamond, Robert Goulet, Claudine Longet, and Oliver just in 1968 and '69. Ian and Sylvia, Buffy Sainte-Marie, and Tom Rush put their stamp on "The Circle Game," and George Hamilton put "Urge for Going" on the country charts. In her June 1969 release, *Clouds*, Mitchell added "Chelsea Morning" (another hit for Judy Collins) and "That Song about the Midway" (later covered by Bonnie Raitt) to her own versions of "Tin Angel" and "Both Sides Now" and the stark "The Fiddle and the Drum." *Ladies of the Canyon*, released early in 1970, contained "The Circle Game" as well as Mitchell's first chart single, "Big Yellow Taxi"(eventually covered by Bob Dylan) with "Woodstock" on the B-side.

After making a big impression on the Beatles in 1968, who then dropped him after one album, James Taylor found solace in the unlikeliest of covers from Brill Building vet Tony Orlando's new trio Dawn ("Rainy Day Man," "Carolina in My Mind"), country warblers B. J. Thomas ("Rainy Day Man") and Bobbie Gentry ("Something in the Way (S)He Moves"), Chad Mitchell replacement John Denver ("Carolina in My Mind"), and the Scottish pop group Marmalade ("Carolina in My Mind"). On the follow-up album, *Sweet Baby James*, "Fire and Rain" was enough to set Taylor up for life, a Top 3 hit on its own in 1970, with eleven covers in 1971, from the likes of Cher, Blood, Sweat and Tears, Richie Havens, Anne Murray, and the Isley Brothers. For good measure, "Steamroller Blues" would collect him an Elvis cover in 1973.

After establishing himself with Judy Collins, Richie Havens, Buffy Sainte-Marie, Dion, and the movie director Robert Altman, who snagged three songs from his first album for use in the movie *McCabe and Mrs. Miller*, Leonard Cohen released *Songs from a Room* in April of 1969 ("Seems So Long Ago, Nancy," "Tonight Will Be Fine"), garnering covers from Joe Cocker ("Bird on a Wire") and Judy Collins ("The Story of Isaac").

The equally dark and brooding Laura Nyro counted among her admirers Peter, Paul and Mary ("And When I Die"), the 5th Dimension ("Stoned Soul Picnic," "Blowing Away," "Sweet Blindness," "Wedding Bell Blues"), Three Dog Night ("Eli's Coming"), and Blood, Sweat and Tears ("And When I Die"). Her November release, *New York Tendaberry* ("Captain for Dark Mornings," "Mercy on Broadway"), added Barbra Streisand, the Supremes, and Petula Clark ("Time and Love"), along with Thelma

Houston, the 5th Dimension, the Raiders, and Julie Driscoll, Brian Augur and the Trinity ("Save the Country").

On the other hand, the surfeit of covers Tim Hardin's "If I Were a Carpenter" delivered, by Joan Baez, Johnny Rivers, Bobby Darin and the Four Tops, among others, seemed to inspire Hardin to even greater depths of darkness and brooding. Instead of thanking Bobby Darin for latching onto "Don't Make Promises" (along with Three Dog Night and Scott McKenzie) and "Misty Roses" (in the company of the 5th Dimension, Sonny and Cher, Johnny Mathis, the Sandpipers, and the Youngbloods) or especially "Reason to Believe" (also covered by Peter, Paul and Mary, Maxine Brown, the Carpenters, Glen Campbell, and Rod Stewart), Hardin accused Darin of stealing his arrangements, his voice, perhaps even his soul. As if to retaliate, he released the dark and brooding *Suite for Susan Moore* ("Susan") with nothing on it remotely coverable and a few months later covered a Bobby Darin song, "Simple Song of Freedom," which was his first and only chart single. Even then, he denied Darin the pleasure of earning further royalties by neglecting or refusing to put it on an album.

Hardin's Hudson Bay publishing cohort John Sebastian's most covered item with the Lovin' Spoonful was the blissfully opposite "Daydream," which found favor in the repertoires of Mercy, Bobby Darin, John Denver, and Gary Lewis and the Playboys, who also covered "You Didn't Have to Be So Nice." The Spoonful's biggest hit, "Summer in the City," was covered by the Ventures and B. B. King, while Cher covered their first and by far their most emblematic hit of the era, "Do You Believe in Magic," in 1972, when both John Sebastian and the era (to say nothing of Cher) were all desperately in the need of some magic. Nothing on his first solo album, *John B. Sebastian*, released in April of 1969 after a year of legal wrangling, was as coverable as even his lesser-known Spoonful hits ("Darling Be Home Soon" was covered by Joe Cocker, Maxine Brown, and the Association), B-sides (Johnny Cash covered "Darlin' Companion"), or album cuts (the Critters had a hit with "Younger Girl").

Although he was also perceived as something of a brooding figure in the 1960s, in later years Paul Simon has allowed a bit of sun to shine on his early career as part of Simon and Garfunkel, especially since it's no longer in question that he alone wrote both the words and the music to all of their songs. Picking up an Elvis cover ("Bridge over Troubled Water," also covered by Peggy Lee, Aretha Franklin, the Jackson 5, and the Ventures) a Dylan cover ("The Boxer") a Sinatra cover ("Mrs. Robinson," also covered, most appropriately, by Billy Paul), a Lana Cantrell cover ("The Sounds of Silence"), a Brenda Lee cover ("59th Street Bridge Song," also a hit for Harper's Bizarre and a jam session for Michael Bloomfield and Al Kooper), and even a cover of "For Emily," a gem from his days as a busker in England (by Johnny Rivers), has to have gone a long way toward reassuring the diffident artist of his enduring worth.

Anything but diffident, Melanie Safka captured the world's attention during the rainstorm of Woodstock, when she sang her only known song at that point, "Beautiful People," later to be covered by the New Seekers, who released it in 1971 as their second of three straight singles written by Melanie, after "Look What They've Done to My Song, Ma" and before "The Nickel Song." By then Melanie would be more known for the song she was inspired to write after her Woodstock performance, the Top 10 hit "Lay Down (Candles in the Rain)."

After winning, as first prize in publisher Don Kirshner's 1966 sweepstakes, the A-side of the Monkees' follow-up single to their No. 1 debut, "Last Train to Clarksville" (written by Boyce and Hart), Neil Diamond delivered "I'm a Believer," which became the top song of 1966 (spawning covers from the Four Tops and the Ventures). As a reward he got to write the Monkees' next single, "A Little Bit Me, A Little Bit You," which peaked at No. 2. His 1969 album, *Brother Love's Traveling Salvation Show*, released in May, had little worth covering save the title track (Peggy Lee, Sonny and Cher). But that changed a few months later, when Neil's biggest hit as a singer to that point, "Sweet Caroline," soared into the Top 5, causing it to be added to later pressings of the album and gaining covers by a spectrum of artists from Elvis Presley to Lawrence Welk, including Neil's old Brill Building neighbor Ron Dante in his studio group, the Cuff Links. Dante was also the voice of the Archies, who derived most of their material from the esteemed team of Jeff Barry and Ellie Greenwich.

As opposed to Neil Diamond, Ellie Greenwich's album career failed to take off after *Composes, Produces and Sings* was a dud in 1968, yielding neither hits nor covers. (Even Tommy Boyce and Bobby Hart, whose albums did equally negligible business, at least scored one hit under their own names, "I Wonder What She's Doing Tonight.") Such was the fate of most songwriters who attempted to make the transition to the stage, among them Jim Webb (beloved by Glen Campbell, the 5th Dimension, and Johnny Rivers), whose *Webb Sings Webb* was a collection of demos released without his permission.

The big song from his 1970 follow-up, *Words and Music*, was the mournful and mysterious "P. F. Sloan," written about the moody and mercurial author of "Eve of Destruction," whose own solo album of 1969, *Measure of Pleasure*, languished in the cut-out bins of the era alongside albums by Webb, Carole King, Randy Newman, and Shel Silverstein.

Like King a former staff songwriter, by early 1970 Newman was already the subject of a creative marketing campaign by his label and had just garnered *Nilsson Sings Newman*, a tribute album of covers from Harry Nilsson ("Love Story," "Cowboy," "Living Without You," "I'll Be Home") as well as a Collins ("Cowboy"), a couple of Dusty Springfields ("Just One Smile," "I Don't Want to Hear It Anymore"), a hit in England courtesy of Alan Price ("Simon Smith and His Amazing Dancing Bear"), a couple of Harper's Bizarres ("Simon Smith and His Amazing Dancing Bear," "The Biggest Night of Her Life"), a Van Dyke Parks ("Vine Street"), and a Peggy Lee ("Love Story"). On *12 Songs* he picked up another Lee ("Have You Seen My Baby") and a cover of "Mama Told Me Not to Come" by Three Dog Night, which would go to No.1. The song was also covered by the Animals and by Lou Rawls, who also covered "Let's Burn Down the Cornfield."

Any normal former staff songwriter would have seen his transition to singer/songwriter a complete success by this point. Not Newman, who told me,

> When I started working for a publisher my only concern was that the lyrics be commercial. We may have said, "What a great lyric," but it was great because Little Peggy March could do it. At the time I liked Carole King and Barry Mann. I liked the music

better than the words. Eventually I became too interested in words to put up with songs that said nothing, or in writing things that embarrassed me. But it was easier when I was writing for other people, when I'd have someone in mind and write a song for them. When I had to think about writing for myself, it was a different matter, what I'd be willing to put in Tom Jones's mouth and what I'd be willing to put in mine.

Shel Silverstein, who made Newman's raspy singing voice sound like Bing Crosby in comparison, came up through the folk ranks with "Hey Nelly Nelly" (covered by Collins), "Boa Constrictor" (covered by the Brothers Four, Peter, Paul and Mary, and Johnny Cash) and "The Unicorn" (a hit for the Irish Rovers). His breakout single for Johnny Cash, "A Boy Named Sue," was contained on *A Boy Named Sue and His Other Country Songs* in 1969. But *Freakin' at the Freakers Ball*, released around the same time, was a more representative collection, featuring "I Got Stoned and I Missed It" (covered by Jim Stafford) and the perennial favorite "Sarah Cynthia Sylvia Stout Would Not Take the Garbage Out," which made it all the way to No. 107 in 1973.

One of the all-time great Brill Building Era composers, Carole King, stepped up in 1969 as a singer on *Now That Everything's Been Said* ("I Wasn't Born to Follow," covered by the Byrds; "Hi De Ho" and "Snow Queen," covered by Blood, Sweat and Tears), although she'd always sung on her demos. On the following year's *The Writer*, her duet with James Taylor on her classic "Up on the Roof" (Little Eva, the Drifters, Dawn, the Cryan Shames, Laura Nyro) foretold the leap she was about to make in *Tapestry*. In the meantime, despite no sales,

The Writer contained "No Easy Way Down" (Dusty Spring-field), "Goin' Back" (the Byrds), and "Child of Mine" (Anne Murray, the New Seekers).

Almost equally accomplished as a composer, Barry Mann had no such luck with his singing career, releasing the lackluster *Lay It All Out* in 1971. For the follow-up, he took a calculated artistic risk. "I cut a classical jazz piece that ran fifteen minutes called 'Long Road to Bethlehem' that was a chronology of the '60s. I thought it was a masterpiece that could have been performed at Carnegie Hall. Then I wrote a song called 'David,' which was the story of my life and ran ten minutes." Clive Davis hated the resulting album and dropped Mann from the label. "Every once in a while," he says, "I still listen to that album. It's a little tedious, but I'm proud of it because it really shows a lot of creativity. Part of me wishes that the rest of humanity could somebody hear it. Another part of me feels relieved."

R&B

In 1969 Motown still ruled the R&B charts, as well as the pop singles chart, but the label's hold on the Sound of Young America was getting shaky. In '68 the Supremes started working on their first album without the guidance and material provided by the team of Holland-Dozier-Holland. When their first post-H-D-H single, "Some Things You Never Get Used To," barely dented the Top 40 in June, the Motown heads of state convened to clone the Holland-Dozier-Holland sound on the single "Love Child," which went to No. 1 in November, once again restoring sanity to a troubled universe—but only for a while. By the end of 1969, Diana Ross would be gone, having spent much of her time on other projects, including her first solo album, *Diana Ross* ("Ain't No Mountain High Enough"), released in 1970. In the meantime, Motown milked their cash cow as much as possible, first with *Love Child*, followed by *Let the Sunshine In* ("I'm Livin in Shame," "Everyday People") in May; then by teaming the Supremes with the Temptations on *TCB*, followed by *The Supremes and the Temptations Together*; and finally by tossing them into a TV tribute to Broadway (*G.I.T. on Broadway*).

If the Supremes were heading toward the Copa in New York City, the Temptations were subject to the psychedelic soul with a touch of funk that Sly and the Family Stone were into in San Francisco, although their James Brown/Sly Stone–influenced single, "Cloud Nine," actually hit the charts two weeks before Sly's "Everyday People" at the end of 1968. Ironically, while Sly, propelled by the success of *Stand!*, released the following April ("Don't Call Me Nigger, Whitey"), and his performance at Woodstock in August, would spend the remainder of 1969 in a drugged-out stupor in L.A., caught between the political agenda of the Black Panthers on the one hand and his personal agenda of "I Want to Take You Higher" on the other, the Temptations were dutifully reporting to work on *Puzzle People*, released in September, which featured, along with the hits "Run Away Child, Running Wild" and "I Can't Get Next to You," some of the angriest messages in the Whitfield-Strong catalog ("Slave" and "Message from a Black Man").

Although preoccupied with thoughts of his singing partner Tammi Terrell's debilitating illness, which would take her life early in 1970, Marvin Gaye also retained the Motown work ethic, coming up with the best-selling album of his career thus far, *M.P.G.* ("Too Busy Thinking About My Baby," "This Magic Moment"), released in April. He also produced *Green Grow the Lilacs* for the Originals, re-titled *Baby I'm for Real* when that single became a hit in November, and took part in the last Marvin Gaye/ Tammi Terrell album, *Easy* ("Good Lovin' Ain't Easy to Come By," "California Soul"), released in September.

Motown veep Smokey Robinson was also hard at work in 1969 moonlighting with his group, the Miracles, but *Time Out* ("Baby, Baby Don't Cry") was hardly his best work. The follow-up, *Four in Blue*, released in November, was just as uninspired. But at least he was still trying his hand at social issues, covering "Abraham, Martin and John" on the former album. Stevie Wonder hadn't put out a relevant single since his cover of Dylan's "Blowin' in the Wind" in 1966. On *My Cherie Amour*, released in August, as well as the title song and "Yester-Me, Yester-You, Yesterday," Steve crooned "Hello Young Lovers" and "The Shadow of Your Smile."

If certain Motown executives took their eyes off the ball as far as Stevie and Smokey were concerned, it was probably because they were all too focused on the next young prodigy in their midst, Michael Jackson, who had moved with his family into Berry Gordy's house in Los Angeles to prepare for the recording and subsequent launch of *Diana Ross Presents the Jackson 5* (although it was really Gladys Knight who discovered them). While the first hit, "I Want You Back," was a Berry Gordy–led collaboration credited to the Corporation, as a corporation Motown was nothing if not communal and collegial in tossing around royalty opportunities for the faithful on the rest of the album. Making the cut was the cherished Smokey Robinson B-side (of his first single, 1960's "Shop Around")

"Who's Lovin' You" (also the first single for Brenda & the Tabulations), as well as the recent hit from Stevie (the former wunderkind) Wonder, "My Cherie Amour." Norman Whitfield got his slice of the action with "I Know I'm Losing You," and even the exiled and reviled Holland-Dozier-Holland claimed a slot with "Standing in the Shadows of Love." Finally, although the Jackson 5 were dubbed by the folks in PR as "Bubblegum Soul," there was a nod on the album to Sly Stone's earlier hit, "Stand!" just to make sure no base was left uncovered.

Astonishing as it sounds, the future of black music lay elsewhere than Motown in 1969, either in the hardworking hands of James Brown or in his opposite number, the notoriously easygoing but just as emotional Rastafarians in Jamaica. While few people had a strong enough radio signal or good enough connections in the import market to have latched onto the early reggae sounds of Bob Marley and the Wailers ("Trenchtown Rock"), Toots and the Maytals ("Pressure Drop"), or the Melodians ("Rivers of Babylon"), if Desmond Dekker's "Israelites" was not their particular cup of tea, everyone could appreciate, if not entirely understand, James Brown.

As a political weathervane representing the voice of the black community, Brown was nothing if not accommodating to both sides, campaigning for Humphrey and appearing at Nixon's inaugural party. He wrote and performed "Say It Loud—I'm Black and I'm Proud" in 1968 after the assassination of Martin Luther King, but by the time the *Say It Loud* album came out in April of 1969, he was no longer singing it, claiming in his biography that "the song cost me a lot of my crossover audience." The album contained the song but nothing else of relevance. In March 1969 he released the single "I Don't Want Nobody

As Aquarius dawned on Broadway, it fell on the heads of the rest of the counterculture. (Photofest)

While the cobra dances: Iggy Stooge makes a career out of self-torture. (Photofest)

Employees of the month at the Motown hit factory, among them Little Stevie, pretty Diana, solid Smokey, Martha and her Vandellas, and the Temptations. (Photofest)

Early in 1970, George Clinton and the mothership called Parliament/Funkadelic freed their minds; soon our asses would follow. (Photofest)

After waiting for eight years in the shadows, Richard Nixon restores American values, welcoming home the astronauts. (NASA)

As the war at home came to a brutal end, the brutality overseas continued. (Photofest)

Speaking for the unsilent minority, the Weathermen failed to bring their umbrellas when the roof caved in. (Photofest)

If I don't get no shelter: Mick Jagger at Altamont, before the deluge. (Cinema 5/Photofest)

No sympathy for the devil—Mick Jagger has a life-imitates-art experience at Altamont. (Photofest)

The Hell's Angels maintain law and order during the Stones' long-awaited performance. (Cinema 5/Photofest)

True believers to the end, John and Yoko stay on message. But the war would slog on for four more years. (Lions Gate Films/Photofest)

to Give Me Nothing (Open up the Door I'll Get It Myself)," which was a plea for equal opportunity, better schools, and better books. But he didn't include it on an album until *Sex Machine* in September 1970. In the meantime he put out an album of standards, *Getting' Down to It* ("All the Way," "It Had to Be You") in May, and three largely instrumental albums based on the Popcorn: *Plays and Directs the Popcorn* in August, *It's a Mother* in September, and *Ain't It Funky* in February 1970.

Other than the sophisticated sound of the Meters, formed by Art Neville in New Orleans, who released *The Meters* ("Cissy Strut," "Sophisticated Cissy") in May, Brown's only competition in the funk arena of 1969–70 was from former Motown staffer George Clinton. Clinton made a lot of noise in Detroit with his Hendrix-inspired Stone/Brown fusion, Funkadelic, whose first album, *Funkadelic* ("I'll Bet You," "I Got a Thing, You Got a Thing, Everybody's Got a Thing," "Mommy, What's a Funkadelic"), charted in March 1970. So influential was the album that the Jackson 5 included a cover of the 1969 single "I'll Bet You" on their second album, *ABC*. Then again, since Clinton was probably un-recouped as a songwriter from his Motown days, the old catalog item might have just been a way for Gordy to save money.

In the Impressions' final release of 1968, the proud "This Is My Country" from the album of the same name, and its successor in June, the thoughtful "Choice of Colors" (from *The Young Mods' Forgotten Story*, with the angrier "Mighty Mighty Spade and Whitey" on the B-side), Curtis Mayfield might have been chiding Brown for his indecisiveness, using Brown's own title phrase from "Say It Loud—I'm Black and I'm Proud" as an indictment of the fence-hopping, audience-counting performer. The single hit No. 1 on the R&B charts at the end of June.

With so much emphasis on black pride, the fate of Motown and the future of funk, and with Aretha Franklin clocking in on the subject as early as January, Stax songwriter Isaac Hayes literally had the field to himself when he was pressed into service by his boss to deliver his second album as an artist, *Hot Buttered Soul*, released in August. As opposed to Aretha's two-, three-, and sometimes four-minute songs, Hayes's languorous approach resulted in an album that consisted of only *four songs*, including a twelve-minute version of "Walk On By" and an eighteen-minute version of "By the Time I Get to Phoenix." When the two were paired as a double A-sided single, they had to represent the buy of a lifetime for the strapped singles fan, if only in terms of total minutes (even considering that "Walk On By" was edited down to 4:20 and "Phoenix" to 6:45).

As a final bookend to the period, 1970 featured a pair of remarkable albums, one sadly looking back to where black music (specifically rock 'n' roll) had been, the other defiantly looking forward to where black music (not necessarily rock 'n' roll) was going. Original Rock and Roll Hall of Famer Chuck Berry's *Back Home* was a comeback album of a sort, a welcome back to Chess Records after not having an album out since 1964 or a single out since '65. Its two best songs, "Tulane" and "Have Mercy Judge," two parts of the same crime-and-capture story, seem to echo the singer's own too recent incarceration. The bluesy "Have Mercy Judge" is almost painfully heartfelt and revealing. Whether or not Berry was planning to get further down in the future, it was a direction he quickly abandoned when his next single, the nonsensical "My Ding a Ling," recorded live in England, became the first No. 1 of his career in 1972.

The prison experience also played a part in the formation of the Last Poets, whose spoken word compositions on their self-titled debut album ("Niggers Are Scared of Revolution," "Wake Up, Niggers," "When the Revolution Comes") came out of a Harlem writing workshop and paved the way for the heightened use of language (especially of the scatological sort) at the core of rap. "With their politically charged raps, taut rhythms, and dedication to raising African-American consciousness," reviewer Jason Ankeny wrote, "the Last Poets almost single-handedly laid the groundwork for the emergence of hip-hop."

And that particular revolution, as the poet/novelist and Harlem contemporary of the Last Poets, Gil Scott-Heron, noted, would be televised—in living color.

AMERICAN POP

From the acid rock of San Francisco to the acid reflux of New York City (it was called acid stomach back then), in 1969 it was still possible for a given region of the U.S. to add its own unique flavor to an album destined for FM radio and the rock audience. Even the provincial world of country music was as big a contributor to the mix as it would ever be, thanks to the legions of rockers who trooped down to Nashville for its lower costs and stellar session players.

Ultimate survivors of the Cambridge folk scene, Geoff and Maria Muldaur met, harmonized, and courted in the town's (and the country's) reigning jug band, led by Jim Kweskin, where Maria made a name and an enduring image for herself with her version of Leiber and

Stoller's "I'm a Woman." Featuring side trips to Georgia ("Georgia on My Mind"), New Orleans ("New Orleans Hop Scop Blues"), and Woodstock by way of Nashville (Dylan's "I'll Be Your Baby Tonight"), the bluesy highlight of the duo's debut album, *Pottery Pie*, is Geoff's workout with guitarist Amos Garrett on "Death Letter Blues." A jug band baby from her days in the Greenwich Village–based Even Dozen Jug Band, Maria is most seductive on "Me and My Chauffeur Blues."

Another member of the Dozen who made the same four-hour journey from Washington Square to Cambridge Square, David Grisman formed Earth Opera with fellow bluegrass scholar Peter Rowan, leading to a brief career on Elektra Records, highlighted by 1968's caustic song "The Red Sox Are Winning" and 1969's *The Great American Eagle Tragedy*, featuring the lengthy title track and the chart single "Home to You." Rowan and Grisman eventually departed for San Francisco, where they teamed up with the like-minded Jerry Garcia in the band and the album *Old & In the Way* in the mid-'70s.

Ending a kind of Golden Age of Filth on the Lower East Side of New York City (to paraphrase the title of a Fugs album), both the Fugs and the Velvet Underground were coming to the end of their reigns in 1969, with the Fugs delivering some appropriate drug-soaked farewell anthems by Tuli Kupferberg ("Flower Children," "Children of the Dream") and bile-soaked Ed Sanders ("Chicago") on *The Belle of Avenue A*. Ironically, the Velvet Underground on *The Velvet Underground* ("Pale Blue Eyes," "I'm Beginning to See the Light") is a far gentler creature than on their earlier, raucous and caustic odes to the Andy Warhol high life and street life, reflecting either the generalized morning-after feeling experienced by the denizens of the counterculture going into 1969 or the loss of John Cale, one of their original guiding lights, or the fact that they recorded the album in Hollywood—or that their amplifiers were stolen before the sessions. In any case, Lou Reed remained the same lovable Lou, addressing the era's problems in "I'm Beginning to See the Light," but concluding, ". . . none of them are mine."

In nearby Hoboken, New Jersey, a hippie refuge of a sort, fulfilling the dream of music journalists everywhere, Robert Palmer, the first full-time rock critic for the *New York Times*, formed Insect Trust, a loopy and collective contingent on whose second album, *Hoboken Saturday Night*, Jeff Ogden put music to a lyric found in the Thomas Pynchon novel *V* ("Eyes of a New York Woman," first warbled on the streets of Norfolk, Virginia by Benny Profane).

Moving inexorably west to Michigan, raspy local legend Bob Seger nearly broke nationwide with his first album, *Ramblin' Gamblin' Man* ("Ramblin' Gamblin' Man," "Ivory"), which hit the charts in February. Unfortunately, he would have to wait seven more years before that massive breakthrough actually came with *Live Bullet* and *Night Moves* in 1976.

After the regional success of the "Ramblin' Gamblin' Man" single, Seger said, "We played the biggest gig of our career in Orlando, Florida. We drew 8500 people and made $10,000 for one night, which was totally ridiculous. About a month after that, when we got back to the normal crummy gigs, the guys got depressed and the group broke up."The fact that Seger prevailed and persisted is almost as inspirational as his eventual success. "The first four years were a fiasco. Nobody knew what they were doing," he said. "The next four years I made some good albums but I had to go through six bands to do it. I had my ups and downs, but I knew sooner or later I'd figure out what I was doing wrong."

Maniacal persistence marked the career of another Detroit legend, Iggy Pop, whose blissfully amateurish self-titled first album with the Stooges ("1969," "No Fun," "I Wanna Be Your Dog") reflected a mind-set particularly at odds with the interesting times preceding it. By loudly admitting that to him 1969 was just "another year with nothing to do," Iggy forever aligned himself with the kind of maladjusted misfit loners (and music critics) for whom punk rock became a panacea in the mid-to-late '70s, with what was left of Iggy still out there hurling himself into crowds from coast to coast.

Born in Fort Worth, Texas, in 1944, Townes Van Zandt moved to Tennessee at the end of the '60s to record for Nashville icon Jack Clement. Described in *Sing Out!* magazine as a "self-destructive hobo saint," Van Zandt released his second and third albums in 1969, *Our Mother the Mountain* ("Be Here to Love Me," "Tecumseh Valley") and *Townes Van Zandt* ("For the Sake of the Song," "Waiting Around to Die"), which found favor mainly in the collections of future country songwriting outlaws like Steve Earle and Jimmie Dale Gilmore. With the appearance of the much-covered "Pancho and Lefty" in 1972 his reputation would be assured. He would, however, remain a "self-destructive hobo saint" until the end, which occurred in 1997.

Having turned from a scene into a business model in the space of two years, San Francisco had become a magnet for maggots by 1969, feasting on the remains of a once oblivious, if not impervious culture. Drifting in on a Greyhound bus from Madison, Wisconsin, gifted vocalist Tracy Nelson made two records with Mother Earth that year before relocating to Nashville, *Living with the Animals* (the first appearance of her mournful, majestic "Down So Low") and *Make a Joyful Noise* (another wrenching performance on "I Need Your Love So Bad").

Ensconced in Wally Heider's new recording studio on Hyde Street between Turk and Eddy in downtown San Francisco for the early part of the year, the Jefferson Airplane hosted a succession of the city's finest musicians as they put together their defining album, *Volunteers* ("We Can Be Together," "Wooden Ships," "Volunteers"), among them Jerry Garcia, David Crosby, and Stephen Stills. By the time the album was released in November, San Francisco had lost its mojo as a mecca and so had the Airplane for original members Marty Balin and Spencer Dryden, who retired from the band soon after.

With Country Joe and the Fish in decline (*Here We Are Again*), Janis Joplin between bands (*I Got Dem Ol' Kozmic Blues Again Mama!*), Moby Grape all but kaput (*Moby Grape '69, Truly Fine Citizen*) and the Grateful Dead falling deep in debt to their label after spending eight months in the recording studio (*Aoxomoxoa*), the mantle of a city's crumbling psychedelic legacy passed, briefly, to John Cippolina in the Quicksilver Messenger Service, who turned *Happy Trails* into a kind of demonic Bo Diddley–inspired guitar opera ("Who Do You Love," "Mona").

Outside of San Francisco life was surely mellower. Jesse Colin Young and the Youngbloods relocated from New York City to Inverness, California, up the coast from San Francisco, where they proceeded to commune with the elements on *Elephant Mountain* ("Darkness, Darkness, " "Sunlight," "Rain Song," "Ride the Wind"). In El Cerrito, just outside of Berkeley, John Fogerty stood far enough outside the counterculture to turn his personal agitation and recent tour of duty in the army into one of the best years a rock band ever had, with *Bayou Country* ("Proud Mary," "Born on the Bayou," "Keep on Chooglin'") released in February, *Green River* ("Bad Moon Rising," "Green River," "Lodi") in August, and *Willy and the Poor Boys* ("Fortunate Son," "Down on the Corner," "It Came out of the Sky") hitting the charts at Christmas.

In Los Angeles, Frank Zappa held the franchise on agitation and on general weirdness, ranging from his own catalog to the artists who appeared on his appropriately named labels, Bizarre (obviously) and Straight (because Zappa was anti-drug use, meaning that, unlike nearly everyone else around him, he actually *knew what he was doing* most of the time). That meant he was in full control of Alice Cooper's campy psychedelic mash-up, *Pretties for You*, which featured such Zappaesque song titles as "10 Minutes Before the Worm," "Earwigs to Eternity," and "Sing Low, Sweet Cheerio." Nothing here was remotely a hit, but Alice later turned "Reflected" into "Elected," which made the Top 40 in 1972.

Zappa also took in Tim Buckley during one of his saddest (although most productive) periods, straight from his April 1969 release of the appropriately titled *Happy/Sad* ("Buzzin' Fly," "Gypsy Woman"). And he let his sometime lead singer Uncle Meat, a.k.a. Essra Mohawk, a.k.a. Sandy Hurvitz, go after throwing her out of the studio during the sessions that resulted in *Sandy's Album Is Here at Last* ("Arch Godliness of Purpleful Magic").

During the next year Buckley worked on and released *Blue Afternoon* ("I Must Have Been Blind"), *Lorca* ("I Had a Talk with My Woman"), and *Starsailor* ("Song to a Siren"), with diminishing financial and, as far as the general consensus, artistic returns. Mohawk, meanwhile, rivaling Buckley's introspective intensity and athletic vocal pyrotechnics, produced *Primordial Lovers* ("I Have Been Here Before," "Thunder in the Morning"), which showed up in 2001 at No. 87 on critic Joe S. Harrington's list of the 100 best albums of all time. "It's incandescent music and hard to describe," he wrote, "but let's just say it was the point between Laura Nyro and Patti Smith, Joni Mitchell and Liz Phair, Erika Pomeranz and Marianna Nowottny."

There was also a point in the history of L.A. between Joni Mitchell and Mama Cass Elliot that the town's and the era's defining 1969 supergroup, Crosby, Stills and Nash (and soon Young) was created (although at one point Crosby and Nash moved from L.A. to San Francisco). Out of the ashes of the Byrds (Crosby), the Hollies (Nash), and especially Buffalo Springfield (Stills and Young) *Crosby, Stills and Nash* gave us the ultimate L.A. sound of sex, drugs, and draft evasion, wrapped around old-fashioned street-corner harmonizing in the face of the apocalypse ("Four Days Gone," "Wooden Ships," "Suite: Judy Blue Eyes," "Marrakesh Express").

Somewhat less ambitious in scope, but possessing the Buffalo Springfield pedigree of Richie Furay and Jim Messina, Poco's first foray into the country rock arena, *Pickin' Up the Pieces* ("Pickin' Up the Pieces," "Grand Junction"), hit the charts the same week in June as the Crosby, Stills and Nash epic, but without the generational weight of expectations; it also sold several million fewer units.

In hindsight, perhaps the Beach Boys in their March 1969 release *20/20* ("I Can Hear Music") should have left the Charles Manson song, rewritten by Dennis Wilson as "Never Learn Not to Love," off the album entirely. Its presence as the B-side of the previous "Bluebirds of Happiness" single should have been Christmas gift enough for the troubled ego of its original progenitor. But such was the level of protectively blissful unconcern going into 1969 that no one around the band, the scene, or the area could have had the presence of mind to see what was coming. After Manson's personal apocalypse unfolded, bringing the good vibrations of the scene down around it, everything seemed so predictable. But nothing would ever be the same.

Manson's own album, *Lie*, was released in 1970. It's still a collector's item.

THINGS FROM ENGLAND

In the great tsunami following the Beatles' U.S. arrival in 1964, so many English artists and bands immediately struck gold on these shores—among them Billy J. Kramer and the Dakotas, Sandie Shaw, Herman and the Hermits, Freddie and the Dreamers, Peter and Gordon, and the Troggs—it seemed like everyone who stood behind a microphone or picked up a guitar in that country in those days must have gotten a record deal and an all-expense paid trip to America, except for Cliff Richard and his backup band, the Shadows (a pretty great guitarist Hank Marvin–led outfit on their own that never made the crossing either).

If not for the Beatles' fortuitous and mammoth takeover of our airwaves, who knows how many of these entities would have gone the way of Richard, into the shadows of history unrequited? For instance, did Domenico

Modugno launch an Italian Invasion with "Volare," or Kyo Sakimoto a Japanese Invasion with "Sukiyaki"? They did not. So there's every reason to believe that without the Beatles there might never have been a scruffy Rolling Stones to forever challenge their authenticity, or eventually a Pete Townshend to rise up from R&B covers to one day tap his inner deaf, dumb, and blind boy. Perhaps Ray Davies would have had to settle for a music hall career, Donovan to count his pennies as a busker, Jimmy Page to remain a searing sideman. Perhaps Dusty Springfield would never have gone to Memphis. And Rod Stewart would never have left the Steampacket. Elton John might have stayed Reg Dwight. *Jesus Christ, Superstar* would have been a big deal only on the West End. With Pink Floyd, Yes, Genesis, and King Crimson mucking about in the midlands, America would have never known the glory that was progressive rock at 6:35 a track. Beyond that, at least half of our FM radio playlists of the 1970s would have remained in the hands of folksingers like David Blue and Carolyn Hester.

By 1969, with many of the original Invasion bands having proven themselves merely singles-oriented AM fodder, FM adherents were in the midst of a second wave of guitar scholars, led by our own Seattle-born but made-in-England Jimi Hendrix. Jeff Beck, Eric Clapton, and Jimmy Page all passed through the school of John Mayall on their way to the Yardbirds. This led to the Jeff Beck Group, Cream, and Led Zeppelin, respectively. The Incredible String Band and Alvin Lee's Ten Years After played Woodstock. The Crazy World of Arthur Brown and Procol Harum played everywhere. The Moody Blues' "Tuesday Afternoon (Forever Afternoon)" was played everywhere, day and night. Manfred Mann played the best covers (Barry and Greenwich, Bob Dylan, and later Randy Newman and Bruce Springsteen). Pink Floyd was in demand for soundtrack work. Out of Belfast and out of his former group, Them, Van Morrison spent his poverty years in New York City and Boston.

A fixture of WNEW-FM's programming was Scott "Scottso" Muni's "Things from England," where we got our daily fix of music from across the pond. Would anyone have heard "Gilbert Street" by Sweet Thursday or "Streets of London" by Ralph McTell or Jimmy Cliff's "Wonderful World" without it? Of course, by then the Beatles and the Stones were no longer thought of as English bands; they belonged to the world. Nevertheless, the competitive fire that burned between these two groups was un-paralleled in music. They closed out 1968 together, with the White Album coming in November and *Beggar's Banquet* in December. Nine months later, they would bookend each other, with the Stones releasing the greatest hits package *Through the Past Darkly* (which contained "Honky Tonk Women") a month before the Beatles put out *Abbey Road* . . . a month before the Stones matched it with *Let It Bleed* (having heard through the grapevine that the Beatles were planning to title their forthcoming album, which arrived the following May, *Let It Be*).

So thoroughly American were these two outfits that the great saying of the time, directed to new bands in the States, was that they all wanted to be either the Beatles or the Stones. Did anyone grow up wanting to be Paul Revere and the Raiders or Gary Lewis and the Playboys, to say nothing of Buddy Holly and the Crickets or the Everly Brothers? Even Levi Stubbs of the Four Tops admitted that by then the decision makers at Motown were taking their cues from the Beatles (when they weren't taking their bass lines from Sly and the Family Stone).

In England, the Bee Gees were the most Beatlesque of the battling bands, releasing their fourth regular album, the underrated *Odessa*, in 1969. Beatles protégée Mary Hopkin released her one and only hit album, *Post Card*, produced by Paul McCartney, early in the year. Like Apple's other rock group, Badfinger, it was a middling trifle.

Traffic had two albums on the charts of 1969, their second and third, *Traffic* and *Last Exit*. They were one of the more unique outfits from England, whose R&B-flavored psychedelia featured Stevie Winwood and Dave Mason, both of whom would have solo careers. Future guitar hero Robin Trower started off in Procol Harum, who were most known for their Bach-based keyboard epic "A Whiter Shade of Pale," played by Gary Brooker. Their 1969 release, *A Salty Dog*, was one of their progressive best. Entering their post–Graham Nash phase, following the appropriately titled 1967 album *Evolution*, the Hollies straddled the line between AM and FM acceptance. In between Dylan covers they were still good for a powerful old-fashioned single like "He Ain't Heavy, He's My Brother," the title tune for their 1970 release.

Proving they were prepared over there for the upcoming era of the singer/songwriter, England was busily developing some strong talents, among them Cat Stevens, whose "Matthew and Son," from the album of the same name, had gotten significant airplay in 1967. The record also contained the future Rod Stewart hit "The First Cut Is the Deepest." "Lady D'Arbanville" came from his third album, *Mona Bone Jakon*, released in April 1970, and stardom arrived with his next album, 1971's *Tea for the*

Tillerman. David Bowie, too, was a couple of years away from his eventual position as spangled avatar of the odd when "Space Oddity" hit the charts in 1969, inspired by the Kubrick film *2001: A Space Odyssey* but propelled by the moon landing. No such luck greeted Nick Drake, who put out the compelling *Five Leaves Left* ("Way to Blue," "Time Has Told Me") in 1969 to little response. Two years after the commercial failures of *Bryter Layter* in 1970 and *Pink Moon* in 1972, Drake was found dead of an overdose.

With his protégés, Led Zeppelin, laying waste to American hotel rooms (to say nothing of good taste), their bluesy forefather, John Mayall, must have felt a certain desperation, putting six albums on the charts in 1968 and 1969, the first three with the Bluesbreakers, as if to disclaim any responsibility whatsoever for Zep's current and future plans for distorting the blues. The three from 1969 were under his own name, including the last and best, *The Turning Point*, which featured the FM hit "Room to Move." In the meantime, Black Sabbath, with Ozzy Osbourne in the lead role, was stirring in the moors of Birmingham, with the dank and blustery *Black Sabbath*, released in 1970, plunging a final dagger into Mayall's bleeding heart (only shortly after John Lennon's *Live in Toronto* came out, via the Plastic Ono Band, effectively doing the same to Paul McCartney).

SOUNDTRACKS OF 1969

Prescient, exploitative, or merely observant moviemakers of the period chipped in with their take on the downfall of the Revolution as early as 1968, which would mean they were conceiving their story lines if not going into production as early as '66 or '67. This reveals them as a far more cynical bunch than the music makers, whose statements had to be relatively immediate, leaving them open to the criticism of being naïve, misinformed, or simply too close to the subject matter—since the subject matter was, by and large, themselves and their plight as pop stars.

Nonetheless, the movies of 1968, making use of songs especially written for their screenplays, ranged from the sublime (the Monkees' quixotic vanity production of *Head*, featuring a dollop of the Monkees oeuvre, mostly written by Carole King and various collaborators) to the ridiculous (the pseudo revolutionary *Wild in the Streets*, with songs by equally old Brill Building hands Barry Mann and Cynthia Weil. Produced by noted conservative activist Mike Curb, this movie's anti-authoritarian zeal might therefore be likened to that of an embedded Fed trying to provoke an otherwise hapless SDS unit). Far more authentically subversive, the mock documentary *You Are What You Eat*, directed by the ubiquitous Barry Feinstein, featured walk-ons by Ringo Starr, David Crosby, the Mothers of Invention, Tiny Tim singing "I Got You Babe," the Electric Flag, Peter Yarrow, Harpers Bizarre, the deejay Rosko, and at least one enduring lost countercultural classic, "My Name Is Jack (and I Live in the Back of the Greta Garbo Home for Wayward Boys and Girls)," covered by no less an authority on lost cultural classics than Manfred Mann (whose single peaked at No. 104 in July of 1968).

While the original Broadway cast album of *Hair!* spent thirteen weeks at the top of the charts in 1968 (out of a total run of 151 weeks), the movie version wouldn't be out until 1979! In England, meanwhile, the critically favored rock band the Pretty Things delivered perhaps the world's first rock opera, *S.F. Sorrow Is Born*, in 1968, to a fairly tepid commercial response. One of the few people who may have heard it was Pete Townshend, whose own rock opera, *Tommy*, made a far bigger splash when it came out in June of '69.

Nineteen-sixty-nine was an especially visible year for Elvis Presley, though it featured the last of his twenty-two movies, *The Trouble with Girls*, easily among his worst. More compelling was the cinematic take on Elvis's real life, starting with *The Comeback Special* on TV and concluding with his triumphant return to Las Vegas, memorialized in *Elvis: That's the Way It Is*, released in 1970.

Although the Beatles put out the ineffably trippy cartoon *Yellow Submarine* in February, *Midnight Cowboy* featured Harry Nilsson's hit version of Fred Neil's "Everybody's Talkin'" in August, and the Kinks score to a British TV drama, *Arthur*, produced the semi-hit "Victoria," 1969 is chiefly remembered for two defining films, *Easy Rider* and *Alice's Restaurant*, each with its own defining soundtrack. But while *Easy Rider*'s soundtrack is a peek into the musical sensibility of its director, Dennis Hopper (the Holy Modal Rounders, the Byrds, the Band, Steppenwolf), the anti-draft spoof *Alice's Restaurant* is more like a two-hour version of the Arlo Guthrie song that was already too long, redeemed by Pete and Arlo singing "Pastures of Plenty" and Joni Mitchell's haunting "Songs to Aging Children Come").

Nineteen-sixty-nine's immediate legacy wasn't on view in movie theaters until 1970, highlighted by Antonioni's polarizing *Zabriskie Point*, an epic statement movie you either hated or didn't see. But, trumping *Easy Rider*'s foray into licensing songs for the soundtrack, the movie did feature music that ranged from Kaleidoscope to Pink Floyd to the Grateful Dead to Patty Page ("The Tennessee Waltz"). *The Strawberry Statement* was nearly all soundtrack, although it was based on the 1968 book that chronicled the student riots at Columbia University. Neil Young was the prize here (with "The Loner" and "Down by the River"), along with CSN ("Four and Twenty") and Buffy Sainte Marie with her version of Joni Mitchell's "The Circle Game."

The reality of the period was far more riveting than fiction, captured in several documentaries, chief among them Haskell Wexler's '69 classic, *Medium Cool*, which took place during the tumult of the Chicago convention of '68, with music by the Mothers of Invention and Michael Bloomfield. *Sweet Toronto*, made by *Monterey Pop* filmmaker D. A. Pennebaker, was ostensibly a document of the mostly oldies-studded Toronto Peace Festival in which John Lennon made his debut appearance as a solo artist, with Eric Clapton on guitar and Yoko Ono rolling around in a bag (and Alice Cooper threw a live chicken into the audience). But the show was stolen by Jerry Lee Lewis, who even played guitar on one number. This is a lucky thing, as Lennon prevailed upon the powers that be to excise his portion from the film a year after its release. Elsewhere the making of *Let It Be* remains probably the most revealing document of the Beatles (and thus the era) in free fall, as Paul and George bicker and Yoko takes it all in, while the band attempts to play on.

Not to be outshone, either by the Beatles or by 1969's mega event, *Woodstock* (whose three-hour chronicle dragged nearly as much as Arlo Guthrie's original rendition of "Alice's Restaurant"), the Rolling Stones had their celluloid comeuppance as well, in 1970's *Gimme Shelter*, the document of the band's 1969 tour that ended with the stabbing at Altamont, filmed by the Maysles Brothers, in which the complicit Stones were as dumbfounded by the events spooling out of control before their eyes as most of the delirious participants in the event and in the era, who slowly and sadly stumbled toward the canvas, down for the count.

CHAPTER TEN

Sky Church

★ ★ ★ ★ ★ ★ ★ ★ ★ ★ ★ ★ ★

FOLLOWING THE SUCCESS OF THE Miami Pop Festival of December 28, 1968, on the heels of the fiasco at Grant Park in Chicago in August (opened by the MC5 and closed by the Chicago police), the summer of 1969 featured the same volatile mix of rock 'n' roll superstars and their riot-hardened college audiences traveling across America as if in a mystic caravan in matching spray-painted VW vans.

The season officially kicked off on April 6 (Easter weekend) at the Palm Springs Pop Festival and San Andreas Boogie, where Timothy Leary made a cameo appearance, Lee Michaels played an exemplary set, Procol Harum headlined, and a crowd over 25,000—or 10,000 more than the legal limit for the venue, a drive-in theater parking lot—showed up. Stoked on Red Mountain wine and Owsley acid, they proceeded to knock down fences to gain free admittance, set bonfires, and rampage through town, leading a local gas station owner to fire a rifle into the crowd, wounding two. This event set the tone for a year in which love and violence, powerful drugs, powerful music, and powerful opposition linked arms at every crossroads of youth and authority in a high-wire grudge match. Perhaps the Jeff Beck Group had it right when they failed to appear at the festival, having broken up in the hotel the night before the event.

Many times the particular lineup had little to do with the success or failure, relative peace, or sudden mayhem at a given event—although you could be sure some configuration of Jimi Hendrix, Santana, the Jefferson Airplane, Creedence Clearwater Revival, and Sweetwater would be on the bill. Admittedly, in the tiny town of Zap, North Dakota, on the banks of the Knife River, on the weekend of May 10, there were no headlined acts at the Zip to Zap Festival, only local bands. But this did not prevent a wild spring break crowd from all over the frozen Midwest from trying to outdo their privileged suntanned brethren who'd been raiding the beaches of Fort Lauderdale and Daytona for their annual post-winter revelries at least since Connie Francis sang about them so poignantly in the 1960 movie *Where the Boys Are*. By Friday evening, there were 2000 kids swarming through Zap. But this was the end of the 1960s, not the beginning; after eight years of freewheeling liberal rule, there was a new sheriff in town.

According to a report published by North Dakota Public Radio,

> Students vomited and urinated in the open—others passed out in the street. Temperatures fell below freezing and wood from a demolished building was used to start a bonfire on Main Street. The party atmosphere disappeared and gradually escalated into a riot. Security was overwhelmed and the café and one

bar were trashed. By dawn, 500 National Guardsman surrounded the town. Two hundred of them moved in and faced about 200 students who were still going. Approximately 1000 others were sleeping wherever they had landed during the night. Their wake-up call was at the point of a fixed bayonet.

For future music executive Clyde Lieberman, a native of Indiana, a festival season highlight was the Michigan Rock and Roll Festival on Memorial Day weekend. He recalled,

A band called the Up opened the show. They were followed by the SRC, the Scott Richardson Case, who had a big hit in 1969 in Indianapolis where I grew up, and was one of the bands we were excited to see. Two bands that stole the day were the Amboy Dukes with Ted Nugent and the Bob Seger System. Lee Michaels, with Frosty on drums, was incredible. Then the Stooges played. They were still called the Psychedelic Stooges at the time and nobody knew what to make of them. People my age (eighteen) were really into great musicianship. And the idea that a band could get up there that could barely play kind of freaked everybody out in my crowd. We understood it. It was raucous. But it kind of reminded us of ourselves. "Our band from Indianapolis is as good as these guys. How come they get to play with all these great bands?" But there was a certain charm to "I Wanna Be Your Dog" and "it's 1969, okay, all across the U.S.A." They were like pre-Ramones. Iggy didn't cut his chest with glass, or any of the stuff I'd see him do later at Max's Kansas City in New York. But he was Iggy; he was completely possessed.

Then the MC5 played. I loved their music, but they were so obviously not good, I remembered getting riled up. But they were incredibly fun to watch and I'd never seen anything like it. They were ripping off their clothes, hanging upside down from the top of the stage, playing one-note solos. At the time everybody's hero was Eric Clapton, and between the Stooges and the MC5 right after them, it was garage band music at its craziest. And you didn't know if it was ever going to become nationally prominent. I had seen Led Zeppelin in Chicago that year, and they were guys who were masters at what they were doing. And then here were bands that broke the whole thing down to the most elemental factors. It was really a confusing time.

And then Sun Ra played, who just took you to a whole other place. Obviously that was his intention. They played the song "Don't you know that yet, it's after the end of the world." I think they knew they had a bunch of stoned hippies in the audience and they just tried to get as trippy as they could. And they made all the other bands seem like fluff. They were wearing thooo oraay costumes and marching around the stage; the guy who played the baritone sax was kind of trailing after Sun Ra, the whole band was chanting, and it was like all of a sudden you had left the planet.

The Newport, California Pop Festival on June 20, featuring Jimi Hendrix, Creedence Clearwater Revival, Ike and Tina Turner, Johnny Winter, and the Byrds, was an eerie precursor to Altamont, looming at the end of the road. It marked the year's first appearance of the Hell's Angels, taking up a little ad hoc crowd control and freelance head busting, standing alongside their usual adversaries, the LAPD, who had been called in to provide the kind of air support that had lately proved so successful in quelling the crowds at People's Park in Berkeley.

The Angels and the LAPD were needed because the crowd had decided, at some point during the first night, that the Newport Pop Festival should be "a free concert!" Toward that politically appealing end, according to Marley Brant in her book *Join Together: Forty Years of the Rock Music Festival*, "a large group scaled the chain link fencing that surrounded the festival grounds, causing the fencing to collapse on those below it. The Hell's Angels . . . began punching those they could catch. The police battled back the mass of people and one of their helicopters hovered overhead, shining a light down on those who were attempting to push their way in."

An audience member, Willie Olmstead, told Brant, "As the crowd got uglier, the security people were told to get out of the way. The crowd tore down the fence and about a hundred people got in for free."

Meanwhile, a canvas draping caught fire near the exit. As Brant reported, "There was no telling what would happen, but most of the raucous people had taken to the streets of suburban Northridge to break windows and cause minor mayhem throughout the upscale business district. That was enough for the LAPD, who determined the event was a 'riot' and thus took what they believed to be appropriate action."

Tear gas made an appearance at the Denver Pop Festival a week later, at which Jimi Hendrix, Johnny Winter, Creedence Clearwater Revival, and the Mothers of Invention played for an otherwise blissful crowd of 50,000. This happened on the second day, when the Denver police faced off against the inevitable crowd of kids who turned their attempts to enter the concert for free into a cause for unified protest. A sudden change in the wind patterns resulted in the tear gas entering Mile High Stadium, causing mass confusion as ticket holders scattered from the stands and took to the field, just as Jimi Hendrix was ending his performance (his last with Experience), causing yet more tear gas to be deployed as the band fled to safety in a waiting van.

On the Fourth of July weekend, a naked man with a wand interrupted Robert Plant's performance with Led Zeppelin at the Atlanta Pop Festival, but was dispatched by a beer bottle to the head. On the same weekend, Led Zeppelin played the historic Newport, Rhode Island, jazz festival. Headlined on the other night by the Modern Jazz Quartet, that year's Newport Jazz Festival was the first and only jazz festival to include electric rock bands, quite an accession to progress by the moldy figs who ran things, even if for the most part these bands played some form of the blues. In many other ways, the younger crowd in attendance felt like "invaders," as rock scene reporter Ethlie Ann Vare recounted:

> I definitely sensed a changing of the guard and a tremendous resistance to our music. In the contrast between Led Zeppelin, who headlined one night, and MJQ, who were the big headliners, you could see the old guard slipping away. People who'd been supporting the festival for many years were trying to acknowledge and incorporate the new but didn't really want it there. Led Zeppelin and Johnny Winter felt like the camel's nose under the tent. This was not that long after Bob Dylan had plugged in for the first time at Newport and shocked and horrified the normally well-behaved crowd. So in a real sense we

were invaders; we weren't really welcome but we had a lot of solidarity.

When we went to Newport we felt like a put-upon minority. We huddled in our little safe spots in the parks, sleeping in sleeping bags and lining up at the few public toilets that would allow us in. It was if everybody was just starting to gather. You would hear little groups saying, "Oh, you're going up to that festival in Bethel? I'll meet you there." These people who felt so alone and different and powerless were starting to meet groups of like-minded people. Soon they were all making a plan to meet up again at the end of the summer. Personally, I never got a sense that Woodstock was going to be any more special than any of the other festivals that year. Woodstock may have been the actual hundredth monkey kind of thing, where youth culture reached critical mass.

Musically, one of the coolest moments at Newport was Johnny Winter and B. B. King performing together on stage, combining their two bands. B. B. was dressed all in white and Johnny was dressed all in black: the white-haired albino dressed in black and the very dark black man dressed in white, and they did the tightest set together—it made me a lover of modern American blues for years after that. Quite frankly, I was not that impressed with Led Zeppelin. I thought Robert Plant was constantly reaching for a note that he could not quite hit. They seemed sloppy, certainly in comparison to B. B. King and Johnny Winter. But although I was not impressed with them as performers, I was very impressed by the energy they created among the crowd. Still, I thought they were overhyped and never imagined they were going to be popular for the next twenty years.

For Ethlie herself, it was the beginning of a legendary summer as well.

> My entire life changed between July and August of 1969. It started with the jazz festival in Newport and ended up with me as a member of the tribe of *Hair!* at the Aquarius Theater in Hollywood . . . watching the moon landing while doing acid with the cast members. Some of the people at *Hair!* were getting on the bus with Wavy Gravy to go out to Woodstock at the end of the summer, but I had to get to Santa Barbara to attend UCSB in the fall.
>
> I never did care for the whole standing in line to use the bathroom in a gas station where the toilet hadn't been cleaned thing. So I did not become a festival person. But I did see a lot of concerts, indoors. I remember on Monday nights when the Aquarius Theater was dark, they had musical performances where anyone might wander in. One night it was the Doors. Jim Morrison was in his fat, bearded, I'm-going-to-recite-some-poetry phase, and everyone was very disappointed.

On the weekend of August 1, the concert caravan reached Atlantic City, New Jersey, where 110,000 fans attended with little incident, as rock journalist Jeff Tamarkin reported:

> It took place at the Atlantic City Race Track and I remember Joni Mitchell famously walked off stage crying after three or four songs, complaining that the audience wasn't paying attention to her. Santana was introduced as the "Santa Ana Blues Band" and Carlos corrected that as soon as he walked on stage. Zappa and the Mothers played a short, all-

instrumental set. There was also the Airplane, Johnny Winter, Buddy Miles, Joe Cocker, Creedence, Chicago, I believe Procol Harum, Dr. John, the Butterfield Blues Band, B. B. King, Janis, and then Little Richard closed it out and I think Janis sang a song or two with him.

The first day, there were surprisingly few people getting high in the stands and then someone made an announcement to the effect that there were only a few "narcs" in the place so it was cool to light up, and then more people did. Because it was a racetrack there was no overnight camping. Since none of my friends had driver's licenses yet my parents dropped us off at the racetrack each day and picked us up at night. I remember my parents being able to walk inside, where they actually saw Janis and Little Richard performing. I'm not sure they were ever the same after that.

Neither were many of the fortunate 400,000 who attended Woodstock on August 15, most of whom had to park their cars along the side of the road and walk the remaining one or two or ten miles to Yasgur's farm with their food, their gear, and their life's possessions on their backs, like the poor evicted souls fleeing the pogroms of Anatevka in the last scene of *Fiddler on the Roof.* Instead of the Russian Army, at the end of the forced march to Woodstock, a lineup of some thirty acts awaited them, along with your regulation swami, your mandatory Hog Farm food, your stage-hogging yippie, your worried representatives from the Concerned Citizens for Walkill, and the omnipresent radical activist theater group the Motherfuckers. Except that twenty-nine of these thirty acts were mired in the same traffic as the concertgoers or waiting for a tardy helicopter to airlift them in from one Catskill Mountain resort or another.

This left a huge gap for a lone troubadour to fill. Luckily, that lone troubadour was Richie Havens, a big-hearted and even bigger-voiced veteran folkie, who knew a thing or two about stream-of-consciousness improvising, although most of his previous magical mystical raps had taken place in half-filled coffee houses on MacDougal Street in Greenwich Village. Havens told me,

> I was absolutely crazy when I walked on that stage. I was supposed to be fifth on the bill and here I am going up first. The concert was three hours late and I'm thinking they're going to throw beer cans at me. I was onstage for three hours. A lot of people don't know that because there's only two songs in the movie. I did about nine or ten encores . . . because I thought I was finished, I went out, and they didn't have anyone to go on behind me, so I had to go back out again. At the same time, the sound was the best I ever played under, and I heard my voice go right out over the hillside to New York City. It was the most amazing thing. It was the perfect marriage of sound and air and environment. So I felt, once I was singing, that it was as small as the Café Wha?

One of those signature songs was "Freedom," which Havens composed spontaneously on the stage at Woodstock as his set approached the three-hour mark. "I'm going, 'What the heck am I going to sing?'" Richie told me for the liner notes to his *Resume* collection.

> I looked down at the audience and I saw there was something we were not talking about yet, and that was that we had already gained our freedom and we

were exercising it by being here together. So I said a few words to that effect. And then I just started playing the guitar. I thought I would play "Motherless Child," but first "Freedom" came out and then I went into "Motherless Child." In the middle of "Motherless Child" a verse from an old spiritual came back to me, so I worked that into it.

Things didn't go as well for John Sebastian, who was there only as a well-connected backstage fan. He explained,

> I was not scheduled to perform, so I accepted an awful lot of acid from Wavy Gravy, who kept saying, "You know, these kids are really having bad trips, but they're not *that* bad." As weird as this sounds, except for the first year or so with the Spoonful, doing eight shows a night and running down to the basement to get stoned between sets, I had begun to discover as I did shows that I couldn't get stoned, because when you become introspective in front of more than 100 people you look like an idiot.
>
> I think I play and sing a lot better than I did that day. I was sort of one with the experience of Woodstock, I guess, so that stood me some sort of short-term good stead, but in the long run I'm sorry that the highest-visibility performance I've ever given was one where I was smashed beyond belief.

As good as the vibes were for those three days, to Sebastian the aftermath was all too predictable. "Somehow every mood that was created at Woodstock was suddenly turned into a marketable item," he said. "No sooner was there was a Woodstock than there were a million natural yogurt companies cropping up. I regret that more of the spirit that existed at that point in time could not carry over into the sort of cocaine and glitter thing that filled the void once it was gone. But I guess those are the jokes."

With the winds of hurricane Camille ripping through Cuba on the fifteenth at 115 mph, heading toward a Sunday night landfall in Mississippi at upwards of 205 mph before lapsing into torrential rains in the hills of Virginia on its way to the Atlantic Ocean, the denizens of Woodstock Nation were lucky to receive only a moderate drenching, resulting in a series of prime time TV moments that made the eventual *Woodstock* documentary so endearing. Unless you were there. Said Kate Marvin, a freelance reporter covering the event for the *Aquarian Weekly* out of New Jersey,

> Camping was a joke. You were completely soaking wet the whole time. After a while you got a little tired of being wet and groggy. We didn't sleep, we hardly ate; the music just went on and basically only stopped for the rain and the thunder. It was kind of like a marathon. I remember eating the goopy gruel the Hog Farm had made. Maybe it was granola but I didn't know it at the time. We didn't bring much food. We had no concept of how big it would be. We thought we'd drive out and get some groceries, or buy a hamburger there. We had no idea there'd be no food because there wasn't any food left in any of the stores.
>
> My friend Joe was the music editor of the *Aquarian Weekly*. He got the tickets and we left for the festival on Friday morning. We had plans to meet our friends there, but once we saw the crowd of cars lined up for miles we knew that was absurd. I was going to call my mother when we got there. I went to

the phone and there were two hundred people on line, so I said, I'm not going to call my mother. I remember my parents freaking out because of the headline in the *Daily News*: "Hippies Mired in a Sea of Mud." There was definitely the sense of "we're locked in and we couldn't get out; we're all trapped here." But it wasn't a bad feeling. It was okay. I didn't feel scared. There were no negative vibes or bad feelings at all. It was very mellow.

It's hard to remember what I saw and what I heard in my tent. What I really remember was thinking, oh my God, there are lots of freaks. I'm not the only one. I went to this conservative Catholic women's college and there were like three hippies on the entire campus. What I remember was thinking, oh my God, there's a whole nation of us.

Oddly enough, this friend of ours who we were planning to meet was going to be sent to Viet Nam on Monday and we were supposed to see him and his girlfriend and say goodbye and it was going to be so sad. And naturally we couldn't find him because the whole thing was just a mob scene and then through some sheer luck we were walking along and we ran into them. And then, for some reason, when he got back he got a last-minute deferment and he didn't go to Viet Nam after all.

The other thing I distinctly remember was coming back wearing my friend's bell-bottoms because I had no dry clothes. He had a little Karman Ghia and we're driving back to New Jersey and I remember really feeling changed. I felt like that song "We Can Change the World." I really felt like I'd been changed by the experience.

When I went back to my college in New Jersey I was like a star. It was my senior year and everyone was going, "She went to Woodstock." It was like I was a celebrity on campus. My campus was pretty quiet. I didn't fit in there, so that's why Woodstock seemed so cool for me. I suddenly didn't feel like I was the only freak on my campus. I felt there's a whole movement out there. There was definitely the sense of "I'm not alone."

As part of his ultimate festival summer, Clyde Lieberman also made the trek to Woodstock, with a buddy, in his buddy's mom's 1968 Camaro. He recalls,

We got there on Thursday, so we were able to get a real parking place. We were about forty rows back, within the main stage area. I don't remember doing anything except listening to music. I don't remember eating anything other than what we had in our sacks, maybe some grapes and nuts. I don't remember ever going to the bathroom the whole time. We did not get in the pond or get naked. We were from Indiana. We had never fully experienced the hippie culture. When I went to California in the summer of '68 and I hitchhiked up and down the California coast, the thing that blew my mind was how people my own age were so advanced, as far as the things they were doing. People were taking VW vans and cutting tops in them and putting moon roofs in them, making instruments, doing organic farming. Back in Indiana we were just trying to escape being Hoosiers. Music was what we lived for. So when I went to these festivals it was always about the music.

Richie Havens played really well. The Airplane kicked ass. The Dead played horribly. They never got comfortable. They weren't used to playing a defined length of time. Apparently Jerry Garcia was getting shocked the whole time, standing in water. Alvin Lee was as good as they made him seem in the movie. He grabbed the moment and he made it electrifying. I remember Crosby, Stills and Nash were really out of tune.

The biggest thing for me and my friend was the Who. They were what we'd come for. We inched our way up to the front and I was literally standing twenty to thirty feet away when the sun came up over the stage and the Who were playing "Tommy," and I will tell you, it was transformational on every level. When Abbie Hoffman got thrown off the stage I was probably yelling as loud as anyone, "Abbie Hoffman, get off the stage. We're trying to watch the music!" The Who and Alvin Lee, because of their time slots, really seized the moment. Santana was a new band to us and obviously it freaked us out that a new band could be that good.

We did not stay for Jimi Hendrix; we'd already seen him plenty. My friend and I had actually met Hendrix in 1967, when I was sixteen. I used to stay with my grandma in Brooklyn for the summer and she'd give me subway fare and I'd go into the city. So my friend and I went to Forty-ninth Street, found Manny's, the famous instrument store, and saw Hendrix inside buying a wah wah pedal.

We followed him out into the street and I said, "Excuse me, I believe you're Jimi Hendrix." He said, "Yeah, man, I am." I said, "We really love your music. What were you buying in there?" "I was buying this," and he showed us this Vox wah wah pedal. He says, "It's brand new, man. It's called a Crybaby." And I said, "That's really cool. Are you playing at all while you're in town?" He goes, "Yeah, man, I'm going to jam tonight down at this club in the Village called Generation." I said, "Well, can we go?" He said, "Yeah, just tell them Jimi Hendrix said it was okay." I gave him a scrap of paper, which he signed, and I put it in my little wallet and my friend and I went to the Village.

We found the club on Eighth Street and knocked on the door. The doorman said, "How old are you guys, sixteen? You can't come in here." So I said, "But Jimi Hendrix is going to play here tonight." He looked at me and he goes, "How'd you know that?" I went, "We were talking to him today over at Manny's." "You were talking to Jimi Hendrix over at Mannys?" I said, "Yeah, how else would we know he was going to play here?" On the bill was Chuck Berry and B. B. King. I go, "He said he was going to be jamming with some guys from B. B. King's band." I just sort of threw that in. He says, "All right, listen, kid, you see those stairs? You walk down those stairs. You get to the bottom of those stairs, you take a left. You sit at the back table, in the back corner, in the dark, where nobody can see you, and if you keep your fucking mouth shut all night, I'll let you see Jimi Hendrix play."

A waitress sat with us and kind of treated us like we were her nephews or something. She brought us sodas out of the kitchen, and we sat there and first B. B. King came out and blew our minds. We'd never seen a horn band like that. I'd seen James Brown when I was twelve or thirteen at the baseball stadium in my hometown. But I'd never seen that kind of thing in a club in New York. And then Chuck came out, in the days when Chuck still cared. It was unbelievable. Then when Chuck got done, instead of people filing out, everybody just kept milling around. Phil Wilson, who was the drummer for the Butterfield band at the time, was up on stage. Paul Butterfield was on stage and Al Kooper was playing organ. Then and all of a sudden we see this guy in a hat with some feathers sticking out of it, carrying what we knew was a Stratocaster case; in his other hand he was carrying a reel to reel tape recorder. It was still kind of dark. He went up on stage and he took the tape recorder apart; he took the speakers and he taped the microphone to each speaker facing toward the bandstand. He still had his back to us and he took out this white left-handed Strat, and then just plugged in. They played "Like a Rolling Stone," for about twenty minutes.

I remember at one point I had to pee and I got up and went to the bathroom. Phil Wilson and Paul Butterfield were standing around and I just remember thinking, "Is this heaven?"

Forever changed or only temporarily, the festival audience next convened at the Dallas International Motor Speedway on August 30, where the emotional highlight was the return of Janis Joplin to her home state.

On September 13, one of the most important festival appearances, if also one of the most agonizing and confounding for the musicians and audience, took place at Varsity Stadium in Toronto when John Lennon's hastily assembled, unrehearsed band, led by Eric Clapton, made it to the stage of the Toronto Pop Festival, ushered in from the airport with great fanfare by the Vagabonds Motorcycle Club, who had the same night provided this service for the Doors. Their ad hoc set, consisting primarily of rock 'n' roll oldies with three chords or less, fit in perfectly on a night when Chuck Berry, Little Richard, Bo Diddley, and Jerry Lee Lewis headlined and the Alice

Cooper band played backup for Gene Vincent. The few sour notes occurred during Yoko Ono's two-song appearance (she'd been rolling around obtrusively in a paper bag prior to her unfortunate emergence) consisting of "Don't Worry Kyoko" and "Oh John (Let's Hope for Peace)." John also sang his forthcoming single "Cold Turkey."

Although huge crowds assembled in many major cities to protest the war at the first World Peace Day on October 15, followed by even huger crowds a month later for Moratorium Day rallies in Washington, D.C., and San Francisco, significantly less of a mob showed up to support the Weather Underground in their nefarious activities outside the Chicago courthouse where the Chicago Eight (later Seven) were ostensibly being tried for inciting the riots at the Democratic Convention of 1968.

Instead, everyone was looking forward to the festival season finale at the Altamont speedway on December 6, less than a week after the draft lottery was announced. The culminating mega-event would more than live up to its advance billing—containing all the elements of self-destruction already embedded in the outdoor concert experience: hard drugs, soft hippies, loud music, the evil if fabricated image of the Rolling Stones, the honest-to-God evil presence of the Hell's Angels, wading into what Lester Bangs' buddy Roger Anderson called "a hippie concentration camp." All you needed for the year's most perfect storm was a man waving a gun.

The appearance of the gun and the Angels' subsequent dispatching of the wielder may have been the climactic scene of the Maysles brothers' documentary, *Gimme Shelter*, shot during the festivities, but it only served to underscore a miserable long day's journey into chaos that started much earlier, with 300,000 street fighting Rolling Stones fans trekking toward a venue straight out of a Lawrence Ferlinghetti poem. As Robert Sam Anson described it in *Gone Crazy and Back Again*, his book about *Rolling Stone* magazine: "Its acres were littered with rotting husks of junked automobiles and thousands of shards of broken glass."

Jim DeRogatis in *Let It Blurt*, the biography of Lester Bangs, provided the soused scribe's eyewitness account.

> A line of drug dealers openly hawked their wares, peddling Seconal by the handful. I remember a naked sobbing girl who came stumbling down past us, shoved by some irate redded-out boyfriend. I remember the freaked-out kid shrieking "kill, kill, kill." I remember the Angels vamping on him too and then seeing him passed in a twitching gel over the heads of the first few rows and then dumped on the ground to snivel at the feet of total strangers who would ignore him because the Stones were coming on in a minute, which would be two hours.

Earlier in the day, the Jefferson Airplane's Marty Balin, rushing to the defense of a stage diver, was socked in the jaw by an Angel, and one of his backup singers was cold-conked by a beer bottle thrown from the audience. Shortly upon the Stones' arrival backstage, Jagger was punched in the face by an angry festivalgoer. This was a bad omen, to be sure, but similar to what had happened to him in Zurich and Warsaw and Berlin, where overzealous fans had broken his arm, dented his chin, and cracked a chair over his head. Starting their set under what the band hoped would be the protective cloak of darkness, Keith Richards implored the audience to settle down, but was forced to give up his microphone to a visiting member of the security crew from Hell, who reemphasized the tone of the proceedings, as far as general crowd control and musician decorum.

"Fuck you," he bellowed.

Where was Pete Townshend of the Who with his guitar when you needed him?

Well before the murder took place it was clear the only ones in control of the stage, their bodies, their instruments, their agenda, and their destinies were the Hell's Angels. Already deified by icons of the counterculture like Ken Kesey, who turned them on to acid in 1965 while Allen Ginsberg took notes in the poem "First Party at Ken Kesey's with Hell's Angels," they were seen by the remnants of the left as a truly noble band of violent revolutionaries and granted much more approbation than the Weathermen were ever able to muster.

In the wake of Altamont, Jann Wenner, who opted to stay home due to problems with his rented helicopter, wrote: "The notion of a counterculture is a myth."

Years later, Lester Bangs expanded on this viewpoint. "It wasn't just Altamont or the Stones," he wrote, "the whole peace brat society was wrongo to the liver. The Stones had expressed it in *Gimme Shelter*, but they were even less prepared to deal with it than we were. Death of innocence in Woodstock nation, my ass. Altamont was the facing up."

Putting all these festivals into better perspective than the self-involved Baby Boom audience was usually capable of doing, Stev Lenon experienced much of 1969 at the Lai Khe base camp in the middle of the Michelin rubber plantation, a damp and dusty place with few opportunities for reflection, let alone revelation. He commented,

The USO offerings I ran across were usually late afternoon performances in some base camp, equivalent
to a small town with a central airstrip and an ammo
dump. The bands were comprised of musicians who
were adept at copying riffs and chords from pirated
albums and learning any lyrics by rote. They were always longhaired and usually greasy-haired, as their
Brylcreme or its analog melted in the tropical heat and
ran down their faces. The costumes were usually
grease-stained copies of what they saw on album
covers. I can recall standing outside an EM club on
a day when the temperature topped out at about
100 degrees, with a matching relative humidity.
This was an after-dinner performance, four men,
two women, trucked in on a six-by-six multi-fueler
two-and-a-half-ton truck with all their gear. They
were covered with dust from the trip. The instrument cases and speakers were, too. Everything took
on a tired orange hue from the red laterite dust that
was ankle deep during the dry season.

The band played about forty-five minutes' worth
of popular rock and soul. The black troops, off in one
part of the audience, were dancing around, and the
rest of us were tapping our feet or clapping when the
tempo pulled us into it. "Galveston" got almost no audience response, "Satisfaction" got a lot, and "Soul
Man" was the most energetic and well-received offering of the evening. The entire audience was locked
into the chorus, screaming it with the band, over and
over. The band actually stretched the chorus out way
past when it should have ended. The women were
dancing, string-fringed minidresses about as short
as possible. They were dripping sweat and tiring
rapidly in the heat. The drummer was having a
hard time holding onto his sticks and the guitars

were detuning. They were starting to try to find the exit for this song when it all came crashing down.

Several 122 mm Katyusha rockets came screaming in. The noise of their descent, faint at first, nearly lost in the music, rapidly grew louder as they neared impact. The troops were suddenly paying no attention at all to the band, the audience area half cleared before the band realized anything was wrong. The USO folks were trying to get the band offstage and under some cover. Troops were running for the nearest bunkers to escape shrapnel from the rockets when they landed. The air was filled with shouts of "Incoming!" and "Where's the fucking bunker?"

The explosions were sharp, louder than anything else in the world for those seconds that it took for all of them to hit. Several hit high in the rubber trees, sending shrapnel scything outward and down. White-hot hunks of rocket warhead and body tore into trees, ground, buildings, tents, and people. Others missed the trees and hit ground, digging fifty-five-gallon drum–sized holes in the hardened earth, throwing their razor-edged fragments up and outward. We could hear them whiz by us, hear the sizzling noise as fragments stuck in trees and boiled the sap.

The rockets finally stopped; probably ten to fifteen in all interrupted the show. Then the first screams of "Medic!" started. That was my cue to leave the relative safety of the bunker I was in and to go take care of the wounded. This time, fortunately, none of them were friends. This time, fortunately, none of the injuries were fatal.

The band would not have filled a small bar in the real world, our term for the continental United

States. But that evening, they brought a small bit of normalcy to several hundred troops who weren't going to see a major music festival, who hadn't heard live music in many months, who didn't care if the women singers looked hard and didn't know the songs well. It may have been the last show some of the audience would ever have the chance to attend. They piled their gear back on the truck, their driver started up and they left in a cloud of diesel smoke. They had sustained no injuries, had no equipment damaged, and had played most of their show. They were going to a bigger and safer location for the night.

I recall reading about Woodstock in *Stars and Stripes*. I saw a picture or two of the crowd. I remember thinking how horrible it would be to be in that crowd, how difficult to find a safe place with overhead cover. I still hate being in crowds. When I attend concerts, I keep close to the exit. Even today, all those miles distant and decades later, part of me is still listening for that first faint scream of incoming artillery, rockets, and mortars.

Hello/Goodbye

★　★　★　★　★　★　★　★　★　★　★　★　★

IDON'T REMEMBER EXACTLY WHERE I was on May 4, 1970, when I heard the news about four dead in Ohio. But I know I wasn't flat on my back on a mattress in a cheap hotel in Chelsea. For one thing, I'd been living in a tiny rent-controlled apartment in Little Italy for more than a year. For another, I'd been moving out of that apartment, shirt by shirt, razor by toothbrush, since January, to spend more time on East Eighth Street with my girlfriend. In September I went back to college; in December we were wed—a pair of events that provided me with the opportunity to say of the early '70s: "I got married and then got my bachelor's degree."

I hung onto the apartment, however, until 1973.

By then the pendulum, having swung all the way to the right with the election of 1972, was in motion again, straight on its way toward Richard Nixon's ass.

"My feeling is it bottomed out about 1971," Paul Simon told me. "People were so angry by 1971 that the ones who had their wits about them and had talent and had enough energy and drive to do something started working."

Manager, publicist, and all-around industry insider Danny Fields agreed. "The counterculture was mercifully becoming the glam-then-punk culture," he said. "In many ways the '70s was our revenge on Nixon. And in New York, it was the best decade of all."

Certainly it was for me, including a couple of writing awards, a job at a national rock magazine, my first book deal, a column in another national magazine, the publication of my first and second novels, the birth of my first child, a weekly newspaper column that ran for seven years, an article for *Playboy*. I feel deeply in love with Bruce Springsteen, Kate Bush, Pere Ubu, Tom Petty, the Roches, Carolyn Mas, Terry Callier, Danny O'Keefe, Steely Dan, Kinky Friedman, Patti Smith, Richard and Linda Thompson, the Funky Kings, Kate and Anna McGarrigle, Blondie, the Flamin' Groovies, Graham Parker, Warren Zevon, Ian Dury and the Blockheads, Garland Jeffreys, the Modern Lovers, Little Feat, Genya Ravan, Tom Waits, Dire Straits, Kirsty MacColl, Motorhead, Rachel Sweet, Tin Huey, and XTC. Since I was a journalist, I didn't have to pay for a single album.

By then the war in Viet Nam was over, disco was on the wane, heavy metal had turned into arena rock, punk had relocated from New York City to Los Angeles, and rap was just a few solitary guys with beat boxes playing parties and local parks in Brooklyn and the Bronx. Meanwhile, the individual Beatles thrived; Bob Dylan came back; the Stones returned, "badder" than ever; Paul Simon, Joni Mitchell, Stevie Wonder, and Marvin Gaye did their best work; "Stairway to Heaven" became the Holy Grail of an air guitar generation; the Parliament/Funkadelic Mothership landed; and *Rolling Stone* magazine relocated to Fifth Avenue. In other words, the rock music business exploded and FM radio flourished, tight playlists and all.

But for the first wave of Baby Boomers, who came of age with Elvis and took the music of Bob Dylan to college, thinking their dominance and their taste and their mission regarding the music (to say nothing of the world) would never end, these developments provided small comfort. The series of endings that began with the election of Nixon in '68 and culminated in 1969 and 1970 on the killing fields of People's Park, Cielo Drive, Altamont Raceway, and Kent State University were devastating. After May 4, the Radical Dream was officially dead, joining on the scrap heap the Revolutionary Dream, the Racial Equality Dream, the Hippie Dream, the Communal Dream of annexing Vermont or Nevada, the innocent Love, Peace, and Flowers Dream, and the LSD in the Drinking Water Dream. After 1972, it was the end of the Liberal Dream, also known as the Kennedy Dream, for the rest of the century.

It was the end of the Beatles, the end of Woodstock Nation, the end of the Greenwich Village folk scene. "The Bus" went into the shop permanently. In San Francisco, Bill Graham got out of the Fillmore business, the Airplane became the Starship, the Dead incorporated. Jimi Hendrix, Janis Joplin, and Jim Morrison reached the end of the road. As Dave Van Ronk told me, "The check was not in the mail." As Tom Wolfe quoted Kesey as saying, "We blew it." And, as Monkee Peter Tork said,

> When they shot them down at Kent State that was the end of the Flower Power era. That was it. You throw your flowers and rocks at us, man, and we'll just pull the guns on you. Essentially, the revolution, which

was sort of tolerated as long as it wasn't a significant material threat, was not tolerated any more. And everybody went "oops" and scurried for cover and licked their wounds. They became isolated, which was the point of it all. Because the less togetherness there is, the more room there is for exploitation. Kent State was an attempt: "Let's try this and see what happens." And what happened was the shooting and vast inflation and a swing to the right. As long as people are educated to believe that isolated self-interest is the only way to go, when the crunch comes, they'll withdraw from each other. Togetherness and flower power alone won't get it. It's got to be togetherness, flower power, plus a willingness to do something pretty stern from time to time. If you're not willing to behave sternly, people who won't stop short of stern behavior are going to keep on going.

With the end of the war bringing the end of the draft, many men rushed to seek a few hours' liberation from their draft-induced marriages and teaching jobs in the one remaining rock 'n' roll–encouraged dream: for a generation approaching thirty, CBGB's, Studio 54, Plato's Retreat, Yankee Stadium, and the set of *Saturday Night Live* held the dream of eternal adolescence. But this was all too soon replaced by the reality of being the oldest cat in a room filled with chicks who "don't remember the Queen of Soul."

At the top of the '80s, the epic soap opera of rock would be handed down again, this time to the MTV Generation, as the pendulum swung madly back to the right, deftly commandeered by former Governor Bloodbath of California.

The revenge of Ronald Reagan was upon us.

A Timeline of the Season

★ ★ ★ ★ ★ ★ ★ ★ ★ ★ ★ ★ ★

Here is a list of some of the signal events of the period documented in this book, with albums listed by date of release and singles listed by the date they hit the charts.

1968

November

December

1969

January

February

March

April

May

July

August

September

October

"Delta Lady" (Joe Cocker)	4
"I'll Bet You" (Funkadelic)	4
Diane Linkletter commits suicide in L.A.	4
John Waters starts filming *The Diane Linkletter Story*	5
The Carpenters release *Ticket to Ride*	9
Yoko Ono has another miscarriage	9
Zodiac killer strikes again	11
"She Belongs to Me" (Rick Nelson)	11
Janis Joplin releases *I Got Dem Ol' Kozmic Blues Again Mama!*	11
Charles Manson arrested for Tate/LoBianco murders	12
Race riots in Springfield, Massachusetts	14
Yes is released	15
Vietnam Moratorium Day	15
Mets defeat Orioles to win the World Series	16
Richard Nader holds first Oldies Revival	18
The Beatles release *Abbey Road*	18
The Band is released	18
"And When I Die" (Blood, Sweat and Tears)	18
"Come Together/Something" (The Beatles)	18
"Na Na Hey Hey Kiss Him Goodbye" (Steam)	18
Jack Kerouac dies	21
"Friendship Train" (Gladys Knight and the Pips)	25
"Jingo" (Santana)	25
"Leaving on a Jet Plane" (Peter, Paul and Mary)	25
"Eli's Coming" (Three Dog Night)	25
Arlo Guthrie releases *Running Down the Road*	25
Supreme Court orders desegregation	30
Race riots in Jacksonville, FL	31

November

1970

January

February

March

April

May

June

Bibliography

★ ★ ★ ★ ★ ★ ★ ★ ★ ★ ★ ★ ★

Anson, Robert Sam. *Gone Crazy and Back Again: The Rise and Fall of the Rolling Stone Generation.* Garden City, New York: Doubleday, 1981.

Anthony, Gene. *Summer of Love.* Millbrae, CA: Celestial Arts, 1980.

Betrock, Alan. *Girl Groups: The Story of a Sound.* New York: Delilah Press, 1982.

Brant, Marley. *Join Together: Forty Years of the Rock Music Festival.* New York: Backbeat Books, 2008.

Burner, David. *Making Peace with the Sixties.* Princeton, New Jersey. Princeton University Press, 1996.

Bronson, Fred. *Billboard Book of Number One Hits.* New York: Billboard Publications, 1985.

Buskin, Richard. *Inside Tracks.* New York: Avon Books, 1999.

Carson, David A. *Grit, Noise, and Revolution: The Birth of Detroit Rock 'n' Roll.* Ann Arbor, MI: University of Michigan Press, 2005.

Cooper, Alice. *Alice Cooper: Golf Monster.* New York: Crown, 2007.

Crenshaw, Marshall. *Hollywood Rock.* New York: Harper-Perennial, 1994.

Dalton, David. *Piece of My Heart: The Life and Times and Legend of Janis Joplin.* New York: St. Martins Press, 1971.

Dannen, Frederic. *Hit Men.* New York: Times Books, 1990.

Denisoff, R. Serge, and Richard Peterson. *The Sounds of Social Change.* Chicago, IL: Rand McNally, 1972.

DeRogatis, Jim. *The Life and Times of Lester Bangs: America's Greatest Rock Critic.* New York: Broadway Books, 2000.

Dickstein, Morris. *Gates of Eden: American Culture in the Sixties.* New York: Basic Books, 1977.

Dimery, Robert. *1001 Albums You Must Hear Before You Die.* New York: Universe, 2006.

Ehrenstein, David, and Bill Reed. *Rock on Film.* San Francisco: Miller Freeman, 1992.

Emerick, Geoff, and Howard Massey: *Here, There and Everywhere: My Life Recording the Music of the Beatles.* New York: Gotham Books, 2006.

Erlewine, Michael, and Scott Bultman. *The All Music Guide.* San Francisco. Miller Freeman, www.allmusic.com.

Farber, David. *The Sixties: From Memory to History.* Chapel Hill, NC: University of North Carolina Press, 1994.

Fariña, Richard. *Been Down So Long It Looks Like Up to Me.* New York: Dell, 1966.

Fisher, Mark. *Something in the Air: Radio, Rock, and the Revolution That Shaped a Generation.* New York: Random House, 2007.

George, Nelson. *Where Did Our Love Go: The Rise and Fall of the Motown Sound.* New York. St. Martin's Press, 1986.

Gilbert, Bob, and Gary Theroux. *The Top Ten, 1956–Present* New York: Fireside Books, 1982.

Giuliano, Geoffrey. *The Beatles: A Celebration.* Ontario, Canada: Methuen Publishing, 1986.

Goldberg, Danny. *Dispatches from the Culture Wars: How the Left Lost Teen Spirit.* New York: Miramax, 2003.

Goodman, Fred. *Mansion on the Hill: Bob Dylan, Neil Young, David Geffen, Bruce Springsteen, and the Head on Collision of Rock and Commerce.* New York: Times Books, 1997.

Gordy, Berry. *To Be Loved: The Music, the Magic, the Memories, a Memoir.* New York: Warner Books, 1994.

Graff, Gary. *Music Hound/Rock: The Essential Album Guide.* Detroit, MI: Visible Ink Press, 1996.

Graham, Bill, and Robert Greenfield. *Bill Graham Presents: My Life Inside Rock and Out.* New York: Dell Publishing, 1992.

Greenfield, Robert. *Timothy Leary: A Biography.* Orlando: Harcourt, 2006.

Guralnick, Peter. *Sweet Soul Music.* New York: Harper & Row, 1986.

Hajdu, David. *Positively Fourth Street: The Lives and Times of Joan Baez, Bob Dylan, Mimi Baez Fariña and Richard Fariña.* New York: Farrar, Straus and Giroux, Inc., 2001.

Hayes, Harold, ed. *Smiling Through the Apocalypse: Esquire's History of the Sixties.* New York: The McCall Publishing Co., 1969.

Hopkins, Jerry. *The Hippie Papers.* New York: New American Library, 1968.

Hopkins, Jerry, and Danny Sugarman. *No One Here Gets Out Alive: The Biography of Jim Morrison.* New York: Warner Books, 1980.

Irvin, Jim. *The Mojo Collection: The Greatest Albums of All Time.* Edinburgh: Mojo Books, 2000.

Jancik, Wayne, and Tad Lathrop. *Cult Rockers.* New York. Fireside Books, 1995.

Lesh, Phil. *Searching for the Sound: My Life with the Grateful Dead.* New York: Little, Brown and Company, 2005.

Lydon, Michael. *Flashbacks: Eyewitness Accounts of the Rock Revolution 1964–1974.* New York: Routledge, 2003.

Marcus, Griel. *Stranded: Rock and Roll for a Desert Island.* New York: Alfred A. Knopf, 1979.

———. *Mystery Train.* New York: Plume Books, 1990.

Marsh, Dave. *Elvis.* New York City: Quadrangle/New York Times Books, 1982.

———. *The Heart of Rock and Soul: The 1001 Best Singles Ever Made.* New York: Plume Books, 1989.

Marsh, Dave, and John Swenson. *The New Rolling Stone Record Guide.* New York: Random House, 1983.

―――. *The Rolling Stone Record Guide.* New York: Random House, 1979.

McAleer, Dave. *British and American Hit Singles, 1960–1990.* London, New York: Omnibus, 1990.

Mungo, Raymond. *Famous Long Ago: My Life and Hard Times with the Liberation News Service.* Boston: Beacon Press, 1970.

―――. *Total Loss Farm: A Year in the Life.* New York: Dutton, 1970.

Murrels, Joseph. *Million Selling Records from the 1900s to the 1980s.* New York. Arco, 1985.

Nite, Norm N. *Rock On: The Illustrated Encyclopedia of Rock 'n' Roll.* New York: Popular Library, 1974.

Olson, Eric, Paul Verna, and Carlo Wolff. *The Encyclopedia of Record Producers.* New York: Billboard Books, 1999.

Palmer, Robert. *Baby That Was Rock and Roll: The Legendary Leiber and Stoller.* New York: Harcourt Brace Jovanovich, 1978.

―――. *Deep Blues.* New York: Penguin, 1982.

Perry, Charles. *Haight-Ashbury: A History.* New York: Random House, 1984.

Pollock, Bruce. *Hipper Than Our Kids: A Rock and Roll Journal of the Baby Boom Generation.* New York: Schirmer Books, 1993.

―――. *Interviews with Great Songwriters.* Port Chester, NY: Cherry Lane Books, 1986.

―――. *In Their Own Words: Lyrics and Lyricists, 1955–1974.* New York: Macmillan, 1975.

―――. *When Rock Was Young.* New York: Holt, Rinehart & Winston, 1981.

―――. *When the Music Mattered.* New York: Holt, Rinehart & Winston, 1983.

―――. *Working Musicians.* New York: Harper Collins, 2002.

Rolling Stone. *The Rolling Stone Record Review.* New York: Pocket Books, 1971.

Romanowski, Patricia, and Holly George-Warren. *Rolling Stone Encyclopedia of Rock and Roll.* New York: Fireside Press, 1996.

Rotolo, Suze. *A Freewheelin' Time: A Memoir of Greenwich Village in the Sixties.* New York: Broadway Books, 2008.

Roxon, Lilian. *Roxon's Rock Encyclopedia.* New York: Workman Publishing, 1976.

Santelli, Robert. *The Sixties: A Listener's Guide.* Chicago, IL: Contemporary Books, 1985.

Stokes, Geoffrey. *The Beatles.* New York: Rolling Stone Press, 1980.

Stone, Robert. *Prime Green: Remembering the Sixties.* New York: Harper Perennial, 2008.

Unterberger, Richie. *Eight Miles High: Folk-Rock's Flight from Haight-Ashbury to Woodstock.* San Francisco: Backbeat Books, 2003.

Walker, Michael. *Laurel Canyon: The Inside Story of Rock-and-Roll's Legendary Neighborhood.* New York: Faber & Faber, 2007.

Weller, Sheila. *Girls Like Us: Carole King, Joni Mitchell, and Carly Simon—and the Journey of a Generation.* New York: Atria, 2008.

Whitburn, Joel. *Bubbling Under, 1959–1981.* Menomenee Falls, WI: Record Research, Inc., 1982.

———. *Rock Tracks.* Menomenee Falls, WI: Record Research, Inc., 1995.

———. *Top Country Hits, 1944–1997.* Menomenee Falls, WI: Record Research, Inc., 1994.

———. *Top Pop Albums, 1955–1999.* Menomenee Falls, WI: Record Research, Inc., 2000.

———. *Top Pop Singles, 1955–1999.* Menomenee Falls, WI: Record Research, Inc., 2000.

———. *Top R&B Hits, 1941–1999.* Menomenee Falls, WI: Record Research, Inc., 2000.

White, Adam, and Fred Bronson. *The Billboard Book of Number One Rhythm and Blues Hits.* New York: Billboard Publications, 1993.

Williams, Paul. *Rock and Roll: The Best 100 Singles.* New York: Carroll & Graf, 1993.

Wolfe, Tom. *The Electric Kool-Aid Acid Test.* New York: Farrar, Straus and Giroux, Inc., 1968.

Wolfe, Tom, and E. W. Johnson, eds. *The New Journalism.* New York: Harper and Row, 1973.

Index

★ ★ ★ ★ ★ ★ ★ ★ ★ ★ ★ ★ ★